Introduction to Documentary

Bill Nichols

Introduction to Documentary

Indiana University Press | Bloomington & Indianapolis

This book is a publication of

Indiana University Press
601 North Morton Street
Bloomington, IN 47404-3797 USA

http://iupress.indiana.edu

Telephone orders   800-842-6796
Fax orders   812-855-7931
Orders by e-mail   iuporder@indiana.edu

The paper used in this publication meets the minimum
requirements of American National Standard for Information
Sciences—Permanence of Paper for Printed Library
Materials, ANSI Z39.48-1984.

MANUFACTURED IN THE UNITED STATES OF AMERICA

Library of Congress Cataloging-in-Publication Data

Nichols, Bill.
    Introduction to documentary / Bill Nichols.
        p.   cm.
    Includes bibliographical references and index.
    Includes filmography.
    ISBN 978-0-253-33954-6 (cl : alk. paper) —
    ISBN 978-0-253-21469-0 (pa : alk. paper)
        1. Documentary films—History and criticism.   I. Title.

PN1995.9.D6 N539   2001
070.1'8—dc21   00-054267

    6   7   8   9   10   12   11   10   09   08   07

For the men and women who make the films

Contents

Acknowledgments

My greatest debt of gratitude goes to the students who have studied documentary film with me over the years. Their curiosity and questions have provided the motivation for this book. I am also greatly indebted to those who have gathered at the Visible Evidence conferences since their inception in 1993 to exchange ideas and pursue debates about documentary film. These conferences, initiated by Jane Gaines and Michael Renov, have proven invaluable to the promotion of a lively dialogue about documentary film in the broadest possible terms.

The Getty Research Institute provided generous support that facilitated the completion of this book during the 1999–2000 academic year, for which I am most grateful.

Without the assistance of the filmmakers who so generously provided still images of their work, this book would be greatly impoverished. I thank them for their willingness to provide superb illustrations, often on short notice.

John Mrozik researched the filmography; Michael Wilson initiated and Victoria Gamburg updated and completed the research for the list of distributors. Their assistance was timely and indispensable.

Joan Catapano helped launch this project at the press, and Michael Lundell saw it to completion. Carol Kennedy did a thorough and felicitous job of copy editing the manuscript. Matt Williamson did the layout and design for the book and designed the cover. I am grateful to them all for helping to produce a work that exceeds my expectations.

No acknowledgment is ever complete without giving thanks to those who make such work possible in the most fundamental sense of all, and from whom the time to do it is inevitably stolen—my wife, Catherine M. Soussloff, and my stepdaughter, Eugenia Clarke. Their contribution is far greater than they will ever know.

Introduction

Organized as a series of questions about documentary film and video, *Introduction to Documentary* offers an overview of this fascinating form of filmmaking. The questions involve issues of ethics, definition, content, form, types, and politics. Because documentaries address *the* world in which we live rather than *a* world imagined by the filmmaker, they differ from the various genres of fiction (science fiction, horror, adventure, melodrama, and so on) in significant ways. They are made with different assumptions about purpose, they involve a different quality of relationship between filmmaker and subject, and they prompt different sorts of expectations from audiences.

These differences, as we shall see, guarantee no absolute separation between fiction and documentary. Some documentaries make strong use of practices or conventions, such as scripting, staging, reenactment, rehearsal, and performance, for example, that we often associate with fiction. Some fiction makes strong use of practices or conventions, such as location shooting, the use of non-actors, hand-held cameras, improvisation, and found footage (footage not shot by the filmmaker) that we often associate with non-fiction or documentary.

Since notions about what is fitting to documentary and what is not change over time, some films spark debate about the boundaries of fiction and non-fiction. At one point Eric von Stroheim's *Greed* (1925) and Sergei Eisenstein's *Strike* (1925) were praised for the high degree of realism or verisimilitude they brought to their stories. At another point Roberto Rossellini's *Rome, Open City* (1945) and John Cassavetes's *Shadows* (1960) seemed to bring lived reality to the screen in ways not previously experienced. Reality TV shows like *Cops, Real TV,* and *World's Most Amazing Videos* have heightened the degree to which television can exploit a sense of documentary authenticity and melodramatic spectacle simultaneously. And films such as *Forrest Gump, The Truman Show, EDTV,* and *The Blair Witch Project* build their stories around the underlying premise of documentary: we experience a distinct form of fascination for the opportunity to witness the lives of others when they seem to belong to the same historical world that we do.

In *The Blair Witch Project* (Eduardo Sanchez and Daniel Myrick, 1999) this fascination not only relies on combining documentary conventions with the gritty realism of camcorder technology to impart historical credibility to a fictional situation, it also makes full use of promotional and publicity channels that surround the film proper and help prepare us for it. These included a Web site with background information about the Blair witch, expert testimony, and references to "actual" people and events, all designed to market the film not as fiction, and not even simply as a documentary, but as the raw footage of three filmmakers who tragically disappeared.

If nothing else, *The Blair Witch Project* should remind us that our own idea of whether a film is or is not a documentary is highly susceptible to suggestion. (Susan Stewart's July 10–16, 1999, *TV Guide* review of a Sci-Fi Channel program, "Curse of the Blair Witch," treats it as a bad but authentic attempt to document the story of an actual witch rather than as a promotional tie-in to this clever fiction story.) Film, video, and now digitally based images can bear witness to what took place in front of the camera with extraordinary fidelity. Painting and drawing seem a pale imitation of reality compared to the sharp, highly defined, precise representations available on film, video, or computer monitors. Yet this fidelity serves the needs of fiction filmmaking as much as it facilitates the work of medical imaging through the use of x-rays, MRIs, or CAT scans. The fidelity of the image may be as crucial to a close-up of Tom Cruise or Catherine Deneuve as it is to an x-ray of a lung, but the uses of that fidelity are vastly different. We believe what we see and what is represented about what we see at our own risk.

As digital media make all too apparent, fidelity lies in the mind of the beholder as much as it lies in the relationship between a camera and what comes before it. (With digitally produced images there may be no camera and nothing that ever comes before it, even if the resulting image bears an extraordinary fidelity to familiar people, places, and things.) Whether what we see is exactly what we would have seen had we been present alongside the camera cannot be guaranteed.

Certain technologies and styles encourage us to believe in a tight, if not perfect, correspondence between image and reality, but the effects of lenses, focus, contrast, depth of field, color, high-resolution media (film with very fine grain, video displays with very many pixels) seem to guarantee the authenticity of what we see. They can all be used, however, to give the *impression* of authenticity to what has actually been fabricated or constructed. And once images are selected and arranged into patterns or sequences, into scenes or entire films, the interpretation and meaning of what we see

Palace of Delights (Jon Else and Steve Longstreth, 1982). Photo by Nancy Roger, courtesy of Jon Else.

A documentary film crew on location. Most of the components of a feature film are replicated on a documentary production, though usually on a smaller scale. The "crew" can be as small as a single camera-sound operator/director. For many documentaries the ability to respond to events that do not unfold entirely as the director intends, to, that is, "real life," plays a central role in the organization of the crew and in its working methods. In this case, Jon Else does the filming, with a 16mm camera, and Steve Longstreth records the sound with a Nagra tape recorder designed to keep the sound synchronized to the image. They are shooting a scene about the "Momentum Machine" at the San Francisco Exploratorium.

will hinge on many more factors than whether the image is a faithful representation of what, if anything, appeared before the camera.

The documentary tradition relies heavily on being able to convey to us the impression of authenticity. It is a powerful impression. It began with the raw cinematic image and the appearance of movement: no matter how poor the image and how different from the thing photographed, the appearance of movement remained indistinguishable from actual movement. (Each frame of a film is a still image; apparent motion relies on the effect produced when they are projected in rapid succession.)

When we believe that what we see bears witness to the way the world is, it can form the basis for our orientation to or action within the world. This is obviously true in science, where medical imaging plays a vital diagnostic role in almost all branches of medicine. Propaganda, like advertising, also relies on our belief in a bond between what we see and the way the world is, or how we might act within it. So do many documentaries when they set out to persuade us to adopt a given perspective or point of view about the world.

Filmmakers are often drawn to documentary modes of representation when they want to engage us in questions or issues that pertain directly to the historical world we all share. Some will stress the originality or distinctiveness of their own way of seeing the world: we will see the world we share as filtered through a particular perception of it. Some will stress the authenticity or fidelity of their representation of the world: we will see the world we share with a clarity or transparency that downplays the style or perceptions of the filmmaker.

In either case, those who adopt the documentary as their vehicle of expression turn our attention to the world we already occupy. They do so with the same resourcefulness and inventiveness that fiction filmmakers use to draw our attention to worlds we would have otherwise never known. Documentary film and video, therefore, displays the same complexity and challenge, the same fascination and excitement as any of the genres of fiction film. Through the course of this book we will explore how the issues involved in representing reality have tested the resourcefulness and inventiveness of documentary filmmakers.

It may be useful to mention as a caveat that this is not a documentary film history. Such a work would bear an obligation to identify the major filmmakers, movements, periods, and schools that have gone into constructing the documentary tradition as we know it today. Several books do this already: Erik Barnouw's highly readable and engaging account of documentary, *Documentary: A History of the Non-Fiction Film,* Richard Meran Barsam's useful overview, *NonFiction Film: A Critical History,* and Jack C. Ellis's carefully organized account, *The Documentary Idea: A Critical History of English-Language Documentary Film and Video.* Although each book has its strengths and weaknesses, in the aggregate they provide a helpful introduction to the historical development of documentary film.

Introduction to Documentary complements these efforts. The historical emphasis of these other books leaves some of the conceptual questions and issues about documentary less carefully developed. What modes of documentary filmmaking exist, for example, is a question that is partly historical (different modes tend to come to prominence at different points in time) but more basically conceptual (the idea of modes, or distinct types, of documentary itself needs to be thought through and developed before it can be applied historically). How should a documentary represent actual people rather than trained actors is another question that is answered implicitly by the record of documentary filmmaking, but it, too, needs to be isolated and scrutinized if we are to come to grips with the ethics of documentary film practice, an issue most histories of the genre neglect.

Introduction to Documentary will provide hints and traces of documentary film history since the issues and practices examined here arise in history and cannot be discussed entirely free from it. The book does not, however, attempt to provide comprehensive and balanced coverage of the various key filmmakers, movements, and national characteristics of the documentary genre over the course of its history. The works chosen for discussion here are indicative of specific questions or exemplify important approaches to certain issues. Although illustrative, they do not amount to a history of the genre.

Identifying some films rather than others immediately suggests the idea of a canon, a list of films that constitute the best of the tradition. I have tried to avoid constructing a canon. Such an approach carries implications about how history works (great artists, great works lead the way). My own view is that certain artists, while extremely influential, are but one part of a larger stew of ideas, values, issues, technologies, institutional frameworks, sponsorship, and shared forms of expression that all contribute to the history of documentary or any other medium.

This book, therefore, runs the risk of constructing a canon through its selective use of examples, but it also tries to indicate that the works chosen, while often extraordinary accomplishments artistically and socially, have little standing as uncontested monuments or icons. It is *how* they solve problems and exemplify solutions, how they are suggestive of trends, practices, styles, and issues rather than any absolute sense of value intrinsic to them that takes priority here.

Many of the works referred to in *Introduction to Documentary* are already part of a canon in that they are works frequently cited in other works and frequently included in courses. It seems more useful to develop the conceptual tools proposed here by referring to familiar works rather than by relying heavily on less accessible ones. This book may therefore reinforce the sense of a canon, but wherever possible I have chosen at least two films to use as examples for a given point. In this way I hope to give a fuller sense of how different films find at least slightly different solutions to common problems and to suggest that no one film deserves the status of best or greatest, certainly not in any timeless, ahistorical sense.

One final point: as an introduction to documentary film and video, this book leaves many similar, sometimes parallel developments to the side. The various forms of realism in fiction films would be one example. Docudrama, which has a complex and even more fascinating history in Britain than in the United States, is another. These alternative ways of addressing and representing the historical world, from photography and photojournalism to radio reports and oral histories, are treated as peripheral to the central focus here. These forms are peripheral only in the sense that they lie somewhat to the side of this study, not that they hold less interest, deserve less attention, or bear less significance. A study revolving around photojournalism or photomontage might treat documentary film and video as peripheral in the same sense as I mean here.

There is a specificity to documentary film and video that revolves around the phenomenon of moving sounds and images recorded in media that allow for a remarkably high degree of fidelity between a representation and what it refers to. Digital forms of representation add to the number of media that fulfill this criteria. Some will see an expansion of documentary into media such as CD-ROMs or interactive Web sites devoted to historical issues and organized according to conventions of documentary representation. I see something closer to cross-pollination than a literal expansion or direct continuation as related media trade conventions and borrow techniques from one another. Web sites, like photography before them, will someday deserve a history and theory of their own. For now we can treat all these related media as very significant but nonetheless peripheral to our central concern.

Digitally based media remind us even more forcefully than film or video how much our belief in the authenticity of the image is a matter of trust to begin with. Digital recording and editing techniques can begin with an image generated without any referent whatsoever in the historical world. Even when there is such a referent, an actual person or event, they can modify sounds and images so that the modification is of exactly the same order and same status as what would be called the "original" version of the sound or image in other media. Copy and original are just strings of 1s and 0s in different locations.

In fact, with digital technology the whole idea of an original begins to fade. Whether this idea is necessary to the belief we tender the documentary image, though, is open to question. This book assumes that the bond between photographic, video, or digital images and what they represent can be extraordinarily powerful even if it can also be entirely fabricated. The questions pursued in this introduction are not intended to allow us to decide whether or to what degree fabrication has taken place so that we can determine what the referent is "really" like or what "really happened." They are designed more to ask how it is that we are willing to trust in the representations made by moving images, when such trust may be more, or less, warranted, and to examine what the consequences of our trust or belief might be for our relation to the historical world in which we live.

Introduction to Documentary pursues the following questions: "Why Are Ethical Issues Central to Documentary Filmmaking?" in Chapter 1. This chapter explores some of the ethical issues surrounding documentary and suggests how they may differ from the types of ethical issues that may arise with fiction. In Chapter 2, we ask, "How Do Documentaries Differ from Other Types of Film?" and examine various, complementary ways in which this question can be answered. This chapter gives our first taste of a historical dimension to documentary but stresses qualities and conditions that recur in different moments.

Chapter 3 asks, "What Gives Documentary Films a Voice of Their Own?" This question introduces concepts from the art of rhetoric to show how documentary remains indebted to the rhetorical tradition and how the documentary filmmaker often resembles the orator of old in his or her efforts to address issues or problems that call for social consensus or solution. Chapter 4 wants to know "What Are Documentaries About?" It looks at some of the characteristics of those issues that tend to provide the content or subject-matter for documentary, especially the degree to which the issues taken up by documentary evade scientific or purely logical solution. They depend on assumptions and values, which, since they vary, then call on representations such as documentaries to persuade us of the worthiness of one approach over others. Chapter 5 asks, "How Did Documentary Filmmaking Get Started?" in order to question some of the prevailing assumptions about documentary being synonymous either with early cinema of the sort Louis Lumière promoted, such as *Workers Leaving the Factory* (1895), or with nonfiction film generally. The chapter identifies four different contributing practices that combined into a documentary film practice by the late 1920s.

Chapter 6 proposes to answer the question "What Types of Documentary Film Are There?" by identifying six different modes, or types, of documentary. Each mode has its exemplary filmmakers, its paradigmatic films, and its own forms of institutional support and audience expectation. All six are available at any given moment to provide the structural organization to a film even if the film freely mixes them together.

Chapter 7 raises the question "How Have Documentaries Addressed Social and Political Issues?" Like Chapters 4 and 5, this chapter also has a historical dimension as it looks at how the central issue of community finds representation in documentary and how this issue has close ties to questions of the nation state, feminism, identity politics, and multiculturalism or hybrid identities.

Finally, Chapter 8 addresses the question "How Can We Write Effectively about Documentary?" Answering this question involves walking through some of the basic steps of constructing an essay, using a hypothetical writing assignment and two possible responses to it. By providing two model essays that take very different views of a classic documentary film, Robert Flaherty's *Nanook of the North* (1922), the chapter tries to indicate how the student's own perspective or thesis becomes a central part of a written response to a given film.

Behind *Introduction to Documentary* lies the assumption that awareness of the central concepts in documentary film practice, along with a sense of the history of documentary filmmaking, provides extremely valuable tools to the filmmaker as well as the critic. A strong link between production and study has been characteristic of much documentary filmmaking in the past. My hope is that it will remain a vital link in the future and that the concepts discussed here will help preserve that vitality.

Introduction to Documentary

Chapter 1

Why Are Ethical Issues Central to Documentary Filmmaking?

TWO TYPES OF FILM

Every film is a documentary. Even the most whimsical of fictions gives evidence of the culture that produced it and reproduces the likenesses of the people who perform within it. In fact, we could say that there are two kinds of film: (1) documentaries of wish-fulfillment and (2) documentaries of social representation. Each type tells a story, but the stories, or narratives, are of different sorts.

Documentaries of wish-fulfillment are what we would normally call fictions. These films give tangible expression to our wishes and dreams, our nightmares and dreads. They make the stuff of the imagination concrete—visible and audible. They give a sense of what we wish, or fear, reality itself might be or become. Such films convey truths if we decide they do. They are films whose truths, insights, and perspectives we may adopt as our own or reject. They offer worlds for us to explore and contemplate, or we may simply revel in the pleasure of moving from the world around us to these other worlds of infinite possibility.

Documentaries of social representation are what we typically call nonfiction. These films give tangible representation to aspects of the world we already inhabit and share. They make the stuff of social reality visible and audible in a distinctive way, according to the acts of selection and arrangement carried out by a filmmaker. They give a sense of what we understand reality itself to have been, of what it is now, or of what it may become. These films also convey truths if we decide they do. We must assess their claims and assertions, their perspectives and arguments in relation to the world as we know it and decide whether they are worthy of our belief. Documentaries of social representation offer us new views of our common world to explore and understand.

As stories, films of both type call on us to interpret them, and as "true stories," films call on us to believe them. Interpretation is a matter of grasping how the form or organization of the film conveys meanings and values. Belief is a question of our response to these meanings and values. We can believe in the truths of fictions as well as those of non-fictions: *Vertigo* (Alfred Hitchcock, 1958) may teach us about the nature of obsession just as much as *The Plow That Broke the Plains* (Pare Lorentz, 1936) may teach us about soil conservation. Belief receives a premium in documentaries since these films often are intended to have an impact on the historical world itself and to do so must persuade or convince us that one point of view or approach is preferable to others. Fiction may be content to suspend *disbelief* (to accept its world as plausible), but non-fiction often wants to instill belief (to accept its world as actual). This is what aligns documentary with the rhetorical tradition, in which eloquence serves a social as well as aesthetic purpose. We take not only pleasure from documentary but direction as well.

This is the appeal and power of documentary. (We'll call documentaries of wish-fulfillment "fictions" from now on and simply use "documentary" as shorthand for non-fiction films of social representation.) Documentaries lend us the ability to see timely issues in need of attention, literally. We see (cinematic) views of the world. These views put before us social issues and current events, recurring problems and possible solutions. The bond between documentary and the historical world is deep and profound. Documentary adds a new dimension to popular memory and social history.

This introduction to the ways in which documentary engages with the world as we know it takes up the series of questions indicated by the chapter titles. These questions are the commonsense sort of questions we might ask ourselves if we want to understand documentary film. Each question takes us a bit further into the domain of documentary; each question helps us understand how a documentary tradition arose and evolved and what it has to offer us today.

Documentary engages with the world by representing it, and it does so in three ways. First, documentaries offer us a likeness or depiction of the world that bears a recognizable familiarity. Through the capacity of film, and audio tape, to record situations and events with considerable fidelity, we see in documentaries people, places, and things that we might also see for ourselves, outside the cinema. This quality alone often provides a basis for belief: we see what was there before the camera; it must be true. This remarkable power of the photographic image cannot be underestimated, even though it is subject to qualification because (1) an image cannot tell everything we want to know about what happened and (2) images can be altered both during and after the fact by both conventional and digital means.

In documentaries we find stories or arguments, evocations or descriptions that let us see the world anew. The ability of the photographic image to reproduce the likeness of what is set before it compels us to believe that it is reality itself re-presented before us, while the story or argument presents a distinct way of regarding this reality. We may be familiar with the problems of corporate downsizing, global assembly lines, and plant shutdowns, but Michael Moore's *Roger and Me* (1989) gives us a view of these issues in a fresh and distinctive way. We may know about cosmetic surgery and the debates surrounding efforts to regain lost youth by these means, but Michael Rubbo's *Daisy: The Story of a Facelift* (1982) adds his own personal perspective to our knowledge.

Second, documentaries also stand for or represent the interests of others. Representative democracy, in contrast to participatory democracy, relies on elected individuals representing the interests of their constituency. (In a participatory democracy each individual participates actively in political decision-making rather than relying on a representative). Documentary filmmakers often take on the role of public representatives. They speak for the interests of others, both for the individuals whom they represent in the film and for the institution or agency that supports their filmmaking activity. *The Selling of the Pentagon* (1971), a CBS news production on the ways in which the American military markets itself and ensures itself a substantial slice of the federal tax dollar, presents itself as a representative of the American people, investigating the use and abuse of political power in Washington. It also represents the interests of CBS news in marketing itself as an institution independent from government pressure and committed to a well-established tradition of investigative journalism.

Similarly, *Nanook of the North* (1922), Robert Flaherty's great story of an Inuit family's struggle for survival in the Arctic, represents Inuit culture in ways that the Inuit were not yet prepared to do for themselves and represents the interests of Revillon Freres, Flaherty's sponsor, at least to the extent of depicting fur hunting as a practice that benefits the Inuit as well as consumers. It also, somewhat less overtly, represents Robert Flaherty's conception of Inuit culture. The emphasis on a nuclear family assembled

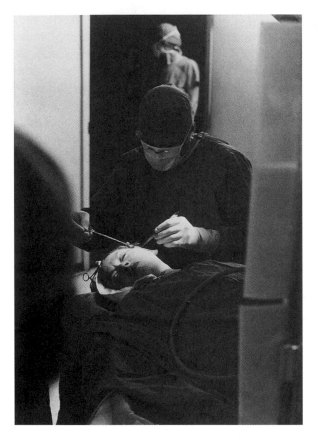

Daisy: The Story of a Facelift (Michael Rubbo, National Film Board of Canada, 1982) Michael Rubbo does not spare us the clinical details. His own voice-over commentary tries to grasp the complexity of the issues while his images detail the realities of the process.

for the sake of the film and on Nanook's own skills as a hunter, despite the fact that most Eskimos living in the 1920s no longer relied on the traditional techniques depicted, for example, belong to the cinema of wish-fulfillment: they are a fiction about the kind of peoples and cultures someone like Flaherty wished to find in the world.

Third, documentaries may represent the world in the same way a lawyer may represent a client's interests: they put the case for a particular view or interpretation of evidence before us. In this sense documentaries do not simply stand for others, representing them in ways they could not do themselves, but rather they more actively make a case or argument; they assert what the nature of a matter is to win consent or influence opinion. *The Selling of the Pentagon* represents the case that the U.S. military aggressively fuels the perception of its own indispensability and its enormous need for continued, preferably increased funding. *Nanook of the North* represents the struggle for survival in a harsh, unforgiving climate as the test of a man's mettle and a family's resilience. Through the valor and courage of this family unit, with its familiar gender roles and untroubled relationships, we gain a sense of the dignity of an entire people. *Daisy: The Story of a Facelift* represents the case for the social construction of an individual's image in novel and disturbing ways that combine the effects of social conditioning, medical procedures, and documentary filmmaking practices.

REPRESENTING OTHERS

Documentaries, then, offer aural and visual likenesses or representations of some part of the historical world. They stand for or represent the views of individuals, groups, and institutions. They also make representations, mount arguments, or formulate persuasive strategies of their own, setting out to persuade us to accept their views as appropriate. The degree to which one or more of these aspects of representation come into play will vary from film to film, but the idea of representation itself is central to documentary.

The concept of representation is what compels us to ask the question, "Why Are Ethical Issues Central to Documentary Filmmaking?." This question could also be phrased as "What Do We Do with People When We Make a Documentary?." For fiction films the answer is simple: we ask them to do what we want. "People" are treated as actors. Their social role in the filmmaking process is defined by the traditional role of the actor. Individuals enter into contractual relations to perform for the film; the director has the right, and obligation, to obtain a suitable performance. The actor is valued for the quality of performance delivered, not for fidelity to his or her own everyday behavior and personality. Both the actor and the filmmaker retain certain rights, receive certain compensation, and undertake to fulfill certain expectations. (Using non-actors begins to complicate the issue. Stories that rely on non-actors, such as many of the Italian neo-realist films or some of the New Iranian cinema, often occupy part of the fuzzy territory between fiction and non-fiction, stories of wish-fulfillment and stories of social representation.)

For non-fiction, or documentary, the answer is not quite so simple. "People" are treated as *social actors:* they continue to conduct their lives more or less as they would have done without the presence of a camera. They remain cultural players rather than theatrical performers. Their value to the filmmaker consists not in what a contractual relationship can promise but in what their own lives embody. Their value resides not in the ways in which they disguise or transform their everyday behavior and personality but in the ways in which their everyday behavior and personality serves the needs of the filmmaker. (One parallel between documentary characters and traditional actors is that filmmakers often favor those individuals whose un-schooled behavior before a camera allows them to convey a sense of com-plexity and depth similar to what we value in a trained actor's performance.)

The director's right to a performance is a "right" that, if exercised, threat-ens the sense of authenticity that surrounds the social actor. The degree to which people's behavior and personality change during the making of a film can introduce an element of fiction into the documentary process (the root meaning of fiction is to make or fabricate). Self-consciousness and modifi-cations in behavior can become a form of misrepresentation, or distortion, in one sense, but they also document the ways in which the act of filmmaking alters the reality it sets out to represent. The famous twelve-hour docu-mentary series on the Loud family televised on PBS, *An American Family* (Craig Gilbert, 1972), for example, raised considerable debate about whether the Louds' behavior and their own family relationships were altered by the act of filmmaking or were simply "captured" on film. (The parents di-vorced, their son declared himself gay; these acts figured heavily in the over-all drama of the series.) And if these events came about because of the watchful eye of the camera and the presence of the filmmakers, were these changes encouraged, even if inadvertently, because they added to the dra-matic intensity of the series?

What to do with people? Put differently, the question becomes, "What responsibility do filmmakers have for the effect of their acts on the lives of those filmed?" Most of us think of the invitation to act in a film as a desir-able, even enviable, opportunity. But what if the invitation is not to act in a film but to *be* in a film, to be yourself in a film? What will others think of you; how will they judge you? What aspects of your life may stand revealed that you had not anticipated? What pressures, subtly implied or bluntly asserted, come into play to modify your conduct, and with what consequences? These questions have various answers, according to the situation, but they are of a different order from those posed by most fictions. They place a different burden of responsibility on filmmakers who set out to represent others rather than to portray characters of their own invention. These issues add a level of ethical consideration to documentary that is much less prominent in fiction filmmaking.

Consider Luis Buñuel's *Land without Bread* (1932). In it, Buñuel repre-sents the lives of the citizens of the Hurdanos, a remote, impoverished re-gion of Spain, and he does so with an outrageously judgmental, if not eth-nocentric, voice-over commentary. "Here is another type of idiot," the narrator tells us at one moment as a Hurdanos man raises his head into the frame. At another moment we see a tiny mountain stream as the narrator informs us, "During the summer there is no water other than this, and the inhabitants

In and Out of Africa (Ilisa Barbash and Lucien Taylor, 1992). Photos courtesy of Lucien Taylor. This film adopts a radically different attitude from *Land without Bread.* A high degree of collaboration occurred between filmmakers and subject. Their interaction gives the viewer a sense of "inside" or "behind-the-scenes" knowledge rather than the impression of parody, or possibly disrespect. Middleman and merchant Gabai Barré assures the filmmakers that this piece of "wood," as he calls it, is a good sculpture. The leap in value that an object takes when it goes from "wood" to "art" is the source of Barré's livelihood and of his client's sense of aesthetic pleasure.

use it despite the disgusting filth it carries." Taken at face value, this abusive representation of people takes our breath away. How profoundly disrespectful; how contemptuous! How little regard for the hardships and difficulties of those who confront an inhospitable environment and whom the filmmaker does not choose to nominate for the myth of noble savage as Robert Flaherty did with Nanook.

On the surface of it, *Land without Bread* seems to be an example of the most callous form of reporting, worse even than the hounding of celebrities by paparazzi or the gross misrepresentations of others in "mondo" films such as *Mondo Cane* (Gualtiero Jacopetti and Franco E. Prosperi, 1965). But Luis Buñuel's film gradually suggests a level of self-awareness and calculated effect that might prompt us to wonder if Buñuel is not quite the insensitive cad we initially thought. In one scene, for example, we are told the Hurdanos eat goat meat only when a goat accidentally dies. What we see, though, is

In and Out of Africa
Art gallery owner Wendy Engel assesses Gabai Barré's wares to choose items for her shop. Much of this film's emphasis is on how objects take on new meanings and values when they cross cultural boundaries. Barré plays a vital but customarily unnoticed role in this process. His willingness to let the filmmakers create meanings and values of their own from his activity led them to give Barré a credit as a co-creator of the film.

a goat that falls off a steep mountainside as a puff of gun smoke appears in the corner of the frame. The film suddenly cuts to an overhead view of the dead goat tumbling down the mountainside. If this was an accident, why was a gun fired? And how did Buñuel jump from one position, at some distance from the point where the goat falls, to another, right above the falling goat, while the goat is still in the midst of tumbling down the mountain side? Buñuel's representation of the incident seems to contain a wink: he seems to be hinting to us that this is *not* a factual representation of Hurdanos life as he found it or an unthinkingly offensive judgment of it but a *criticism* or exposé of the forms of representation common to the depiction of traditional peoples. Perhaps the film's comments and judgments are a caricature of the kind of comments found both in typical travelogues of the time and among many potential viewers of such films at the time. Perhaps Buñuel is satirizing a form of representation that uses documentary evidence to reinforce preexisting stereotypes. *Land without Bread,* from this perspective, might be a highly political film that calls the ethics of documentary filmmaking itself into question.

Seen from this perspective, Buñuel sounds, in 1932, an early and important cautionary note against our own tendency to believe literally what we see and hear. We risk missing the irony of a Buñuel or the manipulations of a Riefenstahl. Leni Riefenstahl constructs as flattering a portrait of the National Socialist Party and its leader, Adolf Hitler, at their 1934 Nuremberg rally in *Triumph of the Will* (1935) as Buñuel constructs an unflattering portrait of the Hurdanos in *Land without Bread.* We accept either as a "truthful" representation at our own peril. Buñuel may be among the first filmmakers to explicitly raise the issue of the ethics of documentary filmmaking, but he is hardly the last.

Ethics exist to govern the conduct of groups regarding matters for which hard and fast rules, or laws, will not suffice. Should we tell someone we film that they risk making a fool of themselves or that there will be many who will judge their conduct negatively? Should Ross McElwee have explained to the women he films, in *Sherman's March* (1985), as they interact with him during his journey through the South, that many viewers will see them as examples of coquettish, heterosexually obsessed Southern "belles"? Should Michael Moore have told the people of Flint, Michigan, he interviews in *Roger and Me* that he may make them look foolish in order to make General Motors look even worse? Should Jean Rouch have warned the Hausa tribesmen whom he films performing an elaborate possession ceremony in *Les Maîtres Fous* (1955) that their actions may seem bizarre if not barbaric to those not familiar with their customs and practices, despite the interpretative spin his voice-over commentary provides? Should Tanya Ballantyne have warned the husband of the down-and-out family she portrays in *The Things I Cannot Change* (1966) that her record of his behavior could serve as legal evidence against him (when he gets into a street fight, for example)?

These questions all point to the unforeseen effects a documentary film can have on those represented in it. Ethical considerations attempt to minimize harmful effects. Ethics becomes a measure of the ways in which negotiations about the nature of the relationship between filmmaker and subject have consequences for subjects and viewers alike. Filmmakers who set out to represent people whom they do not initially know but who typify or have special knowledge of a problem or issue of interest run the risk of exploiting them. Filmmakers who choose to observe others but not to intervene overtly in their affairs run the risk of altering behavior and events and of having their own human responsiveness called into question. Film-

Triumph of the Will (Leni Riefenstahl, 1935)
In contrast to *The City* (see Chapter 2), *Triumph of the Will* celebrates the power of the assembled, choreographed masses. The coordinated *movement* of the troops and the cadence of the sound track's music make it clear that these city dwellers experience not alienation but ecstasy.

makers who chose to work with people already familiar to them face the challenge of representing common ground responsibly, even if it means sacrificing their own voice or point of view for that of others. Carolyn Strachan and Alessandro Cavadini consciously adopt precisely such a collaborative, self-effacing position in *Two Laws* (1981) as they go about making decisions about everything from subject matter to camera lenses through dialogue with the Aboriginal people whose case to regain title to their ancestral land provides the core of their film.

A common litmus test for many of these ethical issues is the principle of "informed consent." This principle, relied on heavily in anthropology, sociology, medical experimentation, and elsewhere, states that participants in a study should be told of the possible consequences of their participation. To invite someone to join in a medical experiment involving a new drug without telling them that the drug has potentially dangerous side-effects, may not prove an effective treatment, and may or may not be, in fact, a placebo breaches medical ethics. The individual may consent to participate, because they cannot afford the standard drug treatment, for example, but they cannot consent on an informed basis without a conscientious explanation of the design and risks of the experiment itself.

To invite someone to participate in a film about their family, unemployment, the possibilities of romance in the nuclear age (as Ross McElwee describes his goal in *Sherman's March*), or to follow someone through the process of obtaining a facelift as Michael Rubbo does with *Daisy,* poses a less clear-cut issue. Of what consequences or risks should filmmakers inform their subjects? To what extent can the filmmaker honestly reveal his or her intentions or foretell the actual effects of a film?

What is a deceptive practice? Is it acceptable to feign interest in a company's achievements to gain evidence of its unsafe labor practices? Is it appropriate to film illegal acts (using cocaine or stealing cars, say) to make a documentary about a successful but severely stressed businessman or an urban gang? What obligation do documentarians have to their subjects relative to their audience or their conception of the truth? Is it all right to make Miss Michigan look foolish by asking for her opinion about local economic conditions in order to mock the irrelevance of beauty pageants to the damage caused by automotive plant shutdowns in Flint, as Michael Moore does in one scene from *Roger and Me*?

One concrete example of such issues involves a scene from *Hoop Dreams* (1994) in which the filmmakers go with Arthur Agee to a local playground. Arthur is one of the two young men whose hopes of making it to the NBA (National Basketball Association) forms the basis of the film. But as Arthur practices his game in the foreground, the camera records his father engaged in a drug deal in the background. Should the filmmakers have included this scene in the final film? Did it compromise Mr. Agee or risk providing legal evidence against him? To answer these questions, the filmmakers consulted their lawyers, who judged the degree of detail in the image was insufficient to serve as evidence in court, and they discussed the matter with the Agee family itself. They were prepared to remove the scene if anyone in the family wanted it removed. In fact, the family, including Mr. Agee, felt it should stay in. Mr. Agee was subsequently arrested on a drug charge, an event that transformed him, on his release, into a far more responsible father. He felt that the scene would help dramatize his own growth as a parent over the course of time.

Given that most filmmakers act as representatives of those they film or of the institution sponsoring them rather than as community members, tensions often arise between the filmmaker's desire to make a compelling film and the individual's desire to have their social rights and personal dignity

No Lies (Mitchell Block, 1973)

    The "production crew" in action. In *No Lies* a single person shoots the film we see. In this case we may end up wondering if we have been deceived when we learn that the cameraman is not the actual filmmaker. On the other hand, we may decide that Mitchell Block has made a wise decision to employ actors to play the role of a filmmaker and his subject, given the highly intrusive nature of the filmmaker's questioning.

respected. Mitchell Block's film, *No Lies* (1973), makes this point exceptionally clear. The film takes place entirely inside the apartment of a young woman whom the filmmaker visits with his handheld camera. He nonchalantly chats with her as he films, seemingly to practice his shooting skills, until a casual question reveals a traumatic event: the young woman was recently raped. What should the filmmaker do? Stop shooting and console her as a friend? Continue shooting and make a film that might aid our understanding of this form of criminal behavior? The filmmaker opts to continue shooting. His questions become increasingly probing and personal. He expresses doubt whether the rape happened at all, causing the woman considerable distress. Finally, as the short film comes to a close, he seems to realize he has pushed too hard and agrees to stop filming.

    What do we make of the young man's conduct? Block's film would seem grotesquely callous if Mitchell were himself the filmmaker and the events we see entirely authentic. But *No Lies* functions something like *Land without Bread:* it works to call into question the values it initially seems to accept. Block practices a calculated deception in order to make this point: we learn in the final credits that the two social actors are, in fact, trained actors and that their interaction was not spontaneous but scripted. *No Lies* functions like a meta-commentary on the very act of filmmaking itself by suggesting that we as an audience are put in a position similar to the young woman's. We are also subject to the manipulations and maneuvers of the filmmaker, and we, too, can be left unsettled and distressed by them. We are unsettled not only by the on-screen filmmaker's aggressive interrogation of the woman but also by the off-screen filmmaker's (Block's) deliberate misrepresentation of the film's status as a fiction with contractual bonds to its actors. The film becomes, in a sense, a second rape, a new form of abuse, and, more importantly, it becomes a comment on this very form of abuse and the risk of turning people into victims so that we can learn about their suffering and misery.

Ethical issues often arise in relation to the question of "In Documentary, How Should We Treat the People We Film?" because of the degree to which the filmmaker is set apart from those he or she films. Filmmakers, especially journalistic filmmakers, belong to organizations and institutions with their own standards and practices. Even independent filmmakers usually see themselves as professional artists, pursuing a career more than dedicating themselves to representing the interests of a particular group or constituency. Conflict is inevitable under these conditions. Developing a sense of ethical regard becomes a vital part of the documentary filmmaker's professionalism.

FILMMAKERS, PEOPLE, AUDIENCES

"How Should We Treat the People We Film?" is a question that also reminds us of the various ways in which filmmakers can choose to represent others. Very different forms of alliance can take shape between the three-fold interaction among (1) filmmaker, (2) subjects or social actors, and (3) audience or viewers. One convenient way to think about this interaction involves a verbal formulation of the three-way relationship. The most classic formulation is

I speak about *them* to *you.*

I. The filmmaker takes on a personal persona, either directly or through a surrogate. A typical surrogate is the Voice of God commentator, whom we hear speaking in a voice-over but do not see. This anonymous but surrogate voice arose in the 1930s as a convenient way to describe a situation or problem, present an argument, propose a solution, and sometimes to evoke a poetic tone or mood. Films like *Night Mail* (1936) and *Song of Ceylon* (1934) rendered the British postal service and Ceylonese culture, respectively, in a poetic tone that made the transmission of information secondary to the construction of a deferential, somewhat romanticized mood. The Voice of God, and a corresponding voice of authority—someone we see as well as hear who speaks on behalf of the film, such as Roger Mudd in *The Selling of the Pentagon* or Michael Rubbo in *Daisy: The Story of a Facelift*—remains a prevalent feature of documentary film (as well as of television news programming).

Another possibility is for the filmmaker him- or herself to speak, either on camera, as in *Sherman's March* and *Roger and Me,* or off-camera, heard but not seen, as in *The Thin Blue Line* (1987), Errol Morris's film about a man wrongfully convicted of murder, and *Reassemblage* (1982), Trinh T. Minh-ha's film about the problems and conventions of ethnographic film. In these cases the filmmaker becomes a persona or character within their own film as well as the maker of the film. Their character may be thinly developed, as in the case of *Reassemblage,* where we learn very little about Trinh herself, or quite richly developed, as in the case of *Roger and Me,* where filmmaker Michael Moore portrays a socially conscious nebbish who will do whatever is necessary to get to the bottom of pressing social concerns, a persona also evident in later work: *TV Nation* (1994), *Pets or Meat* (1992), *The Big One* (1997), and *Bowling for Columbine* (2002).

Speaking in the first person edges the documentary form toward the diary, essay, and aspects of avant-garde or experimental film and video. The emphasis may shift from convincing the audience of a particular point of view or approach to a problem to the representation of a personal, clearly subjective view of things. From persuasion the emphasis shifts to expression. What gets expressed is the filmmaker's own personal perspective and unique view of things. What makes it a documentary is that this expressiveness remains coupled to representations about the social, historical world that are addressed to viewers. Much of the "new journalism" (Hunter Thompson's *Slouching toward Las Vegas,* for example) and documentary filmmaking that was influenced by it, such as Michael Rubbo's, stressed just this combination of an idiosyncratic or personal voice coupled to reporting on a topical issue.

Speak about. The filmmaker represents others. The sense of speaking about a topic or issue, a people or individual lends an air of civic importance to the effort. Speaking about something may involve telling a story, creating a poetic mood, or constructing a narrative, such as the story of how the mail gets to its destination or how Nanook manages to find food for his family, but it also implies a content-oriented desire to convey information, rely on facts, and make points about the world we share. Compared to "What story shall I tell?" the question "What shall I speak about?" turns our minds to the public sphere and to the social act of speaking to others on a topic of common interest. Not all documentaries adopt this posture, but it is among the most common ways of structuring a documentary film.

Them. The third person pronoun implies a separation between speaker and subject. The I who speaks is not identical with those of whom it speaks. We as an audience receive a sense that the subjects in the film are placed there for our examination and edification. They may be rendered as rich, full-rounded individuals with complex psychologies of their own, a tendency particularly noticeable in observational documentaries (discussed in Chapter 6), but just as often they seem to come before us as examples or illustrations, evidence of a condition or event that has happened in the world. This can seem reductive and diminishing, but it can also be highly compelling and effective. Rodney King, for example, does not emerge as a full-blown character in the raw footage of his beating at the hands of the Los Angeles police, but the power and shock of the footage depends more on its claim to authenticity than on its portrayal of a personality. Even in these cases, "they" remain at a remove, not to be represented to us with the complexity we might find in a fiction. For some this diminishes the pleasure of documentary; at the least, it suggests that we look elsewhere for pleasure and satisfaction in documentary representation.

You. Like "them," "you" suggests a separation. One person speaks and another listens. A filmmaker speaks and an audience attends. Documentary, in this sense, belongs to an *institutional* discourse or framework. People with a particular form of expertise, documentary filmmakers, address us as members of a general public or some specific element of it. As an audience we are typically separated from both the act of representation and the subject of representation. We occupy a different social time and space from either; we have a role and identity of our own as viewers and audience members that is itself a distinct aspect of our own social persona: we attend the film as viewers, audience members, even though part of our reason for doing so may be that the film will speak about people and issues whose actual life experience compares or contrasts with our own. "They" too may be husbands and wives, lawyers and accountants, students or athletes, and their actions may prove instructive to our own in more direct ways than we expect from fiction. We need not ask if real army recruits are like Demi

Moore's character in *G.I. Jane* (Ridley Scott, 1997); we can see real recruits in Joan Churchill and Nick Broomfield's documentary, *Soldier Girls* (1980). We may draw analogies about human conduct from the dramatic events in *G.I. Jane,* but we can draw conclusions about human conduct from the actual events represented in *Soldier Girls.*

"You" becomes activated as an audience when the filmmaker conveys a sense that he or she is indeed addressing us, that the film reaches us in some way. Without this sense of activation we may be present *at* but not attend *to* the film. Filmmakers must find a way to activate our sense of ourselves both as the one to whom the filmmaker speaks (about someone or something else) and as members of a group or collectivity, an audience for whom this topic bears importance. The usual means of doing this is by recourse to techniques of rhetoric (discussed in Chapter 4).

Rhetoric is the form of speech used to persuade or convince others about an issue for which no clear-cut, unequivocal answer or solution exists. Guilt and innocence in the judicial process often hinges not simply on evidence but on the convincingness of the arguments made regarding the interpretation of the evidence. The O.J. Simpson trial was a prime example, given that there was a considerable amount of incriminating evidence. Even so, the defense lawyers made a successful argument that this evidence might have been fabricated and that its value was suspect. A judgment about the truth, the verdict, lay outside the realms of science, poetry or story-telling. It came to pass within the arena of rhetorical engagement, the arena in which most documentary operates as well.

Rhetoric differs from reason as used to arrive at a mathematical proof or scientific conclusion; these logical processes contain their own self-evident proof, and they usually address problems for which one and only one solution exists, given a specific set of initial assumptions. Rhetoric also differs from poetic or narrative speech, which aims less to convince us about a social concern than to provide us with an aesthetic experience or involvement in an imaginary world. Rhetoric, though, may readily make use of poetic, narrative, or logical elements. They are, however, put in the service of convincing us about an issue for which more than one point of view or conclusion is possible.

Georges Franju's *Blood of the Beasts* (1949), for example, uses irony and surreal imagery to persuade us of the strangeness of slaughtering cattle, in 1940s France, so that we may enjoy their flesh, whereas Frederick Wiseman's *Meat* (1976) observes the activities in a Midwestern slaughterhouse with considerable detachment, in 1970s America, to show us the routine nature of the human interactions among workers and supervisors, men and animals. Wiseman focuses on issues of labor, Franju on issues of custom.

Wiseman regards the workers as typical or representative wage-earners in a labor-management context, Franju regards the workers as mythical figures who perform astounding feats. Specific stylistic and rhetorical choices operate in both cases to activate our sense of being addressed and engaged in specific ways.

I speak about them to you may be the most common formulation of the three-way relationship among filmmaker, subject, and audience, but it is certainly not the only one. A chart could be made that would include all of the variations in pronouns that this sentence allows for. Each variation would carry a different set of implications for the relationships among filmmakers, subjects, and viewers. A few of the more pertinent ones are sketched out here:

It speaks about them or it to us. This formulation betrays a sense of separation, if not alienation, between the speaker and the audience. The film or video appears to arrive, addressed to us, from a source that lacks individuality. It addresses a subject likewise separated from us, even if it lies within some proximity. This formulation characterizes what we might call an institutional discourse, in which the film, often by means of a voice-over commentary, perhaps even a Voice of God commentator with a deep, male voice, informs us about some aspect of the world in an impersonal but authoritative manner.

The film appears to speak to "us" but addresses itself to a largely undifferentiated audience. We should attend to the film because it assumes we want or need to know about its topic. Informational films and advertising messages, including trailers for forthcoming films, often adopt this framework. *The River,* for example, not only uses a stentorian male commentator, it constantly refers to what "we" have done to the land and what "we" can do to change things, even though the actual culprit is quite removed from you or me today.

Films of this sort seem to arrive from nowhere in particular. They are not the work of a specific individual whom we could call the filmmaker; they are often not even the work of an institution as identifiable as CNN news with its on-camera representatives (anchor men and women, reporters, interviewees). They arrive as the utterances of an "it" that remains impersonal and unidentifiable. (The "it" may be the scientific community, the medical establishment, the government, or the advertising industry, for example.) This "it" speaks to an "us" that may be a function more of demographics than of collectivity. Such works convey information, assign values, or urge actions that invite us to find a sense of commonality within a framework that may be dryly factual or emotionally charged, but it is seldom organized to move beyond a statistical, generic, or abstract conception of who "we" are.

I or We speak about us to you. This formulation moves the filmmaker from a position of separation from those he or she represents to a position of commonality with them. Filmmaker and subject are of the same stock. In anthropological filmmaking the turn to this formulation goes by the name of "auto-ethnography": it refers to the efforts of indigenous people to make their films and videos about their own culture so that they may represent it to "us," those who remain outside. The Kayapo Indians of the Amazon river basin have been exceptionally active in this practice, using their videos to lobby Brazilian politicians for policies that will protect their homeland from development and exploitation.

Often the sense of commonality hinges around the representing of family. Alan Berliner, for example, has made two exceptional films about his own father, *Intimate Stranger* (1992) and *Nobody's Business* (1996). Marlene Booth has made an intriguing film about her family's experience as predominantly assimilated Jews living in Iowa, *Yidl in the Middle* (1998). After discovering in her adulthood that her father was Jewish, Lisa Lewenz travels to Europe to understand how the family lived in 1930s Germany in *Letter without Words* (1999). In a film that mixes staged enactments with documentary representations, Camille Billops describes what happens when she and the now grown daughter whom she gave up for adoption as a child reunite in *Finding Christa* (1991).

By speaking about an "us" that includes the filmmaker these films achieve a degree of intimacy that can be quite compelling.

One of the most striking examples of the first-person voice in a documentary is Marlon Riggs's extraordinary video, *Tongues Untied* (1989). In it Riggs speaks about what it means to be a black, gay male. He and other social actors speak on and off camera about their experiences as black, gay men. Some recite poetry, some recount stories, some participate in sketches and reenactments. These are not the standard voices of authority. They are not stripped of ethnic identity or colloquial idiosyncrasy to approximate the dominant norm of standard, white, non-regional English. Inflection and rhythm, cadence and style attest to the power of individual perception and the strength of personal expression that makes *Tongues Untied* one of the milestones in recent documentary production.

These and other formulations convey some sense of how the filmmaker adopts a specific position in relation to those represented in the film and those to whom the film is addressed. This position requires negotiation and consent. It supplies evidence of the ethical considerations that went into the film's conception. It suggests what kind of relationship the viewer is expected to have with the film by suggesting what kind of relationship we are expected to have with the filmmaker and his or her subjects. To ask what we do with people when we make a documentary film involves asking what we do with filmmakers and viewers as well as with subjects. Assumptions about the relationships that should exist among all three go a long way toward determining what kind of documentary film or video results, the quality of the relationship it has to its subjects, and the effect it has on an audience. Assumptions vary considerably, as we shall see, but the underlying question of what we do with people persists as a fundamental issue for the ethics of documentary filmmaking.

Chapter 2

How Do Documentaries Differ from Other Types of Film?

WORKING OUT A DEFINITION

"Documentary" can be no more easily defined than "love" or "culture." Its meaning cannot be reduced to a dictionary definition in the way that "temperature" or "table salt" can be. Its definition is not self-contained in the way that the definition of "table salt" is contained by saying that it is a chemical compound made up of one atom of sodium and one of chlorine ($NaCl$). The definition of "documentary" is always relational or comparative. Just as love takes on meaning in contrast to indifference or hate, and culture takes on meaning in contrast to barbarism or chaos, documentary takes on meaning in contrast to fiction film or experimental and avant-garde film.

Were documentary a *reproduction* of reality, these problems would be far less acute. We would then simply have a replica or copy of something that already existed. But documentary is not a reproduction of reality, it is a *representation* of the world we already occupy. It stands for a particular view of the world, one we may never have encountered before even if the aspects of the world that is represented are familiar to us. We judge a reproduction by its fidelity to the original—its capacity to look like, act like, and serve the same purposes as the original. We judge a representation more by the nature of the pleasure it offers, the value of the insight or knowledge it provides, and the quality of the orientation or disposition, tone or perspective it instills. We ask more of a representation than we do of a reproduction.

This was quickly realized in photography. Henry Peach Robinson's 1896 guide to good photography, *The Elements of a Pictorial Photograph,* warned beginners that "Imitative illusion is a trap for the vulgar. A scene may, and should be represented truthfully, but some artists can see and represent more and greater truths than every passer-by will notice. . . . The photographer who sees most will represent more truths more truthfully than another." (Robinson himself was a highly regarded photographer who sometimes combined more than one negative to produce the desired effect in his finished prints.)

Documentary is what we might call a "fuzzy concept." Not all films that count as documentaries bear a close resemblance to each other just, as many disparate sorts of transportation devices can count as a "vehicle." As the formulations we looked at in Chapter 1 already suggest, a documentary organized as *It speaks about them to us* will have quite different qualities and affect from one organized as *We speak about us to them.* But these differences are just the beginning. As we will see, there are a number of other ways in which documentaries differ from each other, even though we continue to think of the whole array of films as documentary despite the differences.

Documentaries adopt no fixed inventory of techniques, address no one set of issues, display no single set of forms or styles. Not all documentaries exhibit a single set of shared characteristics. Documentary film practice is an arena in which things change. Alternative approaches are constantly attempted and then adopted by others or abandoned. Contestation occurs. Prototypical works stand out that others emulate without ever being able to copy or imitate entirely. Test cases appear that challenge the conventions defining the boundaries of documentary film practice. They push the limits and sometimes change them.

More than proclaiming a definition that fixes once and for all what is and is not a documentary, we need to look to examples and prototypes, test cases and innovations as evidence of the broad arena within which documentary operates and evolves. The fuzziness of any definition arises partly because definitions change over time and partly because at any given moment no one definition covers all films that we might consider documentary. The usefulness of prototypes as a definition is that they propose generally exemplary qualities or features without requiring every documentary to exhibit all of them. *Nanook of the North* stands as a prototypical documentary even though many films that share its reliance on a simple quest narrative to organize events, its exemplary or representative individual, and its implication that we can understand larger cultural qualities by understanding individual behavior also reject the romanticism, emphasis on a challenging natural environment, and occasionally patronizing elements of *Nanook.* Indeed, some fiction films, like Vittorio De Sica's *Bicycle Thief* (1947), can also share these qualities with *Nanook* without being considered a documentary at all.

New prototypes such as *Night Mail* or the *Why We Fight* (1942–45) series may reject previously dominant qualities in films such as *Nanook* in favor of new ones such as a voice-over commentary or a deflection away from an individual social actor to representative types or groups and the unfolding of an event, process, or historical development in broader, more impersonal terms (poetically or prosaically rendered). Similarly, if we regard *High School* as a prototype or model of observational cinema we can note how it refused to provide any voice-over commentary whatsoever even though voice-over commentary had been considered one of the most characteristic qualities of documentary up until the 1960s.

We can get more of a handle on how to define documentary by approaching it from four different angles: institutions, practitioners, texts (films and videos), and audience.

AN INSTITUTIONAL FRAMEWORK

It may seem circular, but one way to define documentary is to say, "Documentaries are what the organizations and institutions that produce them make." If John Grierson calls *Night Mail* a documentary or if the Discovery Channel calls a program a documentary, then these items come labeled as documentary before any work on the part of the viewer or critic begins. This is similar to saying that the Hollywood feature film is what the Hollywood studio system produces. This definition, despite its circularity, functions as an initial cue that a given work can be considered as a documentary. The context provides the cue; we would be foolish to ignore it even if this form of definition is less than exhaustive. Given that the sponsor is the National Film Board of Canada, Fox TV news, the History Channel, or Michael Moore, we make certain assumptions about the film's documentary status and its degree of likely objectivity, reliability, and credibility. We make assumptions about its non-fiction status and its reference to our shared historical world rather than a world imagined by the filmmaker.

The segments that make up the CBS news program *60 Minutes,* for example, are normally considered examples of journalistic reporting first and foremost simply because that is the kind of program *60 Minutes* is. We assume that the segments refer to actual people and events, that standards of journalistic objectivity will be met, that we can rely on each story to be both entertaining and informative, and that any claims made will be backed up by a credible display of evidence. Shown in another setting, these episodes might seem more like melodramas or docudramas, based on the emotional intensities achieved and the high degree of constructedness to the encounters that take place, but these alternatives dim when the entire institutional framework functions to assure us that they are, in fact, documentary reportage.

Similarly, films that get shown on Public Broadcasting System (PBS) series such as *POV* and *Frontline* are considered documentaries because these series routinely feature documentaries. Shows that appear on the Discovery Channel are, unless proven otherwise, treated as documentaries because this channel is dedicated to broadcasting documentary material. Knowing where a given film or video comes from, or on what channel it is shown, provides an important first cue to how we should classify it.

Films like *This Is Spinal Tap* (Rob Reiner, 1982) build this type of institutional framing into the film itself in a mischievous or ironic way: the film announces itself to be a documentary, only to prove to be a fabrication or simulation of a documentary. If we take its own self-description seriously, we will believe that the group Spinal Tap is an actual rock group. Since one had to be created for the film, just as a "Blair witch" had to be created for *The Blair Witch Project,* we will not be wrong. What we may fail to realize is that neither the rock group nor the witch had any existence whatsoever prior to the production of these films. Such works have come to be called "mockumentaries" or "pseudo-documentaries." Much of their ironic impact depends on their ability to coax at least partial belief from us that what we see is a documentary because that is what we are told we see.

An institutional framework also imposes an institutional way of seeing and speaking, which functions as a set of limits, or conventions, for the filmmaker and audience alike. To say "it goes without saying" that a documentary will have a voice-over commentary, or "everyone knows" that a documentary must present both sides of the question is to say what is usually the case within a specific institutional framework. Voice-over commentary, sometimes poetic, sometimes factual but almost omnipresent, was a strong convention within the government-sponsored film production units headed by John Grierson in 1930s Britain, and reportorial balance, in the sense of not openly taking sides but not always in the sense of covering all possible points of view, prevails among the news divisions of network television companies today.

For a long time, it was also taken for granted that documentaries could

Flower Films presents
Always for Pleasure
A film by **Les Blank**
10341 San Pablo Ave
El Cerrito, California 94530

Chief of the Black Eagles,
New Orleans
Mardi Gras Indian Tribe

Always for Pleasure (Les Blank, 1978). Photo courtesy of Les Blank and Flower Films.

Les Blank's films are difficult to place. Books on documentary and ethnographic film sometimes neglect his work even though films such as this one, on aspects of Mardi Gras in New Orleans, exhibit important characteristics of each of these types of filmmaking. Blank, like most accomplished documentary filmmakers, does not follow rules or protocols; he does not concern himself with where and how his films fit into categories. His avoidance of voice-over commentary, political perspectives, identifiable problems, and potential solutions follows from a descriptive emphasis on affirmative, often exuberant, forms of experience.

talk about anything in the world except themselves. Reflexive strategies that call the very act of representation into question unsettle the assumption that documentary builds on the ability of film to capture reality. To remind viewers of the construction of the reality we behold, of the *creative* element in John Grierson's famous definition of documentary as "the creative treatment of actuality" undercuts the very claim to truth and authenticity on which the documentary depends. If we cannot take its images as visible evidence of the nature of a particular part of the historical world, of what can we take them? By suppressing this question, the institutional framework for documentary suppresses much of the complexity in the relationship between representation and reality, but it also achieves a clarity or simplicity that implies that documentaries achieve direct, truthful access to the real. This functions as one of the prime attractions of the form.

Along with sponsoring agencies for the production of documentary work, a distinct circuit of distributors and exhibitors function to support the circulation of these films. These agencies operate tangentially to the dominant chains of film theaters that specialize in mainstream fiction films. Sometimes one organization, such as the television news networks, produces, distributes, and exhibits documentary work; sometimes the distributors are distinct entities, such as the Discovery Channel to a large degree or specialty film distributors like Women Make Movies, New Day Films, or Third World Newsreel, that acquire the documentaries produced by others. Other agencies, such as the Corporation for Public Broadcasting and the British Film Institute, provide financial support for documentary as well as other types of work. Still others, such as the Film Arts Foundation, the Foundation for Independent Film and Video, the European Documentary Film Institute, or the International Documentary Association, provide professional support for documentary filmmakers themselves, much as the Academy of Motion Picture Arts and Sciences does for Hollywood filmmakers.

A COMMUNITY OF PRACTITIONERS

Those who make documentary films, like the institutions that support them, hold certain assumptions and expectations about what they do. Although every institutional framework imposes limits and conventions, individual filmmakers need not entirely accept them. The tension between established expectations and individual innovation proves a frequent source of change.

Documentary filmmakers share a common, self-chosen mandate to represent the historical world rather than to imaginatively invent alternative ones. They gather at specialized film festivals such as the Hot Springs Documentary Film Festival (U.S.A.), the Yamagata Documentary Film Festival (Japan), or the Amsterdam International Documentary Film Festival (the Netherlands), and they contribute articles and interviews to many of the same journals, such as *Release Print, Documentary,* and *Dox.* They debate social issues such as the effects of pollution and the nature of sexual identity and explore technical concerns such as the authenticity of archival footage and the consequences of digital technology.

Documentary practitioners speak a common language regarding what they do. Like other professionals, documentary filmmakers have a vocabulary, or jargon, of their own. It may range from the suitability of various film stocks for different situations to the techniques of recording location sound, and from the ethics of observing others to the pragmatics of finding distribution and negotiating contracts for their work. Documentary practitioners share distinct but common problems—from developing ethically sound relationships with their subjects to reaching a specific audience, for example—that distinguish them from other filmmakers.

These commonalities give documentary filmmakers a shared sense of purpose despite the ways in which they may also compete for the same funding or distributors. Individual practitioners will shape or transform the traditions they inherit, but they do so in dialogue with others who share their sense of mission. This definition of the documentary contributes to its fuzzy but distinguishable outline. It confirms the historical variability of the form: our understanding of what is a documentary changes as those who make documentaries change their idea of what it is they make. What might begin as a test case or apparent anomaly, as early observational films such as *Les Racquetteurs* (1958), *Chronicle of a Summer* (1960), or *Primary* (1960) did, may fade away as a failed deviation or, as in this example, come to be regarded as transformative innovations leading to a new standard of accepted practice. Documentary has never been only one thing. Later, in Chapter 5, we will trace some of the development of different modes of documentary filmmaking. For now we can use this history of a changing sense of what counts as a documentary as a sign of the variable, open-ended, dynamic quality of the form itself. It is the practitioners themselves, through their engagement with institutions, critics, subjects, and audiences, that generate this sense of dynamic change.

A CORPUS OF TEXTS

The films that make up the documentary tradition are another way to define the form. For a start, we can consider documentary a genre like the western or the science-fiction film. To belong to the genre a film has to exhibit characteristics shared by films already regarded as documentaries or westerns. Norms and conventions come into play for documentary that help distinguish it: the use of a Voice-of-God commentary, interviews, location sound recording, cutaways from a given scene to provide images that illustrate or complicate a point made within the scene, and a reliance on social actors, or people in their everyday roles and activities, as the central characters of the film are among those that are common to many documentaries.

Another convention is the prevalence of an informing logic that organizes the film in relation to the representations it makes about the historical world. A typical form of organization is that of problem solving. This structure can resemble a story, particularly a detective story: the film begins by establishing a problem or issue, then conveys something of the background to the issue, and follows this with an examination of its current severity or complexity. This presentation then leads to a concluding recommendation or solution that the viewer is encouraged to endorse or adopt personally.

The City (Ralph Steiner and Willard Van Dyke, 1939) exhibits a prototypical approach to this idea of a documentary logic. It establishes, through a montage of scenes that include fast motion clips of frenzied city living, that urban existence has become a burden more than a joy. The film presents this as a pervasive problem that saps people of their energy and zest for life. (It also tends to ignore related issues such as whether urban stress correlates with class or race.) What is the solution? The final section provides one: the carefully planned suburban community where every family has the space and tranquility needed as a restorative to the hustle and bustle of urban living (the film assumes the nuclear family and the detached home are the building blocks of community). The City, a classic in the documentary film genre, was sponsored by the American Institute of City Planners, a group with some real stake in the suburbanization of the American landscape, just as The River, which championed the efforts of the Tennessee Valley Authority as the solution to ravages of ruinous floods, was sponsored by the federal government in order to gain popular support for the TVA.

A variation on the problem/solution style of logic occurs in Triumph of the Will (1935). Speeches by Nazi party leaders refer to Germany's disarray following World War I while these same leaders nominate themselves, their party, and, above all, Adolf Hitler as the solution to the problems of national humiliation and economic collapse. The film glosses over the actual problems; instead it devotes the vast amount of its energy to urging its viewers (especially its initial viewers in 1930s Germany) to endorse the efforts of the Nazi party and its leader to redeem Germany and put it on the path to recovery, prosperity, and power. The film assumes that its contemporary audience was well aware of the nature and severity of the problem. More crucial to Leni Riefenstahl than archival footage of Germany's defeat in World War I, a review of the humiliating terms imposed by the Treaty of Versailles, or evidence of the hardships worked by skyrocketing inflation was a vivid, compelling portrait of the Nazi party, and Hitler, at their carefully choreographed best.

The logic organizing a documentary film supports an underlying argument, assertion, or claim about the historical world that gives this genre its sense of particularity. We expect to engage with films that engage with the world. This engagement and logic frees the documentary from some of the conventions relied upon to establish an imaginary world. Continuity editing,

The City (Ralph Steiner and Willard Van Dyke, 1939). Photo courtesy of National Archives.
Images of vast numbers of similar objects, and people, help make *The City*'s point: urban design has fallen behind human need.

for example, which works to make the cuts between shots in a typical fiction
film scene invisible, has a lower priority. We can assume that what is
achieved by continuity editing in fiction is achieved by history in documentary film: things share relationships in time and space not because of the
editing but because of their actual, historical linkages. Editing in documentary often seeks to demonstrate these linkages. The demonstration may be
convincing or implausible, accurate or distorted, but it occurs in relation to
situations and events with which we are already familiar, or for which we
can find other sources of information. Documentary is therefore much less
reliant on continuity editing to establish the credibility of the world it refers
to than is fiction.

Documentary film, in fact, often displays a wider array of disparate shots
and scenes than fiction, an array yoked together less by a narrative organized around a central character than by a rhetoric organized around a controlling logic or argument. Characters, or social actors, may come and go,
offering information, giving testimony, providing evidence. Places and things
may appear and disappear as they are brought forward in support of the

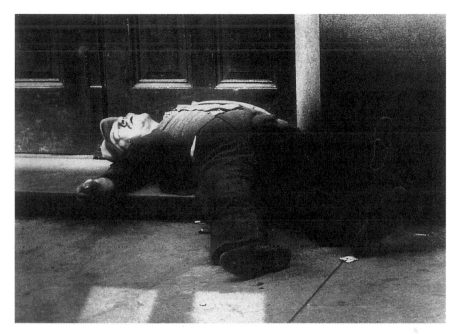

The City (Ralph Steiner and Willard Van Dyke, 1939). Photo courtesy of National Archives.
Images of individuals such as this one do not affirm human triumph in a congested, frenzied environment. They register defeat and prepare for the film's solution: planned, green belt communities.

film's point of view or perspective. A logic of implication bridges these leaps from one person or place to another.

If, for example, we jump from a woman sitting in her home describing what it was like to work as a welder during World War II to a shot from a 1940s newsreel of a shipyard, the cut implies that the second shot illustrates the type of workplace and the kind of work the woman in the first shot describes. The cut hardly seems disruptive at all even though there is no spatial or temporal continuity between the two shots.

Cuts like this occur over and over in Connie Field's *The Life and Times of Rosie the Riveter* (1980); they do not confuse us because they support an evolving story and consistent argument about how women were first actively recruited to fill jobs left vacant by men called into the military and then, when the men returned, actively discouraged from remaining in the work force. The shots fall into place in relation to what the women director Field interviews have to say. We attend to what they say and what we see serves to support, amplify, illustrate, or otherwise relate to the stories they tell and the line of argument Field follows in support of what they say.

Instead of continuity editing, we might call this form of documentary editing evidentiary. Instead of organizing cuts within a scene to present a sense of a single, unified time and space in which we follow the actions of central characters, evidentiary editing organizes cuts within a scene to present the impression of a single, convincing argument supported by a logic. Instead of cutting from one shot of a character approaching a door to a second shot of the same character entering the room on the far side of the door, a more typical documentary film cut would be from a close-up of a bottle of champagne being broken across the bow of ship to a long shot of a ship, perhaps an entirely different ship, being launched into the sea. The two shots may have been made years or continents apart, but they contribute to the representation of a single process rather than the development of an individual character.

Pursuing the example provided by *Rosie the Riveter,* some choices for documenting a given topic, such as shipbuilding, can be sketched out. The film may (1) describe a process like shipbuilding poetically or simply chronologically, (2) present an argument about shipbuilding—that women were urged to take up work and then discouraged from continuing it during and after World War II, for example, (3) stress the filmmaker's response to the process of shipbuilding, representing it as an awesome feat of technical skill or a nightmare of hazards and hardships, or (4) tell the story of a particular, perhaps typical, worker in a shipyard, hinting at the larger meanings this one story implies. In each case editing serves an evidentiary function. It not only furthers our involvement in the unfolding of the film but supports the kinds of claims or assertions the film makes about our world. We tend to assess the organization of a documentary in terms of the persuasiveness or convincingness of its representations rather than the plausibility or fascination of its fabrications.

A great deal of this persuasiveness stems from the sound track in documentary, whereas a great deal of our identification with a fictional world and its characters depends on the literal views we have of them. Arguments call for a logic that words are better able to convey than are images. Images lack tense and a negative form, for example. We can make a sign that says, "No Smoking," but we typically convey this requirement in images by the convention of putting a slash through an image of a cigarette. To decide to *not* show an image of a cigarette at all would not in any way communicate the same meaning as a sign declaring the injunction, "No Smoking." The convention of a slash mark through an image to mean "No" or "Not" is very hard to adapt to filmmaking. Whether it is through what we hear a commentator tell us about the film's subject, what social actors tell us directly via interviews, or what we overhear social actors say among themselves as the camera observes them, documentaries rely heavily on the spoken

The Life and Times of Rosie the Riveter (Connie Field, 1980). Women welders at the Landers, Frary and Clark Plant, Connecticut, 1943. Photograph by Gordon Parks.

Rosie the Riveter is a brilliant example of a film that uses historical film material not to confirm the truth of a situation but to demonstrate how truth claims can be made to serve political goals. In this case the historical footage was designed to encourage women to enter the work force during World War II and then to leave the work force when the soldiers returned from the war. Thanks to Field's editing, the contortions of logic required for this task are often hilariously blatant. (Few government films even acknowledged the presence of African-American women in the work force, giving this particular photo extra value.)

word. Speech fleshes out our sense of the world. An event recounted becomes history reclaimed.

Like other genres, documentaries go through phases or periods. Different countries and regions have different documentary traditions and styles of their own. European and Latin American documentary filmmakers, for example, favor subjective and openly rhetorical forms such as we find in Luis Buñuel's *Land without Bread* or Chris Marker's *San Soleil* (1982), whereas British and North American filmmakers have placed more emphasis on objective and observational forms such as the "two sides of every argument" tone to much journalistic reporting and the highly non-interventionist approach of Frederick Wiseman in films like *High School* (1968), *Hospital* (1970), and *Model* (1980).

Documentary, like fiction film, has had its movements. Among them we could include the documentary work by Dziga Vertov, Esther Shub, Victor Turin, and others working in the Soviet Union in the 1920s and early 1930s; the Free Cinema of 1950s Britain, when Lindsay Anderson, Karel Reisz, Tony Richardson, and others took a fresh, unadorned look at contemporary British life in films such as *Every Day except Christmas* (1957),

Momma Don't Allow (1956), and *We Are the Lambeth Boys* (1958), and the observational filmmaking of people such as Frederick Wiseman, the Maysles brothers, and Drew Associates (principally Richard Drew, D. A. Pennebaker, and Richard Leacock) in 1960s America.

A movement arises from a group of films made by individuals who share a common outlook or approach. This is often done consciously through manifestoes and other statements such as Dziga Vertov's "WE: Variant of a Manifesto" and "Kino Eye," which declared open warfare on scripted and acted films. These essays defined the principles and goals to which films like *The Man with a Movie Camera* (1929) and *Enthusiasm* (1930) gave tangible expression. Lindsay Anderson's essay in *Sight and Sound* magazine in 1956, "Stand Up! Stand Up!" urged a vivid sense of social commitment for documentary filmmaking. He defined the principles and goals of a poetic but gritty representation of everyday, working-class reality freed from the sense of civic responsibility for "solutions" to class difference itself that had made work produced by John Grierson in the 1930s seem a handmaiden of the British government's policies of limited amelioration.

Free Cinema advocates and practitioners sought a cinema free of a government's propaganda needs, a sponsor's purse strings, or a genre's established conventions. Their movement helped stimulate the revival of the British feature film built around similar principles of the unvarnished representation of working people and an irreverent attitude toward social and cinematic conventions. The "Angry Young Men" of 1950s Britain gave us *Saturday Night and Sunday Morning* (Karel Reisz, 1960), *The Loneliness of the Long Distance Runner* (Tony Richardson, 1962), and *This Sporting Life* (Lindsay Anderson, 1963) in a spirit that drew on sensibilities quite similar to the Free Cinema of the time. (Many of those who began in documentary production went on to make the feature films that were characterized as "kitchen sink" dramas of working-class life.)

Documentary falls into periods as well as movements. These, too, help give it definition and differentiate it from other types of films with different movements and periodizations. The period of the 1930s, for example, saw much documentary work take on a newsreel quality as part of a Depression-era sensibility and a renewed political emphasis on social and economic issues. The 1960s saw the introduction of lightweight, hand-held cameras that could be used together with synchronous sound. Filmmakers acquired the mobility and responsiveness that allowed them to follow social actors in their everyday routines. The options to observe intimate or crisis-laden behavior at a distance or to interact in a more directly participatory manner with their subjects both became highly possible. The 1960s were thus a period in which the ideas of a rigorously observational and of a far more participatory cinema predominated.

In the 1970s, documentary frequently returned to the past through the use of archival film material and contemporary interviews to put a new perspective on past events or events leading up to current issues. (Historical perspective was an element found missing from observational and participatory filmmaking.) Emile de Antonio's *In the Year of the Pig* (1969) provided the model or prototype that many others emulated. De Antonio combined a rich variety of archival source material with trenchant interviews to recount the history of Vietnam and the war there in a way radically at odds with the American government's official version of the war. *With Babies and Banners* (1977), about a 1930s automobile factory strike but told from the women's point of view; *Union Maids* (1976), about union organizing struggles in different industries; and *The Life and Times of Rosie the Riveter* (1980), about women's role in the work force during and after World War II, are but three examples that draw on de Antonio's example and inflect it to address issues of women's history. As such they were also part of a broad tendency in the 1960s and 1970s to tell "history from below," as lived and experienced by ordinary but articulate people rather than "history from above," based on the deeds of leaders and the knowledge of experts.

Periods and movements characterize documentary, but so does a series of modes of documentary film production that, once in operation, remain a viable way of making a documentary film despite national variations and period inflections. (Observational filmmaking may have begun in the 1960s, for example, but it remains an important resource in the 1990s, long after the period of its greatest prevalence.) Modes, too, distinguish documentary film from other types of film. Modes come close to movements in that a new mode usually has its champions as well as its principles or goals, but it also tends to have a broader base of support so that different movements can derive from a single mode. In fact, this book will identify six primary modes of documentary filmmaking. They are discussed further in Chapter 6.

Poetic Mode: emphasizes visual associations, tonal or rhythmic qualities, descriptive passages, and formal organization. Examples: *The Bridge* (1928), *Song of Ceylon* (1934), *Listen to Britain* (1941), *Night and Fog* (1955), *Koyaanisqatsi* (1983). This mode bears a close proximity to experimental, personal, or avant-garde filmmaking.

Expository Mode: emphasizes verbal commentary and an argumentative logic. Examples: *The Plow That Broke the Plains* (1936), *Trance and Dance in Bali* (1952), *Spanish Earth* (1937), *Les Maîtres Fous* (1955), television news. This is the mode that most people identify with documentary in general.

Observational Mode: emphasizes a direct engagement with the everyday life of subjects as observed by an unobtrusive camera. Examples: *High School* (1968), *Salesman* (1969), *Primary* (1960), the *Netsilik Eskimo* series (1967–68), *Soldier Girls* (1980).

Participatory Mode: emphasizes the interaction between filmmaker and subject. Filming takes place by means of interviews or other forms of even more direct involvement. Often coupled with archival footage to examine historical issues. Examples: *Chronicle of a Summer* (1960), *Solovky Power* (1988), *Shoah* (1985), *The Sorrow and the Pity* (1970), *Kurt and Courtney* (1998).

Reflexive Mode: calls attention to the assumptions and conventions that govern documentary filmmaking. Increases our awareness of the constructedness of the film's representation of reality. Examples: *The Man with a Movie Camera* (1929), *Land without Bread* (1932), *The Ax Fight* (1971), *The War Game* (1966), *Reassemblage* (1982).

Performative Mode: emphasizes the subjective or expressive aspect of the filmmaker's own engagement with the subject and an audience's responsiveness to this engagement. Rejects notions of objectivity in favor of evocation and affect. Examples: *Unfinished Diary* (1983), *History and Memory* (1991), *The Act of Seeing with One's Own Eyes* (1971), *Tongues Untied* (1989), and reality TV shows such as *Cops* (as a degraded example of the mode). The films in this mode all share qualities with the experimental, personal, and avant-garde, but with a strong emphasis on their emotional and social impact on an audience.

Modes come into prominence at a given time and place, but they persist and become more pervasive than movements. Each mode may arise partly as a response to perceived limitations in previous modes, partly as a response to technological possibilities, and partly as a response to a changing social context. Once established, though, modes overlap and intermingle. Individual films can be characterized by the mode that seems most influential to their organization, but individual films can also "mix and match" modes as the occasion demands. Expository documentaries, for example, remain a staple form, particularly on television, where the idea of a voice-over commentary seems obligatory, be it for A&E's *Biography* series, nature films on the Discovery Channel, or the evening news.

The texts in the corpus we call documentaries share certain emphases that allow us to discuss them as members of a genre (characterized by norms and conventions such as an organizing logic, evidentiary editing, and a prominent role for speech directed at the viewer) that in turn divides into different movements, periods, and modes. In these terms, documentary proves to be one of the longest-lived and most richly varied of genres, offering many different approaches to the challenge of representing the historical world. These approaches share many of the qualities of standard fiction films, such as story telling, but remain distinct enough to constitute a domain of their own.

A CONSTITUENCY OF VIEWERS

The final way to consider documentary is in relation to its audience. The institutions that support documentary may also support fiction films; the practitioners of documentary may also make experimental or fiction films; the characteristics of the films themselves can be simulated in a fictional context, as works like *No Lies* (1973), *David Holzman's Diary* (1968), and *Bontoc Eulogy* (1995) make clear. In other words, what we have taken some pains to sketch out as the domain of documentary exhibits permeable borders and a chameleon-like appearance. The sense that a film is a documentary lies in the mind of the beholder as much as it lies in the film's context or structure.

What assumptions and expectations characterize our sense that a film is a documentary? What do we bring to the viewing experience that is different when we encounter what we think of as a documentary rather than some other genre of film? Most fundamentally, we bring an assumption that the text's sounds and images have their origin in the historical world we share. On the whole, they were not conceived and produced exclusively for the film. This assumption relies on the capacity of the photographic image, and of sound recording, to replicate what we take to be distinctive qualities of what they have recorded. That this is an *assumption,* encouraged by specific qualities of lenses, emulsions, optics, and styles, such as realism, becomes increasingly clear as we bear in mind the ability of digitally produced sounds and images to achieve a similar effect: the sound we hear and the image we behold seem to bear the trace of what produced them.

Recording instruments (cameras and tape recorders) register the imprint of things (sights and sounds) with great fidelity. It gives them documentary value, at least in the sense of a document as something caused by the events it records. The notion of a document is akin to the notion of an image that serves as an index of what produced it. The indexical dimension of an image refers to the way in which the appearance of an image is shaped or determined by what it records: a photo of a boy holding his dog will exhibit, in two dimensions, an exact analogy of the spatial relationship between the boy and his dog in three dimensions; a fingerprint will show exactly the same pattern of whorls as the finger that produced it; markings on a fired bullet will bear an indexical relationship to the specific gun barrel through which it was shot. The bullet's surface "records" the passage of that bullet through the gun barrel with a precision that allows forensic science to use it as documentary evidence in a given case.

Similarly, cinematic sounds and images enjoy an indexical relationship to what they record. What they record, together with the creative decisions and interventions of the filmmaker, is what produces them. The filmmaker may shoot the boy and his dog with a telephoto lens or a wide-angle one, with a camera fixed to a tripod or hand-held and moving slowly to the left, with color film and a red filter or with black and white film. Each variation will tell us something about the filmmaker's style. The image is a document of this style; it is produced by it and gives vivid evidence of the nature of the filmmaker's engagement with a subject, but each variation also tells us something about the boy and his dog that depends directly on the actual, physical relation between these two entities: it is a document of what once stood before the camera as well as of how the camera represented them. As an audience we are particularly attentive, in watching documentaries, to the ways in which sound and image attest to the look and sound of the world we share. It is this quality of an intimate relationship to an actual environment and its inhabitants, particularly to the two central characters, Arthur Agee and William Gates, that made *Hoop Dreams* a work of considerable significance.

This indexical relationship, however, is true of fictions as well as nonfiction. The distributor of *Hoop Dreams,* in fact, mounted a campaign to have the Motion Picture Academy of Arts and Sciences nominate the film not for Best Documentary but for Best Picture. The campaign failed, but it underscored the permeable and often arbitrary nature of sharp distinctions between fiction and documentary film. The camera documents the grain of an individual's voice, whether it is of Dustin Hoffman in *The Death of a Salesman* or of Paul Brennan in the Maysles brothers' *Salesman.* This is why we can say all films are documentaries, whether they represent documentaries of wish-fulfillment or of social representation. In fiction, however, we turn our attention from the documentation of real actors to the fabrication of imaginary characters. We suspend our disbelief in the fictional world that opens up before us. In documentary, we remain attentive to the documentation of what comes before the camera. We uphold our belief in the authenticity of the historical world represented on screen. We continue to assume that the indexical linkage of sound and image to what it records attests to the film's engagement with a world that is not entirely of its own design. Documentary *re*-presents the historical world by making an indexical record of it; it

LARRY MARCUS 1995   FINELINE FEATURES

<u>William Gates</u>, at age 23, (L) and from his senior year at St. Joseph High School (R) in
"Hoop Dreams." This award-winning documentary film follows Gates and his best friend
Arthur Agee from high school to college as they pursue their dreams of scoring big in the
NBA. **"Hoop Dreams"** premieres on PBS Wednesday, November 15, 1995, at 8PM (ET)
(check local listing).

Hoop Dreams (Steve James, Fred Marx, Peter Gilbert, 1994). Photos courtesy of Fine Line Features.

  William Gates is one of the two young men we follow in *Hoop Dreams*. These publicity shots, which
signal a significant passage of time (from high school to the age of 23), promise a "coming of age" tale
in which we will witness how these two individuals develop as basketball players and mature as men.

represents the historical world by shaping this record from a distinct perspective or point of view. The evidence of the *re*-presentation supports the
argument or perspective of the *representation*.

  We assume that documentary sounds and images have the authenticity of evidence, but we must be wary of this assumption. We must always
assess the argument or perspective on grounds that include but go beyond
factual accuracy. The shots of concentration camp victims and survivors in
Alain Resnais's *Night and Fog* bear the same appearance as what we would
have seen had we been there because the cinematic image is a document
of how these individuals appeared at the moment when they were filmed

during and at the end of World War II. The perspective of the film on these events, however, differs considerably from Beryl Fox's *Memorandum* (1965), Claude Lanzmann's *Shoah* (1985), or James Moll's *The Last Days* (1998). Even if we can rule out special effects, digital manipulation, or other forms of alteration that could allow a photographic image to give false evidence, the authenticity of the image does not necessarily make one argument or perspective superior to another.

When we assume that a sound or image bears an indexical relationship to its source, this assumption carries more weight in a film we take to be a documentary than in a film we take to be a fiction. It is for this reason that we may feel cheated when we learn that a work we thought was nonfiction proves to be a fiction after all. The line dividing the two may be imprecise or fuzzy, but we tend to believe in its reality all the same. *No Lies,* therefore, angers some who consider it bad faith for the director to create a fiction that pretends to be a documentary: we believe we could have observed this historical occurrence for ourselves, only to learn that what we would have observed was the construction of a fiction, even if it is a fiction designed to imitate the qualities of a documentary.

The weight we grant to the indexical quality of sound and image, the assumption we adopt that a documentary provides documentary evidence at the level of the shot, or spoken word, does not automatically extend to the entire film. We usually understand and acknowledge that a documentary is a *creative treatment* of actuality, not a faithful transcription of it. Transcriptions or strict documentary records have their value, as in surveillance footage or in documentation of a specific event or situation, such as the launching of a rocket, the progress of a therapeutic session, or the performance of a particular play or sports event. We tend, however, to regard such records strictly as documents or "mere footage," rather than as documentaries. Documentaries marshal evidence but then use it to construct their own perspective or argument about the world, their own poetic or rhetorical response to the world. We expect this transformation of evidence into something more than dry facts to take place. We are disappointed if it does not.

Among the assumptions we bring to documentary, then, is that individual shots and sounds, perhaps even scenes and sequences will bear a highly indexical relationship to the events they represent but that the film as a whole will stand back from being a pure document or transcription of these events to make a comment on them or to offer a perspective on them. Documentaries are not documents in the strict sense of the word, but they are based on the document-like quality of elements within them. As an audience we expect to be able both to trust to the indexical linkage between what we see and what occurred before the camera *and* to assess the poetic or rhetorical transformation of this linkage into a commentary or perspective on the world we occupy. We anticipate an oscillation between the recognition of historical reality and the recognition of a representation about it. This expectation distinguishes our involvement with documentary from our involvement with other film genres.

This expectation characterizes what we might call the "discourses of sobriety" in our society. These are the ways we have of speaking directly about social and historical reality such as science, economics, medicine, military strategy, foreign policy, and educational policy. When we step inside an institutional framework that supports these ways of speaking, we assume an instrumental power: what we say and decide can affect the course of real events and entail real consequences. These are ways of seeing and speaking that are also ways of doing and acting. Power runs through them. An air of sobriety surrounds these discourses because they are seldom receptive to whim or fantasy, to "make-believe" characters or imaginary worlds (unless they serve as useful simulations of the real world, such as in flight simulators or econometric models of business behavior). They are the vehicles of action and intervention, power and knowledge, desire and will, directed toward the world we physically inhabit and share.

Like these other discourses, documentary claims to address the historical world and to possess the capacity to intervene by shaping how we regard it. Even though documentary filmmaking may not be accepted as the equal partner in scientific inquiry or foreign policy initiatives (largely because, as an image-based medium, documentaries lack important qualities of spoken and written discourse, such as the immediacy and spontaneity of dialogue or the rigorous logic of the written essay), this genre still upholds a tradition of sobriety in its determination to make a difference in how we regard the world and proceed within it.

For this reason, the notion of the "history lesson" functions as a frequent characteristic of documentary. We expect more than a series of documents; we expect to learn or be moved, to discover or be persuaded of possibilities that pertain to the historical world. Documentaries draw on evidence to make a claim something like, "This is so," coupled to a tacit "Isn't it?" This claim is conveyed by the persuasive or rhetorical force of the representation. *The Battle of San Pietro,* for example, makes a case that "war is hell" and persuades us of this with evidence such as close-ups of a series of dead soldiers rather than, say, a single long shot of a battlefield that would diminish the horror and perhaps increase the nobility of battle. The impact of such a sight, in close-up, carries an impact, or "indexical whammy," that is quite different from the staged deaths in fiction films, such as *The Thin*

Red Line (Terrence Mallick, 1998) or *Saving Private Ryan* (Steven Spielberg, 1998), that also ponder the human price of waging war. The representations may be similar, but the emotional impact of close-up images of the dead and dying changes considerably when we know that there is no point at which the director can say, "Cut" and lives can be resumed.

Audiences, then, encounter documentaries with an expectation that the desire to know more about the world we already occupy will find gratification during the course of the film. Documentaries invoke this desire-to-know when they invoke a historical subject and propose their individual variation on the history lesson. How did a given state of affairs come to pass (poverty among migrant farm workers in *Harvest of Shame* [1960], the degradation of farm land in *The Plow That Broke the Plains*)? How does this institution work (in *High School* or *Herb Schiller Reads the New York Times* [1982])? How do people conduct themselves in situations of stress (female army recruits during basic training in *Soldier Girls* [1980], experimental subjects during tests of obedience that might cause harm to others in *Obedience* [1965])? What kind of interpersonal dynamics take place in a concrete historical context (during the campaigns of John F. Kennedy and Herbert Humphrey for the Democratic presidential primary of 1960 in *Primary,* among family members all trying to make a go of a marginal pizza parlor in *Family Business* [1982])? What is the source of a given problem and how might we address it (inadequate housing for working people in *Housing Problems* [1935], colonial history and exploitation in Argentina in *The Hour of the Furnaces* [1968])? For what reasons should men fight (the *Why We Fight* series on the reasons for the United States' entry into World War II, *People's War* [1969] on the North Vietnamese reasons for trying to unify Vietnam and oppose American intervention)? How do members of a different culture organize their lives and express their social values (among the Dani of the New Guinea Highlands in *Dead Birds* [1963], among the Turkana of Kenya in *Wedding Camels* [1980])? What happens when one culture encounters another, notably when western, colonial powers encounter so-called primitive people (for the first time in 1930s New Guinea in *First Contact* [1984], on a recurring basis along the Sepic River in New Guinea as tourists meet indigenous people in *Cannibal Tours* [1988])?

Documentary film and video stimulates epistephilia (a desire to know) in its audience. It conveys an informing logic, a persuasive rhetoric, or a moving poetics that promises information and knowledge, insight and awareness. Documentary proposes to its audience that the gratification of these desires to know will be their common business. He-Who-Knows (the agent has traditionally been masculine) will share knowledge with those who wish to know. We, too, can occupy the position of The-One-Who-Knows.

They speak about them to us and we gain a sense of pleasure, satisfaction, and knowledge as a result.

This dynamic may pose questions as well as resolve them. We may ask, Who are we that we may come to know something? What kind of knowledge is the knowledge documentaries provide? To what kind of use do we, and others, put the knowledge a film provides? What we know, and how we come to believe in what we know, are matters of social importance. Power *and* responsibility reside in knowing; the use we make of what we learn extends beyond our engagement with documentary film as such to our engagement with the historical world represented in such films. The engagement we have with this world provides the vital foundation for the experience and challenge of documentary film itself.

Chapter 3

What Gives Documentary Films a Voice of Their Own?

THE QUALITIES OF VOICE

If documentaries represent issues and aspects, qualities and problems found in the historical world, they can be said to speak about this world through both sounds and images. The question of speech raises the question of "voice." Since documentaries are not lectures, questions of speech and voice are not meant entirely literally.

The spoken word, of course, does play a vital role in most documentary film and video: some films, like *Portrait of Jason* (1967), *Frank: A Vietnam Veteran* (1984), or *Shoah* (1985), seem, at first glance, to be nothing but speech. And yet, when documentaries speak about the historical world, they do so with all the means at their disposal, especially with sounds and images in relation to each other, or, in silent films, with images alone.

When Jason tells us about his life in *Portrait of Jason,* a key avenue to understanding his words involves what we see of his inflections, gestures, and behavior, including his interaction with Shirley Clarke, the filmmaker, as she orchestrates their dialogue. And when Frank, in *Frank: A Vietnam Veteran,* or the various interviewees in *Shoah* speak to us about their past, a key aspect of understanding the force and severity of that past lies in registering its effect on their way of speaking and acting in the present. Even the most speech-oriented of documentaries—often referred to as "talking head" films—convey meanings, hint at symptoms, and express values on a multitude of levels apart from what is literally said. What does it mean, then, to raise the question of "voice" in documentary?

In Chapter 2 we said that documentaries *represent* the historical world by shaping its photographic record of some aspect of the world *from a distinct perspective or point of view. As such they become one voice among the many voices in an arena of social debate and contestation.* The fact that documentaries are not a reproduction of reality gives them a voice of their own. They are a *representation* of the world, and this representation stands for a particular view of the world. The voice of documentary, then, is the means by which this particular point of view or perspective becomes known to us.

The voice of documentary can make a case or present an argument as well as convey a point of view. Documentaries seek to persuade or convince us: by the strength of their argument or point of view and the appeal, or power, of their voice. The voice of documentary is the specific way in which an argument or perspective is expressed. Like a plot, an argument can be presented in different ways. "Freedom of choice is vital for women who must decide whether to have an abortion." This is an argument, or point of view, but one documentary might work performatively to convey what women in such a position feel or experience, as *Speak Body* (1987) does, with its array of women's voices heard off screen as we see fragments of female bodies on screen, while another work might rely on interviews with women in different countries to underscore the social impact that access or impediments to abortion procedures create, as *Abortion Stories: North and South* (1984) does, with its array of women who testify on camera to their experience in various North and South American countries. *Speak Body* and *Abortion Stories* make basically the same argument, but they do so from distinctly different perspectives and hence with distinctly different voices.

The idea of voice is also tied to the idea of an informing logic overseeing the organization of a documentary compared to the idea of a compelling story organizing a fiction. Not mutually exclusive, there is nonetheless the sense that an informing logic, conveyed by a distinct voice, has dominance in documentary compared to the compelling story, conveyed by a distinct style, that has dominance in narrative fiction. Voice, then, is a question of *how* the logic, argument, or viewpoint of a film gets conveyed to us.

Voice is clearly akin to style, the way in which a film, fiction or non-fiction, inflects its subject matter and the flow of its plot or argument in distinct ways, but style operates differently in documentary than in fiction. The idea of the voice of documentary stands for something like "style *plus.*" Style in fiction derives primarily from the director's translation of a story into visual form; it gives the visual manifestation of a plot a style distinct from its written counterpart as script, novel, play, or biography. Style in documentary derives partly from the director's attempt to translate her perspective on the historical world into visual terms, but it also stems from her direct involvement with the film's actual subject. That is, fictional style conveys a distinct, imaginary world, whereas documentary style or voice reveals a distinct form of engagement with the historical world.

When Robert Flaherty films Nanook biting into a phonograph record to see what kind of thing this strange disc that produces sound is, the inclusion, duration, and specific placement of the shot—elementary questions of style—reveal a willingness on Flaherty's part to let Nanook be the butt of a joke: Nanook "erroneously" uses his mouth where he should use his ear. The trust and collaboration between filmmaker and subject may appear in jeopardy, especially when viewed across the chasm of post-colonial studies that take some pains to examine the ways in which patterns of hierarchy persist in the everyday encounters between peoples of different cultures. The voice of the film betrays its maker's form of engagement with the world in a way that even he might not have fully recognized.

In another example, Jon Silver uses a long take at the opening of *Watsonville on Strike* (1989) (about a farm-worker strike in the California coastal town of Watsonville) while we hear him arguing with the union director about whether he can continue to film inside the union hall. This stylistic choice (long take over editing) also bears witness to an existential necessity: Silver must actually negotiate his own right to be there, his own right to film, in this specific moment. Everything is at risk at a precise instant of historical time that anything other than a long take could represent but not authenticate in quite so direct a manner. The long take is a record of that moment seen from Silver's literal, and political, point of view as it gradually but dramatically reveals itself to us.

When the director threatens to have Silver thrown out of the hall, he responds by panning his camera to the on-looking Chicano/Chicana workers and asks them, in Spanish rather than in the English he uses with the Anglo director,—What do you say? Is it all right for me to film? The record of his question and their enthusiastic response, all within the same shot as the director's intransigent refusal to grant permission, testifies to Silver's desire to represent himself as a straight-forward, above-board activist whose spontaneous loyalty lies with the workers rather than union representatives. We *see* him display this spontaneous loyalty when he pans the camera away from the director and toward the workers rather than cutting to another discussion at another time or place. He does not cut until the director has

Watsonville on Strike (Jon Silver, 1989)

In this opening scene, the union manager points and stares directly at the camera held by filmmaker Jon Silver. Such moments cause embarrassment within an observational framework or self-consciousness within a fictional framework. Here the manager's direct confrontation with the filmmaker testifies to Silver's active, participatory role in the shaping of events. What we see would not have occurred had the camera, and the filmmaker, not been there to record it.

wagged his finger at him and warned, "If you put my picture on television, I'll sue you."

The voice of the film reveals Silver's willingness to acknowledge the reality of the moment rather than slip into the illusion that people act as if the camera, and filmmaker, were not there. His voice, represented in the long take and camera movement, as much as in what he actually says, reveals *how* he makes his argument on behalf of the worker's cause. Like style, but with an added sense of ethical and political accountability, voice serves to give concrete embodiment to a filmmaker's engagement with the world.

The voice of documentary testifies to the character of the filmmaker like Robert Flaherty or Jon Silver, to *how* he acquits himself in the face of social reality, as much as to his creative vision. Style takes on an ethical dimension. The voice of documentary conveys a sense of what the filmmaker's social point of view is and of how this point of view becomes manifest in the act of making the film.

The voice of documentary is not restricted to what is verbally said, either by voices of unseen "gods" and plainly visible "authorities" who represent the filmmaker's point of view—who speak *for* the film, or by social actors who represent their own points of view—who speak *in* the film. The voice of documentary speaks with all the means available to its maker. These means can be summarized as the selection and arrangement of sound and image, that is, the working out of an organizing logic for the film. This entails, at least, the following decisions: (1) when to cut, or edit, and what to juxtapose and how to frame or compose a shot (close-up or long shot, low or high angle, artificial or natural lighting, color or black and white, whether to pan, zoom in or out, track or remain stationary, and so on), (2) whether to record synchronous sound at the time of shooting, and whether to add additional sound, such as voice-over translations, dubbed dialogue, music, sound effects, or commentary, at a later point, (3) whether to adhere to an accurate chronology or rearrange events to support a point, (4) whether to use archival or other people's footage and photographs or only those images shot by the filmmaker on the spot, and (5) which mode of representation to rely on to organize the film (expository, poetic, observational, participatory, reflexive, or performative).

When we represent the world from a particular point of view we do so with a voice that shares qualities with other voices. Genre conventions are one way to cluster such qualities. Some conventions are not specific to film but are shared with the essay, diary, notebook, editorial, evocation, eulogy, exhortation, description, or report. (These kinds of categories or forms constitute the chapter headings for Erik Barnouw's highly informative history of documentary film, *Documentary: A History of the Non-Fiction Film,* where he mentions "reporter," "advocate," "prosecutor," and "guerilla," among others.) Other conventions, such as the ones that characterize the various modes of documentary—expository and observational documentary, for example—are specific to the medium.

Together, generic forms and modes establish some of the constraints that identify a given voice, but they do not wholly determine that voice. Each voice retains a uniqueness. This uniqueness stems from the specific utilization of forms and modes, of techniques and style in a given film, and from the specific pattern of encounter that takes place between filmmaker and subject. The voice of a documentary serves as evidence of a perspective, an argument, or an encounter. Our recognition that such a voice addresses us in a distinct way is a key part of our recognition of a given film as a documentary.

The fact that the voice of a documentary relies on all the means available to it, not just spoken words, means that the argument or point of view

Bontoc Eulogy (Marlon Fuentes, 1995). Photo courtesy of Marlon Fuentes.

Finding a voice. On first viewing we do not know that the person sitting in front of the old phonograph player is the filmmaker; nor do we know that the scratchy sounds dominating the sound track will eventually become the voice of the filmmaker's grandfather. In the course of the film, Fuentes embarks on his own voyage of discovery to learn more about his grandfather and his turn-of-the-century encounters with colonial anthropology. He combines archival footage, staged events (such as this one), and his own voice-over commentary to give to his film a voice that seeks to recover both family and Filipino history.

carried by a documentary can be more or less explicit. The most explicit form of voice is no doubt the one conveyed by spoken, or written, words. These are words that stand for the point of view of the film directly and are what we typically refer to as "voice-of-God" or "voice-of-authority" commentary.

Commentary is a voice that addresses us directly; it lays out its point of view explicitly. The comments can be passionately partisan, as it is in bold graphic intertitles of *Salt for Svanetia,* made in the Soviet Union in 1930 as Stalin was implementing a Five Year Plan to accelerate industrialization and agricultural production. These titles proclaim the arrival of the road that will bring much-needed salt to this remote region as a massive triumph of the highest order. In other cases, comments can be seemingly impartial, as in the reportorial style of most television journalists. In both cases, this voice of direct address to the viewer argues for a position that says, in effect, "See it this way." This can be a galvanizing voice or a reassuring one, but its tone provides us with a ready-made point of view to which we will, it is hoped, subscribe.

Some documentaries eschew this type of explicitness, even in poetic modalities where comments hint and suggest rather than declare or explain. The point of view becomes implicit. The voice of the film does not address us directly. There is no voice of God or authority to guide us through what we see and to suggest what we should make of it. Evidence accrues, but evidence of what? The argument and voice of the film lie embedded in all the means of representation available to the filmmaker *apart from* explicit commentary. In contrast to the voice of commentary, we might call this the voice of perspective.

Perspective is what the specific decisions made about the selection and arrangement of sounds and images convey to us. This voice advances an argument by implication. The argument operates on a tacit level. We have to infer what the filmmaker's point of view, in fact, is. The effect is less "See it this way" than "See for yourself."

Although invited to see for ourselves, and to infer what is left tacit or unspoken, what we see is not a reproduction of the world but a specific form of representation with a specific perspective. The sense of a perspective, that is, an informing logic and organization, separates a documentary from mere footage or photographic records, where this sense of perspective is minimal. (It may still exist: surveillance footage from a store that focuses on transactions at a cash register implicitly says something about which elements of customer/personnel interaction hold the highest priority.)

Once we infer a perspective we know that we are not confronted by value-free replicas of the historical world. Even if the voice of the film adopts the guise of nonjudgmental, impartial, disinterested, or objective witness, it nonetheless offers a perspective on the world. At the least, a strategy of self-effacement testifies to the significance of the world itself and to a particular filmmaker's sense of solemn responsibility to report on it fairly and accurately.

The Thin Blue Line (1987), for example, uses no voice-over commentary at all, and yet through the perspective it offers it makes a clear argument for the innocence of a man convicted of murder. The voice of the film speaks to us through the juxtaposition of interviews with images that affirm or undercut what is said, in a spirit of critical irony similar to *The Life and Times of Rosie the Riveter*'s critical irony toward the official propaganda films that celebrated women's work during World War II. A key witness against the accused has her validity undercut by Errol Morris's decision to cut to scenes from a 1940s series of films about Boston Blackie, a former thief turned crime stopper who operates independently from the police. A scene of Blackie capturing a crook with the aide of his loyal female companion adds a comic note to the witness's solemn claims: through the juxtaposition of a light-hearted entertainment film with what was presumably decisive legal testimony, Morris gives voice to a point of view that, although tacit and indirect, remains hard to miss.

DOCUMENTARY AND THE VOICE OF THE ORATOR

The voice of documentary is most often the voice of oratory. It is the voice of a filmmaker setting out to take a position regarding an aspect of the historical world and to convince us of its merits. The position addresses those aspects of the world that are subject to debate. They are issues and topics that do not lend themselves to scientific proof. As issues of understanding and interpretation, value and judgment about the world we actually occupy, they require a way of speaking that is fundamentally different from logic or story telling. The rhetorical tradition provides a foundation for this way of speaking. It can embrace reason and narrative, evocation and poetry, but does so for the purpose of inspiring belief or instilling conviction about the merit of a particular viewpoint on a contentious issue.

How do we proceed when we proceed rhetorically? In what forms, with what conventions do we speak? Classic rhetorical thinking identified three divisions (discussed in the next chapter) and five "departments," each of which carries over to documentary film: invention, arrangement, style, memory, and delivery. Cicero described their connection this way:

> [S]ince all the activity and ability of an orator falls into five divisions, . . . he must first hit upon what to say; then manage and marshal his discoveries, not merely in orderly fashion, but with a discriminating eye for the exact weight as it were of each argument; next go on to array them in the adornments of style; after that keep them guarded in his memory; and in the end deliver them with effect and charm. (*De oratore,* I.xxxi)

We can review the usefulness of these five divisions in turn.

Invention

Invention refers to the discovery of evidence or "proofs" in support of a position or argument. (The word "proof" occurs in classic texts, but we should remember that rhetoric and documentary film address aspects of human experience where the certainty of scientific proof is unavailable. What counts as proof is subject to social rules and conventions rather than to something as conclusive as the scientific method.) Aristotle proposed two types of evidence. They correspond to the division between appeals to the facts of the matter—inartistic or non-artificial proofs—and appeals to the feelings of the audience—artistic or artificial proofs.

Inartistic proof involves the facts or evidence that can be brought to bear and that lies beyond dispute (although the *interpretation* of this factual evidence may be very much in dispute). Examples of inartistic proof include witnesses, documents, confessions, physical evidence, and scientific analyses of fingerprints, hair or blood samples, DNA, and so forth. These types of evidence lie outside the reach of the orator or filmmaker's artistic power to create, although very much within her power to evaluate or interpret.

More pertinent to our discussion of how documentaries speak or acquire a voice of their own is the idea of artistic or artificial evidence or proof. These are the techniques used to generate the *impression* of conclusiveness or proof. They are a product of the orator or filmmaker's inventiveness rather than something found elsewhere and introduced intact. In his *Rhetoric,* Aristotle divided artistic proofs into three types. Each strives to convince us of an argument's or perspective's validity. All three have relevance to documentary film and video:

- ethical: generating an impression of good moral character or credibility;

- emotional: appealing to the audience's emotions to produce the desired disposition; putting the audience in the right mood or establishing a frame of mind favorable to a particular view;

- demonstrative: using real or apparent reasoning or demonstration; proving, or giving the impression of proving, the case.

If real reasoning or logic were totally satisfactory, the issue would probably be scientific or mathematical in nature rather than rhetorical. The mixture of hunks of real reasoning with veiled pieces of apparent, faulty, or misleading reasoning characterizes rhetorical address. This can be seen as a flaw, from the point of view of pure logic, or as a necessary consequence of taking up issues for which there is no final proof or single solution. In this case, decisions will hinge on values and beliefs, assumptions and traditions rather than the weight of reason alone. For example, deciding whether to restrict land development because it will harm the environment or to promote land development because it will stimulate the economy admits, partially, of scientific or factual evidence, but the final decision will hinge heavily on values and beliefs. Rhetoric facilitates giving expression to these quite real and very fundamental factors.

These three strategies call on the orator or filmmaker to honor the three "C's" of rhetorical discourse by being credible, convincing, and compelling. An important tendency within documentary film since the 1970s has been to shift the focus of these strategies from supporting representations of the historical world by experts and authorities to supporting representations that convey more personal, individual perspectives. This lessens the requirement for the filmmaker to produce effective artistic proofs to a minor key since a work like Rea Tajiri's *History and Memory* (1991) does not claim to be an overarching history of the internment of Japanese Americans during World War II but a more personal account of her own family's experience. It can be credible, convincing, and compelling without being definitive or conclusive.

The best of these personal works, such as Tajiri's; Alan Berliner's two films, *Intimate Stranger* and *Nobody's Business,* on his own hard-to-know and often absent father; Deborah Hoffmann's *Complaints of a Dutiful Daughter,* on the filmmaker's relation to her mother after she succumbs to Alzheimer's disease; Emiko Omori's *Rabbit in the Moon,* on her family's internment during World War II and its consequences; Su Friedrich's *The Ties That Bind,* on her relation to her German-born mother and to German history mediated through her mother; Marilu Mallet's *Unfinished Diary,* on her life in Canada as a Chilean exile married to a Canadian documentary filmmaker (Michael Rubbo); Ngozi Onwurah's *The Body Beautiful,* on her relation to her white British mother and her black African father; Marlon Riggs's *Tongues Untied,* on the filmmaker's experience as a gay, black male; and Marlon Fuentes's *Bontoc Eulogy,* on his relation to his grandfather and the legacy of colonialism in the Philippines, all successfully couple their accounts of personal experience to larger social, historical ramifications.

This coupling itself often serves to establish credibility and conviction since the filmmaker starts from what she or he knows best—family experience—and extends outward from there. These works also gain a compelling quality thanks to the intensity with which the filmmaker approaches aspects of his or her own life. The frankness and intimacy of the approach contrasts quite dramatically with the aura of detached objectivity that marked more traditional documentaries. Subjectivity itself compels belief: instead of an aura of detached truthfulness we have the honest admission of a partial but highly significant, situated but impassioned view.

An example of a more traditional approach to oratorical address is television news broadcasting. The anchor person, at one end of a spectrum from the sensationalist talk show host, establishes a basic ethical proof: here is an honest, trustworthy person, free of personal biases and hidden agendas; you can trust this person to relay the news to you without distor-

History and Memory (Rea Tajiri, 1991)

   This image of a woman's hands holding a canteen beneath a stream of tap water recurs throughout Tajiri's film. It is, in one sense, an impossible image (for a documentary), since it is an image, Tajiri tells us, that appears in her dreams as if it were a memory of what living in the Japanese-American internment camps during World War II was like for her mother. In her voice-over commentary Tajiri refers to this image as one of the inspirations for her effort to return to this suppressed history, a history that no one in her family wished to reexamine as much as she did. How could she build on this small scrap of a larger experience with its references to the desert, the primacy of water, the hands of her mother, and the sense of isolation or fragmentation that haunted the interred citizens? *History and Memory* is an eloquent answer to this question.

tion. A Jerry Springer or Geraldo Rivera, the other hand, serves more as a stereotype than a credible speaker: we expect certain forms of excess and outrage to occur because "that's the kind of person he is." There is a certain predictability, far more than credibility, attached to their images.

   On broadcast news shows, emotional proof operates in reverse fashion from usual: the show works to quiet, not arouse, emotion. What happened in the world need not perturb even if it does interest us. We need not take any specific action other than to attend to the news. The packaging and management of world affairs, the reassurance that almost any event, no matter how extraordinary, can be encapsulated within the daily format of a news item assures us that things may change but the news

Rabbit in the Moon (Emiko Omori, 1999). Photos courtesy of Emiko Omori.

A very personal film, *Rabbit in the Moon* involves the reflections of filmmaker Emiko Omori and her sister on their experience as young girls in the detention camps built during World War II to house citizens of Japanese ancestry on the West Coast of the United States and Canada. The film couples family interviews and the filmmaker's voice-over commentary with historical footage to place the personal story in a larger framework of lingering racism and government policies of "national security."

can consistently assimilate them. If there is an effort to compel belief, it lies in the news broadcast's effort to convince us of its own powers of reportage. We can feel safe and secure because the news carries on. Events happen, people die, leaders change, nations fall, but the news provides a constant reference point. We can trust it to give us a window onto the world indefinitely.

News broadcasts also must convince us. They must resort to demonstrative proofs, with their traditional mix of real and apparent proof. The real proofs come from the factual evidence brought before us: statistical information on inflation or unemployment, eyewitness accounts of specific events, documentary evidence of a certain occurrence, and so on. One kind of apparent proof lies in the way such evidence may be interpreted to support a particular case. News coverage in the United States of the Gulf War against Iraq, for example, might provide authentic images of a speech by Saddam Hussein on Iraqi television but edit it and position it to support representations of his anti-American attitude and defiant belligerence, whether that was the main point of his speech or not.

A more extensive source of apparent proof lies in the structure of news programs as such. The convention of situating the anchor in a TV studio that seldom has a specified geographic location works to give the sense that "the news" emanates from somewhere apart from the events it reports, that it is above or beyond such events, and is, therefore, free from partisan involvement in the events. At the same time, a second convention calls on the anchor person to sketch out the broad outline of a story or news item and then to call on a reporter for substantiation.

Unlike the anchor, who sets the tone of impartiality, hovering in a space without geographic coordinates, the reporter is always "on the scene." This convention operates as if to say, I have told you about this event but lest you doubt, I will prove the truth of what I said by inviting a reporter to provide further detail from the very place where the story is unfolding. When we cut to reporters, they invariably occupy the foreground of the shot while the background serves to document, or prove, their location on the spot: oil fields in Kuwait, the White House in Washington, the Vatican in Rome, cable cars on the streets of San Francisco, and so on.

In this case physical presence serves a rhetorical function. It functions as a metonymy. Whereas metaphors link together physically disconnected phenomena to suggest an underlying similarity (love is a battlefield, or marriage is a piece of cake, for example), metonymies make associations between physically linked phenomena. They typically use an aspect of something to represent the whole thing: fresh fish goes with seafood restaurants set along the shore because the ocean is only yards away, for example. The restaurant's physical proximity to the sea serves as a metonymy for fresh fish. Similarly, reporters standing on the scene of a news event will get the true story because they are there, in physical proximity to the event itself.

Metaphor and metonymy are rhetorical or figurative devices rather than logical or scientific forms of proof. They need not be true. Not all love is necessarily a battlefield, just as not all fish prepared in seaside restaurants is fresh. Similarly, not all commentary heard from reporters on the scene is true. This may do little to detract from its convincingness. The value of figures of speech like metaphor and metonymy is precisely that they offer a more vivid and compelling image of something, whether this image corresponds to any larger truth or not.

Television news is a sober business. It adopts the solemn airs of those other discourses of sobriety that address the world as it is, such as economics, business, medicine, or foreign policy. This sobriety, and the three

"C's" of rhetorical engagement, can be treated ironically as well. Films like *Land without Bread* (1932), *Blood of the Beasts* (1949), and *Cane Toads* (1987), about the rampant growth of a toad population in Australia, exemplify an ironic use of the three artistic proofs. The credibility of the commentators in all three films, for example, seems assured by their solemn intonation and objective style. They are also male voices, tapping into a culturally constructed assumption that it is men who speak of the actual world and that they can do so in an authoritative manner. But credibility unravels as *what* they say begins to undercut *how* they say it. Why is the commentator pointing out "another idiot," or praising a slaughterhouse worker as if he were a god, or describing cane toads as if they were an invading army?

Conviction also erodes as we begin to sense that the ostensibly objective tone is itself a mock-scientific one. Is the commentator serious about his claims of a toad menace when we see the Australian landscape pass by from the literal point of view of a solitary toad inside a wooden crate set inside a railroad freight car? Is the heroism of the abattoir worker genuine when we see the still twitching heads of slaughtered cows piled in a corner? Can we be getting a full picture of the life of the Hurdanos when the commentator likens their customs to those of "barbaric" people elsewhere?

Finally, the films consciously refuse to compel belief in the truthfulness of their representations. The hints of partiality and exaggeration build to a conviction that what we see is *not* what careful scrutiny of the facts would reveal, that what we see is an intensified emphasis on how these films see the historical world from a particular point of view. The particularity of the point of view captures our attention; its idiosyncrasy compels us to believe in it as a representation that deliberately undercuts believability in order to question our usual willingness to believe films that adopt the very conventions these films subvert.

Irony involves *not* saying what is meant or saying the opposite of what is meant. Just as the ironic use of television's journalistic conventions provides an important clue that *This Is Spinal Tap* is a mock documentary, the ironic use of authoritative commentary in these three films is a vital clue that they want to provoke suspicion of documentary conventions themselves more than they want to persuade us of the validity of their actual representations about the world.

Land without Bread, Blood of the Beasts, and *Cane Toads* all serve to remind us that beliefs stem from shared values and that shared values take on the form of conventions. These include conventional ways of representing the world in documentary (sober-minded commentators, visual evidence, observational camera styles, location shooting, and so on) as well as conventional ways of seeing and thinking about the world itself. Subvert the conventions and you subvert the values that compel belief.

Arrangement

Arrangement involves the usual order of parts in a rhetorical speech or, in this case, film. One typical arrangement already discussed is the problem/solution structure. A more comprehensive treatment of arrangement, as recommended by classic orators, is

- an opening that catches the audience's attention,

- a clarification of what is already agreed as factual and what remains in dispute, or a statement or elaboration of the issue itself,

- a direct argument in support of one's case from a particular viewpoint,

- a refutation that rebuts anticipated objections or opposing arguments, and

- a summation of the case that stirs the audience and predisposes it to a particular course of action.

These parts can be subdivided in various ways. Aristotle, for example, stressed two parts, stating an issue and making an argument about it, whereas Quintilian favored five parts that elaborated on Aristotle's scheme. However subdivided, the classic rhetorical speech retains two characteristics. First, the alternation of pro and con arguments inclines traditional rhetoric to place issues within a black or white, either-or frame such as right or wrong, true or false, guilty or innocent. It is particularly conducive to a problem/solution approach or the balanced, "both sides of the question" convention of journalism that still allows for right and wrong, good and bad views. Open-ended, both-and perspectives, such as the sense of perplexity and wonder conveyed by Errol Morris's *Fast, Cheap and Out of Control* (1997) or the sense of complex interaction between the art and life of R. Crumb in Terry Zwigoff's film *Crumb* (1994) call for more radical departures from traditional rhetorical form.

Second, all of the various ways of subdividing stress an alternation between appeals to evidence and appeals to audience, factual appeals and emotional appeals. Given that the types of issues addressed by rhetoric always involve questions of value and belief as well as evidence and fact, this alternation makes good sense. It allows the speech, or the voice of a doc-

Solovky Power (Marina Goldovskaya, 1988). Photos courtesy of Marina Goldovskaya.

A monastery in the Middle Ages, the buildings became one of the first prisons in the Soviet Gulag. It is approximately 3500 kilometers north of Moscow. The spirituality of the former monastery became appropriated by government propaganda made about the virtues of the prison.

umentary, to add flesh to fact, to locate its arguments not in the abstract domain of impersonal logic but in the concrete domain of embodied experience and historical occurrence.

Much of the power of documentary, and much of its appeal to governments and other institutional sponsors, lies in its ability to couple evidence *and* emotion in the selection and arrangement of its sounds and images. How powerful it is to show images of the dead and dying as evidence of the Holocaust; how compelling it is to give as evidence of backward custom an image of someone drinking from a stream in which we just saw a pig wallowing. Such images not only provide visible evidence, they pack an emotional punch, boosted by the indexical whammy of our own belief in their authenticity. They locate an argument all the more forcefully in relation to the historical world and in relation to our own engagement with the world.

Style

Style involves all the uses of figures of speech and codes of grammar to achieve a specific tone. Introductory film books usually cover elements of film style under the broad categories of camera, lighting, editing, acting, sound, and so on. These same elements clearly come into play in documentary film and video, tempered by the forms (diary, essay, etc.) and modes (expository, reflexive, etc.) most characteristic of documentary. Since other introductions cover these elements quite thoroughly, they will be referred to in particular contexts here rather than reviewed in their entirety.

Solovky Power

Director Marina Goldovskaya discovered a 1927–28 Soviet propaganda film that presented Solovky prison as a model of clean living, wholesome food, and redemptive hard work. The authorities had to withdraw the film from circulation: their enthusiasm to deceive led them to fabricate an environment better than that of most of the viewers. Citizens began to wonder why prisoners had nicer rooms and better food than they did!

Memory

Memory held crucial importance for speech delivered on the spot, such as in the heat of a debate. One could memorize a speech by sheer force of will, or one could develop a "memory theater" as a way to remember what was to be said. This involved imaginatively placing the components of the speech in different parts of a familiar space such as one's house or a public place. This mental image then facilitates retrieval of the speech's components as the speaker "moves" through the imagined space, in a set order, retrieving the arguments deposited there.

Since films are not delivered as spontaneous speech, the role of memory enters in more fully in two ways: first, film itself provides a tangible "memory theater" of its own. It is an external, visible representation of what was

Solovky Power

Marina Goldovskaya excavates the story of the prison through interviews with survivors, prisoner diaries, and official records that attest to the living conditions of extreme hardship. We see here some of the family photographs and letters of a Solovky prisoner.

said and done. Like writing, film eases the burden to commit sequence and detail to memory. Film can become a source of "popular memory," giving us a vivid sense of how something happened in a particular time and place.

Second, memory enters into the various ways by which the viewers draw on what they have already seen to interpret what they presently see. This act of retrospection, of looking back, remembering what has come before during the course of a film, and making a connection with what is now present, can prove crucial to an interpretation of the whole film just as memory can prove crucial to the construction of a coherent argument. Although not part of rhetorical *speech* as such, it is part of the overall rhetorical *act*. When Errol Morris begins *The Thin Blue Line* with exterior, evening shots of abstract, impersonal Dallas skyscrapers coupled to the accused man's comment that Dallas seemed like "hell on earth," these images serve a metaphorical function that hovers over the remainder of the film, if we activate our memory of them in an appropriate manner. Similarly, our recall of the opening image of a man sitting on the floor playing a phonograph record becomes crucial to an overall understanding of Marlon Fuentes's *Bontoc Eulogy* (1995). As the film unfolds we learn the identity of the man and the significance of his act. We gradually come to understand why the film begins as it does. We can only arrive at this understanding by re-membering, by thinking back to the beginning with the addition of later knowledge. This form of re-view is often crucial to a full grasp of a film's meaning.

Delivery

Originally, delivery divided into voice and gesture, which represents some-thing akin to our division between commentary and perspective as ways of advancing an argument or point of view. Gesture involves non-verbal com-munication; it is also a key aspect of what is meant by performance or style. Other vital aspects of delivery are the ideas of eloquence and decorum. Al-though these words now have a feel of the drawing room about them, this is a particular piece of historical baggage that degrades their original im-portance. We can consider eloquence, for example, as an index of the clar-ity of an argument and the potency of an emotional appeal, and decorum as the effectiveness of a particular argumentative strategy, or voice, for a specific setting or audience. Eloquence and decorum measure "what works" and reflect the pragmatic, effect- or result-oriented nature of rhetoric itself. They are not by any means restricted to polite (or overly polite) speech. They can apply to any form of speech or voice that seeks to achieve results in a given context.

The five departments of classic rhetoric provide a useful guide to the rhetorical strategies available to the contemporary documentarian. Like the orator of old, the documentarian speaks to the issues of the day, propos-ing new directions, judging previous ones, measuring the quality of lives and cultures. These actions characterize rhetorical speech not as "rhetori-cal" in the sense of argumentative for the sake of being argumentative, but in the sense of engaging with those pressing matters of value and belief for which no facts and no logic provide a conclusive guide to proper conduct, wise decisions, or insightful perspectives. The voice of documentary testifies to its engagement with a social order and to its assessment of those val-ues that underlie it. It is a specific orientation to the historical world that gives a documentary film a voice of its own.

Chapter 4

What Are Documentaries About?

THE TRIANGLE OF COMMUNICATION

For every documentary there are at least three stories that intertwine: the filmmaker's, the film's, and the audience's. These stories are all, in different ways, part of what we attend to when we ask what a given film is about. That is to say, when we watch a film we become aware that the film comes from somewhere and someone. There is a story about how and why it got made. These stories are often more personal and idiosyncratic for documentary and avant-garde film than they are for feature films. Leni Riefenstahl's production of *Triumph of the Will,* for example, remains a controversial story of Riefenstahl's artistic ambitions to make great films of emotional power but free of propagandistic intent—according to her own accounts—together with the story of Nazi party pressure for a film that would generate a positive image at a moment when its power was not fully consolidated and its leadership not fully concentrated in Hitler—from the point of view of most film historians. Interpretations of the film often pick up the thread of one or the other of these stories, praising the film as a great piece of film art or condemning the film as a blatant piece of Nazi propaganda.

We often want to consider how a film relates to the previous work and continuing preoccupations of the filmmaker, to how the filmmaker might un-

Triumph of the Will (Leni Riefenstahl, 1935)
   This dramatically choreographed entrance by the three Nazi leaders stresses the utter centrality of the all-powerful leader in relation to the attendant masses of troops. George Lucas replicated
this choreography at the end of *Star Wars* as if the hero-worship could be extracted from its fascist context and applied to Han Solo, Chewbacca, and Luke Skywalker as "good old boys."

derstand and explain her intentions or motives, and how these considerations relate to the general social context in which the work was made. This
reference back to the filmmaker and the context of production is one of the
ways in which we can discuss what a film is about. Such background stories do not exhaust our curiosity, however, and we need to take statements
of intention with a grain of salt since the effect of a work on others, and its
interpretation, may be quite different from the intentions of its maker.

   There is also the story of the text itself and our understanding and interpretation of this story. This is the standard task of critical analysis and
the usual focus of film history and criticism. We now concentrate on what
the film itself reveals to us about the relation between filmmaker and subject and what, for documentary, the film reveals to us about the world we
occupy.

Triumph of the Will
By shifting to a different angle, Riefenstahl draws the leaders into closer proximity to the masses while still maintaining a vivid sense of physical distance and hierarchical distinction.

Finally, there is the story of the viewer. Every viewer comes to new experiences, such as watching a film, with perspective and motives based on previous experience. Jean-Luc Godard's great film *Contempt* (1963) refers to this phenomenon directly. A screenwriter, Paul, is given the task of revising an adaptation of Homer's *The Odyssey* for the screen. Meanwhile, his wife feels that he has betrayed their relationship by his complicity with the producer's advances toward her. The writer slowly becomes defensive and jealous. In the midst of his own marital conflict he claims that the central theme of *The Odyssey* is infidelity. Why? Because, according to Paul, Penelope has cheated on Odysseus for some time. He is, however, fully aware of it; he deliberately delays his return to postpone the moment of necessary confrontation when he must face the full consequences of this betrayal! Paul has reversed the usual interpretation of this classic text, where Penelope faithfully awaits her husband's return, as a result of projecting his own experiences onto the story itself. Although aberrant as an interpretation, this projection of personal experience onto Homer's story achieves a certain level of credibility. It is a perfect example of how the story of the viewer or audience changes the meaning of the story of the work itself.

As audience members we often find what we want, or need, to find in films, sometimes at the expense of what the film has to offer others. Different audiences will see different things; introducing or promoting a film in a particular way can coach viewers to regard it one way rather than others; this practice can help filter out interpretations that project stories of personal experience onto the story of the film. The practices of members of other cultures can seem bizarre and "unnatural" to viewers from a different culture, for example. Watching, without any preparation, *Les Maîtres Fous* (1955), in which Hauka tribesmen enter into a trance and become Hauka spirits, during which they froth at the mouth, drool, sacrifice a live chicken, and eat the flesh of a dog, or *The Nuer* (1970), in which a Nuer boy has several cuts made across the width of his forehead as a rite of passage into male adulthood, can prompt some viewers to feelings of revulsion or nausea. These feelings tell us about the story of the audience. They say more about the audience's understanding of appropriate conduct, control of the body, and the sight of blood than they do about another culture's practices. Placing these films within an ethnographic frame that draws attention to the larger issues of cross-cultural interpretation and of cultural bias encourages a focus on the story told by the film over the story we may be inclined to project onto it.

Our own predispositions and experiences cannot be screened out entirely, nor should they be. Documentaries often pitch themselves to tap into the stories we bring to them as a way of establishing rapport rather than revulsion or projection. They may appeal to our sense of curiosity or our desire for an explanation of American policy toward the war against Vietnam, or Iraq, or Grenada, or Haiti, or Serbia, for example. Our desire to hear a story that strengthens our preexisting assumptions and predispositions often draws us to particular documentaries. Skill in the use of the rhetorical techniques for creating credible, convincing, compelling accounts depends on knowing one's audience and knowing how to enlist its common sense attitudes and pre-existing stories for specific ends.

For example, a film such as *Operation Abolition,* which describes protests against a set of hearings by the House Un-American Activities Committee (HUAC) into Communist agitation in the San Francisco Bay Area in May 1960 as the work of dangerous extremists, readily taps into the stories some audience members will already bring with them about a looming, sinister Communist menace to American society.

By contrast, *Operation Correction* (1961), which recounts the same events and uses much of the same footage, argues that the violence surrounding the protests was instigated by the police. By showing the actual chronology of occurrences, it further claims that *Operation Abolition* deliberately reverses chronology and falsely juxtaposes events to blame the protestors for what the police provoked. *Operation Correction* has more ready-made appeal to audience members who come to film already suspicious of the perpetrators of the Red Scare in postwar America.

The assumptions and expectations we bring to a film, particularly a documentary, can have a significant effect on our reception of the film. They are one dimension of what we need to take into account as we ask what a documentary is about. The bulk of this book looks at the stories told by documentary films themselves, but alongside the subjects spoken about within the films hover the stories of filmmakers and their preoccupations, on the one hand, and of audiences and their predispositions, on the other.

CONCRETE EVENTS
AND ABSTRACT CONCEPTS

Before considering some specific topics that documentaries have frequently addressed, we should note that the concepts and issues we say documentaries are about are themselves invisible. We cannot see poverty as a concept, for example; we can see only specific signs and symptoms of a deprived or debased existence, to which we then assign the concept "poverty." (Some viewers, following other dispositions, might assign other concepts to the same images such as "white trash" or "ghetto life.") That is to say, the documentary value of non-fiction films lies in how they give visual, and audible, representation to topics for which our written or spoken language gives us concepts. Photographic images do not give us the concepts; they give us examples. (This is why so many documentaries rely on a spoken commentary to guide the viewer to the "correct" interpretation of the images that illustrate what's said.) Documentaries offer the sensuous experience of sounds and images organized in such a way that they come to stand for something more than mere passing impressions: they come to stand for qualities and concepts of a more abstract nature.

Frederick Wiseman's *Hospital* (1970), for example, observes a series of encounters between patients and staff in a generic urban hospital (New York City's Metropolitan Hospital), but amounts to more than an informational or instructional account of how the hospital works. The film becomes a representation of, or perspective on, how *hospitals* work. It possesses its own distinct voice or point of view. Wiseman's organization of these specific encounters come to stand for a perspective on basic concepts such as "medical ethics," "bureaucracy," "class difference," and "quality of life." We derive these concepts, intangible and invisible themselves, from the scenes Wiseman puts before us, just as we infer from his editing and organization of the film what Wiseman's views are on how well this particular hospital fulfills its duties and obligations.

Similarly, John Huston could say, in written English, "War is hell" or "The ordinary soldier pays with his life for what generals decide," but his film *The Battle of San Pietro* shows us what war is like so that we may arrive at such thematic abstractions ourselves from the immediate experience of Huston's choice of specific moments of war. Huston's act of showing becomes more than a mere record or display because it is organized through specific acts of selection and arrangement, such as a voice-over comment, by Huston himself as the narrator, to "Note the interesting treatment of the chancel" of the San Pietro town church when what we see is its bombed-out ruins. The "incidental" reference to carnage in the tone and vocabulary of architectural design creates a vivid sense of irony: it is as if Huston were saying, "War is hell—and even more so when we do not even see it as such."

Put differently, documentary films usually contain a tension between the specific and the general, between historically unique moments and generalizations. Without generalizing, potential documentaries would be little more than records of specific events and experiences. Were they nothing but generalizations, documentaries would be little more than abstract treatises. It is the combination of the two, the individual shots and scenes that locate us in a particular time and place and the organization of these elements into a larger whole, that gives documentary film and video its power and fascination.

Most of the topics that we identify as common topics in documentary filmmaking, such as war, violence, biography, sexuality, ethnicity, and so on, are abstractions derived from but not identical to specific experiences. They are ways of bundling experience into larger categories, or gestalts, that have distinct qualities of their own. This is what we mean when we say that the whole is greater than the sum of the parts. Documentary films do precisely this: they bundle shots and scenes into larger categories or gestalts, what we call concepts. This is what allows us to treat them as something other than straightforward records or mere footage. Documentaries are *organized* sequences of shots that are about something conceptual or abstract because of this organization (such as a problem/solution structure, a story with a beginning and end, a focus on a crisis, an emphasis on a tone or mood, and so on).

What specific kind of concepts or issues do documentaries address? In general, they address those concepts and issues over which there is ap-

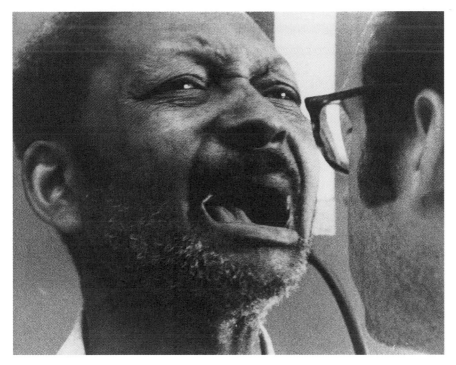

Hospital (Frederick Wiseman, 1970). Photo courtesy of Zipporah Films, Inc., Cambridge, Massachusetts.

Frederick Wiseman exhibits a relentless empiricism that carries hints of surrealism and the theater of the absurd for some viewers. His focus on institutions and social practices from high schools to department stores provides a remarkable study of contemporary American life. His mosaic-like pattern of numerous events that do not follow a single character or issue and that are not united by a voice-over commentary demands that the viewer respond to the often intense charge of the immediate moment and discern the larger patterns of power and control, need and response within the specific social framework that the film addresses.

preciable social concern or debate. If a concept is not in doubt, such as the condensation of liquids as temperatures fall or the evaporation of liquids as temperatures rise, there is little call for a documentary film to address it. An informational or instructional film may still be of use to explain and exemplify the concept, but its organization is strictly devoted to conveying factual information and consolidating our grasp of an undisputed concept rather than coloring or inflecting our very understanding of the concept itself. Their interest as documentaries is close to nil. It is *debated concepts* and *contested issues* that documentaries routinely address.

Debates and contestation surround the basic social institutions and practices of our society. Social practices are precisely that: the conventional way of doing things. They could be otherwise. For example, many serious issues of law are resolved by juries in the United States and by judges in Europe. A different judge or jury may very well come to a different conclusion about the same issue. Children may feel they owe a debt to their parents after they become adults themselves, or not, depending on the conventions of a culture and an individual's own relation to those conventions and to their actual parents. A woman may feel she deserves, and be prepared to demand, opportunity and treatment equal to that given men, or not, depending on the prevailing social practices and her personal attitude toward them.

Social practices gain support from the ways in which various ideals get attached to them. These ideals or values are then adopted by those engaged in a specific social practice. We believe women should remain at home and men work because this fulfills an ideal we have about family life and the raising of children, for example; or, conversely, we believe men and women should contribute to child-raising equally because this fulfills an ideal we have about equality between the sexes.

With most social practices, where more than one way of doing things is possible and where more than one set of values or ideals can be attached and adopted, different approaches must contend with each other. Dominant values must struggle to remain dominant. Alternative values must struggle to gain legitimacy. We enter contested terrain where different ideals and values compete for our allegiance. This competition gets played out in an ideological arena rather than by coercive means. Dominant and alternative practices seek to persuade us of their value rather than physically force us to comply. (Force remains a last resort.) Persuasion, though, requires a means of representing an acceptable way of doing things, a desirable course of action, a preferable solution that makes these options ones we will feel disposed to make our own. Persuasion requires communication, and communication depends on a means of representation, from written languages to dress codes, from television to film, from video to the web. These sign systems are the fundamental means of persuasive representation.

THE CHALLENGE OF PERSUASION

In the Western tradition, the different uses to which spoken and written language can be put has led to a classification scheme that sketches out three broad categories: poetics and narrative (for telling stories and evoking moods), logic (for matters conducted in the spirit of scientific or philosophic inquiry), and rhetoric (for creating consensus or winning agreement on issues open to debate). Each of these three great divisions of language has a particular sphere to which it is most appropriate, but they are not mutually exclusive: elements of narrative (suspense or point of view) and poetic figures of speech (metaphor or simile) color both scientific and rhetorical discourse; persuasive tactics sometimes play a central role in both story telling and scientific reasoning. (Galileo, for example, had to couch much of his argument against considering the earth as the center of the universe in terms that would persuade the Church hierarchy and not seem blasphemous; this challenge called for rhetorical skill as much as for logical proof.)

In general, then, we can say documentary is about the effort to convince, persuade, or predispose us to a particular view of the actual world we occupy. Documentary work does not appeal primarily or exclusively to our aesthetic sensibility: it may entertain or please, but does so in relation to a rhetorical or persuasive effort aimed at the existing social world. Documentary not only activates our aesthetic awareness (unlike a strictly informational or training film), it also activates our social consciousness. This is a disappointment to some, who yearn for the pleasure of escaping into the imaginary worlds of fiction, but it is a source of stimulation for others, who hunger for imaginative, passionate engagement with the pressing issues and concerns of the day.

In ancient times rhetoric, or oratory, garnered less respect than logic, or philosophy, because it seemed to be a concession to those aspects of human affairs not yet subject to the rule of reason. Our experience of the course of some two thousand years of additional history, our acquaintance with Sigmund Freud and the idea of the unconscious, and our awareness of the links between power and knowledge, belief and ideology give us reason to suspect that rhetoric is not the bastard child of logic but more likely its master. At the very least we can say that rhetoric is an indispensable ally in those situations where we must speak about issues for which widespread agreement does not exist. Put differently, if an issue has not yet been definitively decided, or if agreement cannot be definitively achieved, documentary film is one important means for disposing us to see that issue from a specific perspective. Most social practices—from family life to social welfare, from war to urban planning—occupy contested territory. Documentary film and video engages us on just such territory.

Rhetoric, or oratory, then, is the use of language of particular interest to the study of documentary film and video. The topics that documentary is about often belong to the three kinds of issues that were considered the proper domain of rhetoric. These issues fall into the three classic divisions of rhetoric. These divisions identify most, but not all, of the issues documentaries address.

Legislative or Deliberative

This is the domain of encouraging or discouraging, exhorting or dissuading others on a course of public action. Political issues of social policy such as war, welfare, conservation, abortion, artificial reproduction, national identity, and international relations belong to this domain. Deliberations face toward the future and pose questions of what is to be done. A problem/solution structure fits deliberation comfortably; it allows the expediency or harmfulness of different choices to receive careful scrutiny. Films from *Smoke Menace,* favoring gas heat over smog-producing coal, and *Housing Problems,* favoring government-sponsored housing to eliminate slums, to *Why Vietnam?,* supporting American involvement in Vietnam, and *It's Elementary: Gay Issues in School,* attacking homophobia and supporting efforts to eliminate stereotyping and violence, exemplify the deliberative use of rhetoric in documentary.

Judicial or Historical

This is the domain of evaluating (accusing or defending, justifying or criticizing) previous actions. The judicial orator looks toward the past and poses questions of "What really happened?" These are questions of fact and interpretation, where guilt or innocence is at stake in relation to the law and truth or falsehood at stake in relation to history. The orator sets out to see justice done or to establish the truth, matters that would call for definitive resolution, although such resolution is seldom achieved in undisputed form (verdicts are appealed, laws changed, and histories revised).

In judicial as in deliberative rhetoric, public issues of morality and tradition, value and belief are put to the test. These are cases where "the truth" in any definitive sense is not entirely certain. The issue is open to doubt. Trials exist to put doubt to rest, but do so on the basis of evidence and argument that is, in its totality, less than scientific.

Were logic to prevail, the outcome of trials would not be subject to appeal, and questions of guilt and innocence would not persist despite the verdict of a jury. That we rely on verdicts rather than scientific proofs, and turn to the judgment of our peers rather than allow experts and specialists to decide, hints at the fundamental undecidability of issues involving the past.

Similarly, history writing functions like a trial, putting the past into the witness box to tell its story of what happened while we, the readers or viewers, attend, noting the point of view or line of argument of the historian as we arrive at a judgment. That we turn to more than one account of events to form our own view hints at the fundamental undecidability of the past. *Shoah,* on questions of guilt and responsibility for the Holocaust, *The Thin*

FAR FROM POLAND
a film by JILL GODMILOW

Beach Street Productions
135 Hudson Street, NY,NY 10013
(212) 226-2462

TOP: Anna Walentynowicz, Gdansk, 1980
BOTTOM: Ruth Maleczech in the role of
Anna Walentynowicz

Far from Poland (Jill Godmilow, 1984). Photos by Mark Magill, courtesy of Jill Godmilow.

Jill Godmilow explores the dilemma facing the documentarian who cannot be there, on the spot where events occur. The Solidarity movement transformed Polish society, but Godmilow could not secure a visa to enter Poland as a filmmaker. How could she represent the movement and her own dilemma? She opted for a technique older than Flaherty's *Nanook of the North:* reenactment.

Instead of treating reenactments as if they were fully authentic, however, Godmilow makes it clear to us that what we see represents situations and events we cannot see directly. Godmilow recruits individuals to play the roles of Solidarity participants for her film. She herself plays the role of a filmmaker trying to make a film about the Solidarity movement.

Blue Line, on an individual case of guilt or innocence, *The Fall of the Romanov Dynasty,* on the history of Russia leading up to the revolution of 1917, and *Eyes on the Prize,* about the history of the civil rights movement in the United States, exemplify the range of documentary filmmaking in the judicial or historical domain.

Ceremonial or Panegyric

This is the domain of praising or blaming others, of evoking qualities and establishing attitudes toward people and their accomplishments. This rhetoric of assessment complements deliberative and judicial rhetoric to enhance the moral weight of an argument. The orator often looks to the present but may draw heavily on the past to prove worthiness or unworthiness. Rules of evidence and argumentative procedure, however, are less firmly established for ceremonial rhetoric than for deliberative or judicial. Character can be made, or unmade, by a variety of means; fairness and impartiality are not always honored.

Much of what we can categorize as ceremonial rhetoric could also be called biographical, essayistic, or poetic: it addresses a person or situation and sets out to supply an affective, moral coloration to it. It seeks to render people, places, and things in pleasing or displeasing tonalities.

In some ways ceremonial rhetoric is similar to description in narrative: at times description seems extraneous to the primary business of advancing the plot; at other times it seems vital if the plot is to have any texture or resonance at all. "Boy meets girl" is altogether too bare-boned a plot to hold interest until descriptive strategies give some distinctiveness and life to a particular "boy" and "girl."

Similarly, commemorative rhetoric can give life to deliberative and judicial rhetoric as well as stand on its own as a more poetic form of description. In this way it differs from a prosaic biography that sketches the chronological details of a given life. Commemorative rhetoric sets out to give moral coloration to a person's life so that we may deem it worthy of emulation and respect or of demonization and rejection. That we remain uncertain of our final judgment of others, that no single, agreed-upon set of standards exists in our society, and that no one set of procedures for consistently applying such standards enjoys universal acceptance are factors that make rhetoric necessary. We are once again in the realm of the contested or undecidable. It is the task of rhetoric to move us toward decision and judgment.

Nanook of the North, with its portrait of Nanook as a worthy hunter and father; *N!ai: Story of a !Kung Woman,* as the portrait of a hard-pressed but strong-willed !Kung woman over a period of some twenty years; *Lonely Boy,* on Paul Anka as a dubious example of the making of a young male singing sensation; and *Paris Is Burning,* as a sympathetic and respectful description of the lives of individuals within a black and Latino urban gay subculture of masquerade and performance, give some idea of the range of films that take up topics for which commemorative rhetoric is appropriate.

THE POWER OF METAPHOR

One final generalization about the topics of documentaries is that they are about those concepts and issues that we need metaphors to describe. That is to say, some topics lend themselves to straightforward description; few issues are involved, and a prosaic, linear account is all we want or need. The manufacture of silicon chips might be such a topic, and the use of various grips and strokes in tennis another. Love, war, and family, on the other hand, are topics that a straightforward, dictionary-style definition does not exhaust. We may know what these subjects mean in a dictionary sense ("strong affection for or attraction to another," "armed, hostile conflict between states," "the basic unit in society, having as its nucleus at least one parent and one child"), but still debate whether they are a blessing or a curse, heaven or hell. We may debate such questions about love, war, family, and other topics in general, or we may focus on specific instances: Perhaps war is a necessary evil, but is America justified in bombing Vietnam, or Kosovo? Maybe families are a sacred form of union, but is the Loud family exemplary of such union? (The Louds are the family at the center of the multiple-part documentary *An American Family.*) Documentary films enter into the debate to offer persuasive accounts or arguments. They furnish us with a way of saying, "War is hell" or "Families are snake pits" or "a haven." These metaphors enrich and enliven our grasp of dictionary definitions and give them a moral, social, and political coloration.

Social practices, basic domains of human experience, lend themselves to metaphor. We can know what a family is in a dictionary sense and still want to know what family is *like* in a more metaphorical sense. Metaphors come into service to give us ways of likening war or love or family to something else that has similar qualities or values. Depending on whether we say that a family is a haven in a heartless world, as *The Adventures of Ozzie and Harriet* suggests, or a family is a battlefield, as *A Married Couple* (1970) suggests, our view of family life will differ considerably. Similarly, if war is a kind of hell and if hell is a painful, undesirable state, then war must be something to avoid, as *The Battle of San Pietro* suggests. If war is a rite of passage or test of manhood, and if such rites and tests provide a sense of identity and even glory, then war must be something to embrace, as *The Spanish Earth* suggests. It all depends on the values we assign to war in general or to a specific war or a given side in a war. The values we favor or reject are often indicated by metaphor.

Documentary film as an organized sequence of sounds and images constructs metaphors that assign or infer, affirm or contest values that surround social practices about which we as a society remain divided. They use deliberative, judicial, and panegyric rhetoric, among other strategies, to persuade us of their orientation, judgment, or particular argument.

Metaphors help us define or understand things in terms of how they look or feel; they establish a likeness that involves our own physical or experiential encounter with a situation rather than our knowledge of a standard dictionary definition. Metaphors draw on basic forms of personal experience like physical orientation (up, down, above, below) to assign values to social concepts. Success, for example, may be represented as *rising* to a *higher* station in life, not literally moving to a place of greater altitude but metaphorically moving to a social position of greater esteem.

Such representations are readily available to film, where we can show someone ascending an actual slope as a metaphor for success or show images of dead bodies as a metaphor for war as hell. The selection and arrangement of sounds and images are sensuous and real; they provide an immediate form of audible and visual experience, but they also become, through their organization into a larger whole, a metaphorical representation of what something in the historical world is like.

What is it like to negotiate the marriage of a young woman in Turkana society? It is *like this* when, in *Wedding Camels,* we see the particular negotiations surrounding a particular wedding but understand them to stand for a representation of wedding negotiations in the culture as a whole. Love is *like this* in *A Married Couple, Sherman's March,* or *Silverlake Life;* war is *like this* in *Frank, A Vietnam Veteran, The Anderson Platoon,* or *Victory at Sea;* family is *like this* in *Finding Christa, The Body Beautiful,* or *Nobody's Business.*

We may know the dictionary definition for these social practices and still hunger for metaphorical representations to help us understand what values to attach to these social practices. Documentaries give us the sense that we can understand how other social actors experience situations and events that fall into familiar categories (family life, health care, sexual orientation, social justice, death, and so on). Documentaries offer an orientation to the experience of others and, by extension, to the social practices we share with them.

Whether we accept the perspectives and arguments of documentary films as our own or not will depend heavily on the stylistic and rhetorical power of the film. The oscillation between the specific and the general in documentary, though, results from the effectiveness of allowing a particular representation to (metaphorically) stand for a general orientation or assessment of a given issue or topic. Metaphorical understanding is often the most meaningful and persuasive way of convincing us of the merit of one perspective over others. A definition of genocide may sound appalling ("the deliberate and systematic destruction of a racial, political, or cultural group"), but the sound and image of a specific bulldozer pushing a large mass of individual naked bodies into an open trench at a given, historical moment *is* appalling in a more vivid, indelible way. If genocide is *like this,* as the representation of it in *Night and Fog* suggests, the metaphor presents us with a perspective and orientation of formidable power.

What we speak about in documentary then are those subjects that engage us most passionately, and divisively, in life. These subjects follow the pathways of our desire as we come to terms with what it means to take on an identity, to have intimate, private connection to an other, and to belong in the public company of others. Personal identity, sexual intimacy, and social belonging are another way of defining the subjects of documentary film.

Along the paths marked out by our desires in these three directions we find such basic subjects as biography and autobiography, gender and sexuality, family and intimate relationships, labor and class, power and hierarchy, violence and war, economics, nationality, ethnicity, race, social justice and social change, history and culture. Documentaries provide us with representations of what encounters with these different forms of social practices have been like for other people in other places from a perspective designed to predispose us toward a particular perspective of our own.

The Fall of the Romanov Dynasty (1927), for example, recounts the story of the final years of Romanov rule in Russia and the early days of the Soviet revolution. It sets up a series of striking parallels and contrasts between life for the Czar, his family, and his court and life for the majority of the Russian people. Life under the Romanovs becomes a world of vivid oppositions: leisure or labor, wealth or poverty, elegance or necessity. Esther Shub provides this perspective by way of archival film material that she reassembles into an indictment. She accentuates the contrasts with intertitles, juxtapositions, and individual shots that sometimes ironically and sometimes caustically declare the moral bankruptcy of a regime indifferent to the condition of its subjects.

In one shot, for example, a count and his wife take tea at an outdoor table. After they rise to leave, a servant appears to remove the tea service. The class relation is clearly revealed through these actions alone, but Shub's archival clip goes one step further: when we look closely we see that the servant is standing in the deep background of the shot all along, waiting for his cue to move forward and reclaim the tea service. Shub has found an early home movie that this count staged to document his estate life in the way that landscape paintings documented the wealth of the landed gentry, only now the document's moral value is reversed: it stands as a condemnation of what it once celebrated. The very act of staging the rituals of domination and servitude, which was perhaps meant to pass unnoticed originally, becomes, itself, evidence of the willingness to use others to maintain privilege that Shub argues brought the Romanovs down.

In another documentary of social change, Jill Godmilow provides an account of the rise of the Solidarity movement in Poland and the collapse of Communist rule. In contrast to Shub, Godmilow does not have access to a bounty of archival footage, nor does she even have access to events as they unfold. Various obstacles keep her in New York as Solidarity makes its advances toward power. How can Godmilow represent what she cannot witness? *Far from Poland* (1984) adopts a reflexive rather than an expository strategy. Godmilow makes the film into a work that is, all at once, *about* the difficulties of representation, about the convention of "being there" as testament to the truth of what is said, about the motivations filmmakers have for representing others when this act distorts as readily as it reveals, and about this specific historical moment of social transformation. The perspective is one that warns us about the powers of documentary representation at the same time as it expresses a clear solidarity with the social movement it can only partially and incompletely represent.

Similarly, *Dead Birds* is an ethnographic account of life among the Dani of the New Guinea Highlands, a tribe still living in a nearly pre-contact state at the time of this expedition in 1961. The film has as a central preoccupation ritual violence among the Dani. Adopting a poetic, reflective tone, Gardner suggests that the rigors and hazards of ritual warfare, in which large contingents of men from neighboring groups hurl spears and shoot arrows at each other until someone is wounded or killed, play a vital role in defining individual and cultural identity. Life is *like this,* Gardner suggests, when we engage in regulated forms of social aggression, the better to maintain a sense of social coherence.

By contrast, Mitchell Block's *No Lies,* like Godmilow's *Far from Poland,* takes a more reflexive view of ritual violence. Block uses the psychic violence of an intrusive, tactless filmmaker who persists in drawing out, and judging, the story of how his friend was raped as a commentary not only on the problem of rape and our social attitudes toward it, as men and women, but also on the problem of the ritual violence of representing the

The Fall of the Romanov Dynasty (Esther Shub, 1927)

This documentary image of a count and his wife clearly required not simply its subjects' consent but their active orchestration: as a home movie, it demonstrates their everyday ritual, in pre-revolutionary Russia, of taking tea in the garden. The couple leaves the frame, and we may assume the shot has fulfilled its usefulness. But no; the shot continues, and a pair of servants enters to remove the used tea service. Shub converts the home movie into a social document of class structure and hierarchy. In a good print it is even possible to see the male servant waiting in the background, behind the shrubs, for his cue to enter the foreground, or, no doubt in Shub's mind, the historical stage.

Far from Poland. Photo by David Dekok, courtesy of Jill Godmilow.

Shooting "on location" for the film, but with Shamokin, Pennsylvania, standing in for the coal mines of Poland. Through her self-conscious style, Godmilow adds a reflexive note that makes us aware of the substitutions. This may prompt us to question the limitations and values of the trade-off between a sense of authenticity and the forms of truth it supports. Her tactics, at the very least, contrast strikingly with those of the television newscasts of the same events.

victims of rape as targets for a medium that perpetuates the victimization of the original act. The filmmaker psychically abuses his subject just as her assailant physically abused her. By representing this process of abuse as a function of documentary representation, Block calls into question the ethical underpinnings of the relation between filmmaker and subject in a direct and pointed way. He asks whether the act of filming an interview with a woman who has been raped in *this* way is *like* the actual rape she has already experienced.

As a final example, consider two representations of family relations. In *Four Families* (1959), Margaret Mead adopts the expository mode (a voice-over commentary) to compare and contrast family life among four families from four different cultures: France, India, Japan, and Canada. She applies conceptual categories such as child raising, discipline, male and female roles, and so on to make points about the many similarities and some of the differences among cultures. The specific families we see serve as examples. We do not get to know individual family members in any complex sense. Examples of their behavior and interaction are selected to illustrate qualities of the culture as a whole rather than of the social actors as individuals. Margaret Mead informs us that family life in these cultures is *like this.*

This representation of the family as a culturally homogenous entity, best understood when compared to families from another culture, contrasts sharply with the view we have in Ngozi Onwurah's *The Body Beautiful* (1991). Onwurah adopts a performative approach to the subject of her relationship to her own mother. The filmmaker is the product of a mixed-race marriage between her African father and her British mother. Via a poetic voice-over and reenacted childhood scenes that feature her actual mother, the filmmaker describes the ambivalence she felt as a child toward her working-class and, from her youthful perspective, unattractive mother. Only in retrospect does she come to recognize the hardship her mother experienced and the sacrifices she made, beginning with the choice to see her pregnancy with Ngozi to term, even when it meant that she would have to undergo a radical mastectomy for a cancer that might have been treated without removing her breast had she done so during the pregnancy, but at risk to her growing fetus.

Onwurah enacts a drama of reconciliation and love that is highly performative in its emphasis on the filmmaker's own subjective investment in the subject. (At one point, Onwurah stages an imaginary seduction and love scene between her mother and a younger black man that would not have occurred had Onwurah not chosen to stage it.) We learn no statistical facts about mixed-race marriages or the complexities of identifying differences in family structure at the level of national cultures. Instead, *The Body Beautiful* immerses us in a representation that suggests, "An ambivalent relationship to one's own mother is *like this.*" The metaphor is all the more rooted and powerful when based on her own specific family.

The affective power of these two films is radically different, as are the claims to general social knowledge that each makes. Mead's film suggests that families can be understood in terms of a cross-cultural, comparative examination of categories that are given concrete exemplification via the four families selected to stand for the four cultures, whereas Onwurah's film suggests that families can be understood in terms of a highly localized, embodied sense of what the conflicts and dilemmas in one particular family, her own, were like. Just as Mead's film allows for particularization through the four families selected, but downplays it, Onwurah's film allows for generalization to issues of race, class, and nationality, but downplays that di-

The Body Beautiful (Ngozi Onwurah, 1991). Photo courtesy of Women Make Movies.

Sian Martin poses during a fashion shoot in Onwurah's film about her relation to her own mother. The world of fashion photography represents an escape from the drab existence associated with her mother. An imaginary seduction scene that Onwurah stages with her own mother as one of the participant/actors suggests an attempt to transport her mother out of her ordinary existence into a world of fantasy. The larger theme of the film, however, is the process by which Onwurah comes to accept both her mother and all of the blunt realities of her mother's own life.

mension in favor of specificity. Both films adopt a "Family life is *like this*" form of metaphorical assertion, but they do so in very different ways.

In sum, documentary films and videos speak about the historical world in ways designed to move or persuade us. They tend to dwell on those aspects of experience that fall into the general categories of social practices and institutionally mediated relations: family life, sexual orientation, social conflict, war, nationality, ethnicity, history, and so on. They take up these issues from a particular point of view; they represent one way of seeing, and valuing or assessing, their subject. As such they become one voice among the many voices in an arena of social debate and contestation. This is the arena in which we vie for the support and belief of others in the name of a particular cause or system of values. It is, ultimately, an ideological arena that establishes our commitment to or detachment from the dominant practices and values of our culture. Rhetorical techniques are crucial in this arena since neither logic nor force can readily prevail. The arena is a small but compelling one in *The Body Beautiful* and a large but galvanizing one in *The Fall of the Romanov Dynasty*. In either case, documentary film and video moves us to understand and engage the historical world in ways that matter.

Chapter 5

How Did Documentary Filmmaking Get Started?

THE MYTHIC ORIGIN IN EARLY CINEMA

The voice of documentary relates to the ways in which documentary film and video speaks about the world around us, but from a particular perspective. When a documentary makes a case or advances an argument, "voice" refers to how it does so. Our discussion of voice would not be complete without some consideration of how this form of speech about the world arose. When did it begin; what relation does it enjoy to other forms of cinema? How, in other words, did documentary find its voice?

We should note that no one set out to build a documentary film tradition. No one set out to "invent" documentary film as such. The effort to construct the history for documentary film, a story with a beginning, way back then, and an end, now or in the future, comes after the fact. It comes with the desire of filmmakers and writers, like myself, to understand how things got to be the way they are now. But to those who came before us, back then, how things are now was a matter of idle speculation.

Their interest was not in providing a clean, clear path for the development of a documentary tradition that did not yet exist. Their interest and passion was in exploring the limits of cinema, in discovering new possibilities and untried forms. That some of these efforts would jell into what we now call documentary obscures the blurred boundaries between fiction and non-fiction, documenting reality and experimenting with form, showing and telling, narrative and rhetoric that fueled these early efforts. The continuation of this tradition of experimentation is what allows documentary itself to remain a lively, vital genre.

A standard way of explaining the rise of documentary involves the story of the cinema's love for the surface of things, its uncanny ability to capture life as it is, an ability that served as a hallmark for early cinema and its immense catalog of people, places, and things culled from around the world. Like photography before it, the cinema was a revelation. People had never seen images that possessed such extraordinary fidelity to their subject, and they had never witnessed apparent motion that had imparted such a convincing sense of motion itself. As film theorist Christian Metz noted in the 1960s in a discussion of the phenomenology of film, to duplicate the impression of movement is to duplicate its reality. Cinema achieved this goal at a level no other medium had ever attained.

The capacity of photographic images to render such a vivid impression of reality, including movement as a vital aspect of life that painting and sculpture had been able only to allude to but not to duplicate, prompts two complementary stories to unfold—one about the image and one about the filmmaker.

The remarkable fidelity of the photographic image to what it records gives such an image the appearance of a document. It offers visible evidence of what the camera saw. The underlying sense of authenticity in the films of Louis Lumière made at the end of the nineteenth century, such as *Workers Leaving the Lumière Factory, Arrival of a Train, The Waterer Watered, The Gardener,* and *Feeding the Baby,* seem but a small step away from documentary film proper. Although they are but a single shot and last but a few minutes, they seem to provide a window onto the historical world. (Fiction films often give the impression that we look in on a private or unusual world from outside, from our vantage point in the historical world, whereas documentary films often give the impression that we look out from our corner of the world onto some other part of the same world.) The departing workers in *Workers Leaving the Lumière Factory,* for example, walk out of the factory and past the camera for us to see as if we were there, watching this specific moment from the past take place all over again.

These early works have typically served as the "origin" of documentary by maintaining a "faith in the image" of the sort the influential French critic André Bazin admired when he tried to answer the question "What Is Cinema?" through a series of important essays in the 1940s. Lumière's films seemed to record everyday life as it happened. Shot without adornment or editorial rearrangement, they reveal the shimmering mystery of events. They appear to reproduce the event and preserve the mystery. A note of humility was in the air. The cinema was an instrument of extraordinary power; it required no exaggeration or spectacle to win our admiration.

The second story involves the filmmaker. The remarkable accuracy of the image as a photographic representation of what the camera saw fascinated those who took the pictures. A compelling need to explore this source of fascination drove early cinematographers to record diverse aspects of the world around them. Even if they staged aspects of the action or decorated the scene, as Georges Méliès did in works such as his *A Trip to the Moon* (1902), a fascination with the power of the photographic image to record whatever came before it and to present the product of this power to an audience by means of the film strip, capable of projection over and over, took precedence over the niceties of story telling or character development.

We have, then, two stories, (1) the uncanny capacity of film images and photographs to bear the physical imprint of what they record with photomechanical precision thanks to the passage of light energy through lenses and onto a photographic emulsion, combined with (2) the compulsion that was ignited in early film pioneers to explore this capacity, form, for some, the foundation for the rise of documentary film. The combination of a passion for recording the real and an instrument capable of great fidelity attained a purity of expression in the act of documentary filming.

This conventional story culminates in the dual attainments of the narrative polish with which Robert Flaherty brought Inuit life to the screen in *Nanook of the North* (1922) and of the marketing skill with which John Grierson established an institutional base for what, by the late 1920s, had become known as documentary film. Grierson spearheaded the government sponsorship of documentary production in 1930s Britain as Dziga Vertov had done throughout the 1920s in the Soviet Union and as Pare Lorentz would do in the mid-1930s in the United States. In point of fact, Vertov promoted documentary quite a bit earlier than Grierson but remained more of a maverick within the fledgling Soviet film industry; he did not attract a corps of like-minded filmmakers nor gain anything like the solid institutional footing that Grierson achieved. John Grierson became the prime mover of the British and, later, the Canadian documentary film movements. Despite the valuable example of Dziga Vertov and the Soviet cinema generally, it was Grierson who secured a relatively stable niche for documentary film production.

Coupling the uncanny power of film to document pre-existing phenomena with the rise of an institutional base corresponds to the four-way definition of documentary discussed in Chapter 2. These developments provide a group of practitioners, an institutional frame, a body of films with common characteristics, and, presumably, an audience attentive to these distinguishing qualities. These developments, though, amount to necessary but not sufficient conditions. Their use to tell the story of documentary film's beginnings presumes too clear a set of intentions and too straightforward a march from the origins of cinema to the achievements of documentary. This story amounts to a myth.

The capacity of film to provide rigorous documentation of what comes before the camera leads in at least two other directions: science and spectacle. Both directions begin with early cinema (roughly from 1895 to 1906, when narrative cinema begins to gain dominance). Both have contributed to documentary film development but are hardly synonymous with it. The differences can be noted briefly.

First, the capacity of the photographic image (and later of the recorded soundtrack) to generate precise replicas of certain aspects of their source material forms the basis for scientific modes of representation. These modes rely heavily on the indexical quality of the photographic image. An indexical sign bears a physical relation to what it refers to: a fingerprint replicates exactly the pattern of whorls on the fleshy tips of our fingers; the asymmetrical shape of a wind-swept tree reveals the strength and direction of the prevailing wind.

The value of this indexical quality to scientific imaging depends heavily on minimizing the degree to which the image, be it a fingerprint or x-ray, exhibits any sense of a perspective or point of view distinctive to its individual maker. A strict code of objectivity, or institutional perspective, applies. The voice of science demands silence, or near silence, from documentarian or photographer. Documentary flourishes when it gains a voice of its own. Producing accurate documents or visual evidence does not lend it such a voice. In fact, it can detract from it.

Documentary film practice allows for the image to generate an appropriate impression rather than guarantee full-blown authenticity in every case. Just as a photograph can be "doctored," so can a documentary. The "father" of documentary, Robert Flaherty, for example, created the impression that some scenes took place inside Nanook's igloo when, in fact, they were shot in the open air with half an oversized igloo as a backdrop. This gave Flaherty enough light to shoot but required his subjects to act as if they were inside an actual igloo when they were not. *Hoop Dreams* adds music to enhance the power of the story, just as a fiction film might do. For *The Thin Blue Line* Errol Morris shot a series of reconstructions that represent the murder of a Dallas police officer as various figures in the film describe it. Not only are the reconstructions discrepant from each other, raising the question of "What really happened?" but every one of them was shot not in Dallas but in New Jersey. These choices all represent tactics by the filmmaker to generate the effect they desire on an audience. They may amount to bad science, but they are part and parcel of documentary representation.

When we believe in something without conclusive proof in the validity of our belief, this becomes an act of fetishism, or faith. Documentary film often invites us to take on faith that "what you see is what there was." This act of trust, or faith, may derive from the indexical capabilities of the photographic image without being fully justified or supported by it. For the filmmaker, creating trust, getting us to suspend doubt or disbelief, by rendering an *impression* of reality, and hence truthfulness, corresponds to the priorities of rhetoric more than to the requirements of science. We accept the evidentiary value of images as an article of faith with some peril.

Early cinema not only supported the scientific use of images, it also led to what film historian Tom Gunning has termed a "cinema of attractions." His term refers to the idea of circus attractions and their open delight in showing us a wide variety of unusual phenomena. Such attractions could both whet the curiosity and satisfy the passion of early cinematographers and audiences alike for images that represented aspects of the world around them. A tone of exhibitionism prevailed that differed radically both from the sense of looking in on a private, fictional world and from documenting material that would serve as scientific evidence. This exhibitionism also differs from documentary.

The cinema of attractions relied on the image as document to present viewers with sensational sketches of the exotic and lingering depictions of the everyday. The "cinema of attractions" paralleled the excitement surrounding the great world fairs and exhibitions of the time, such as the St. Louis World Exhibition in 1904 with its "authentic" recreation of a Filipino village populated by Filipinos imported into the United States more as specimens than citizens. (The exhibit was presented as an anthropological display of native culture.) The "cinema of attractions" pitched its appeal directly to the viewer and took delight in the sensationalism of the exotic and bizarre.

But the voice of the filmmaker was again noticeably silent. The discovery of a celluloid world remarkably similar to the physical world invited us to behold what the camera could put on display. The distinctive point of view of the filmmaker took second place. Louis Lumière sent scores of camera operators around the world armed with his newly patented cinématographe (an invention that not only shot film like a modern motion picture camera but also served to develop and project it!). We remember the names of only a handful of them. What they shot mattered more than how they shot it.

Aspects of this tradition of a "cinema of attractions" linger on just as sci-

Copyright © 1963, by Times Film Corporation. Permission granted for newspaper and magazine reproduction when credit given to Filmruns Prod. | MONDO CANE TECHNICOLOR Produced by GUALTIERO JACOPETTI — A TIMES FILM RELEASE | "Property of National Screen Service Corp. Licensed for display only in connection with the exhibition of this picture in your theatre. Must be returned immediately thereafter." | 63/197

Mondo Cane (Gualtiero Jacopetti, 1963)

A slew of "Mondo" films has followed in the wake of *Mondo Cane.* The sense of spectacle and sensationalism goes back to early cinema and clearly carries over to contemporary "reality TV" shows from *Cops* to *Survivor.*

entific uses of the photographic image remain strong. It is vividly on display in a variety of films that peek into the underbelly of everyday life. We find it, for example, in "mondo" movies, beginning with the classic tour of outrageous customs and bizarre practices, *Mondo Cane* (1963), with its catalogue of bare-breasted women, the mass slaughter of pigs, and august pet cemeteries in different corners of the world. We find a similar display of "attractions" in the hard-core scenes in pornography, where an exhibitionist tone seems to know no limits. Safari films and travelogues on everything from surfing to architecture also rely heavily on this exhibitionist impulse to appeal to us directly with the wonders of what the camera discovered. In addition, reality TV shows such as *Cops* or *Rescue 911* flourish by presenting a succession of images and scenes, as if to say little more than, "Isn't that amazing!" Clearly an element of documentary film, this "cabaret of curiosities" is often an embarrassing fellow-traveler more than a central element.

THE 1920s: DOCUMENTARY FINDS ITS LEGS

Neither an emphasis on showing off (a "cinema of attractions") nor one on gathering evidence (scientific documentation) provides an adequate basis for documentary film. A direct line does not exist from Louis Lumière's train arriving in a station to Hitler arriving at Nuremberg (in *Triumph of the Will*) nor from the fascination with movement itself to fascination with moving audiences to action. We continue to lack a sense of the filmmaker's oratorical voice in these early tendencies. If there were a linear path from these qualities of early cinema to documentary, we would expect documentary to develop in parallel with narrative fiction through the 1900s and 1910s rather than gain widespread recognition only in the late 1920s and early 1930s.

If we couple these two directions that go back to early cinema—display and documentation—into one "leg" of documentary, we need to consider three more legs before we can speak of the arrival of a documentary film genre: (1) poetic experimentation, (2) narrative story telling, and (3) rhetorical oratory. The recognition of documentary as a distinct film form becomes less a question of the origin or evolution of these different elements than of their combination at a given historical moment. That moment came in the 1920s and early 1930s. We can review the nature of these additional three elements here briefly.

Poetic Experimentation

Poetic experimentation in cinema arises largely from the cross-fertilization between cinema and the various modernist avant-gardes of the twentieth century. This poetic dimension plays a vital part in the emergence of a documentary voice. The poetic potential of cinema, though, remains largely absent in the "cinema of attractions," where "showing off" took higher priority than "speaking poetically." Poetry flourished most vividly in the practices of the modernist avant-garde that began after the turn of the century and flourished through the 1920s. Classic examples would include the work of 1920s French impressionist artists and critics such as Jean Epstein (*L'Affiche* [*The Poster*], 1925), Abel Gance (*La Roue* [*The Wheel*], 1922), Louis Delluc (*Fièvre* [*Fever*], 1921), Germaine Dulac (*The Smiling Madame Beudet,* 1923), and René Clair (*Paris Qui Dort,* aka *The Crazy Ray,* 1924) and the experimental work of Dutch filmmaker Joris Ivens (*The Bridge,* 1928; *Rain,* 1929), the German artist Hans Richter (*Rhythmus 23,* 1923; *Inflation,* 1928), the Swedish artist Viking Eggling (*Diagonal Symphony,* 1924), French artist Marcel Duchamp (*Anemic Cinema,* 1927), the Ukranian filmmaker Alexander Dovzhenko (*Zvenigora,* 1928), and the expatriate American Man Ray (*Retour à la Raison,* 1923).

It was within the avant-garde that the sense of a distinct point of view or voice took shape in ways that refused to subordinate perspective to showing off attractions or creating fictional worlds. This work often began with photographic images of everyday reality, although some, such as Man Ray's "rayograms," were made without a lens by exposing undeveloped film to various objects. These images of a recognizable world quickly veered in directions other than fidelity to the object and realism as a style. The filmmaker's way of seeing things took higher priority than demonstrating the camera's ability to record what it saw faithfully and accurately.

Voice came to the fore in modernist works such as Dimitri Kirsanov's *Menilmontant* (1924), a tale of love betrayed, murder, and contemplated suicide told from a woman's point of view; Alberto Cavalcanti's *Rien que les Heures* (1926), a day in the life of Paris that flips whimsically between images of reality and the reality of images (images of a woman descending a staircase become a strip of film that is torn up and tossed into the street, for example); Joris Ivens's *The Bridge* (1928), with its "story" of the rise and fall of a bridge told primarily through carefully composed but fragmented shots of the bridge's structure, and Man Ray's *L'Etoile de Mer* (1928), a surreal series of scenes involving events in the everyday life of a Parisian woman.

The empirical ability of film to produce a photographic record of what it recorded struck many of these artists as an impediment or handicap. If a perfect copy was all that was desired, what room was left for the artist's desire, for the impulses and idiosyncrasies of vision that saw the world anew? A film technician would do. French impressionist theory in the 1920s celebrated what Jean Epstein termed *photogénie,* whereas Soviet film theory championed the concept of montage. Both were ways of overcoming the mechanical reproduction of reality in favor of the construction of something new in ways only cinema could accomplish.

Photogénie referred to what the film image offered that supplemented or differed from what it represented. A machine-governed, automatic reproduction of what came before the camera became secondary to the magic worked by the image itself. Details of reality could become wondrous when projected onto a screen. The image offered a captivating rhythm and a seductive magic all its own. The experience of watching film differed from looking at reality in ways that words could only imperfectly explain.

Abel Gance's *La Roue,* for example, used single-frame flashbacks and numerous motifs of wheels, rotation, and movement to capture the delirium of a train engineer caught up in an impossible love. Robert Flaherty, in a spirit different from the French impressionists, also suggests what this sense of wonder can be like when he begins *Louisiana Story* with a slow,

Berlin: Symphony of a City (Walter Ruttmann, 1927)

This publicity still for the film uses photomontage to celebrate the dynamism and energy of the modern city but does so without the sharp, political edge that photo-and film-montage achieved elsewhere in 1920s Germany and in '20s Soviet cinema and constructivist art. Montage can stress formal relationships or political associations. The editing of *Berlin,* like the photomontage in this still, opts for the poetic over the political.

enchanting journey through the Louisiana bayou as seen from the pirogue of a young boy.

The idea of *photogénie* and editing, or montage, allowed the filmmaker's voice to take center stage. Ruttmann's *Berlin: Symphony of a City* (1927), for example, has a poetic but non-analytic voice; it celebrates the diversity of daily life in Berlin unrelated to any clear social or political analysis of urban life. Dziga Vertov's *The Man with a Movie Camera* (1929), by contrast, adopts a poetic but also reflexive, analytic voice to examine the transformative power of the coordinated masses as they, like the machinery of cinema, go about the business of producing a new, post-revolutionary Soviet society.

The avant-garde flourished in Europe and Russia in the 1920s. Its emphasis on seeing things anew, through the eyes of the artist or filmmaker, had tremendous liberating potential. It freed cinema from replicating what came before the camera to celebrate how this "stuff" could become the raw material not only of narrative filmmaking but of a poetic cinema as well. This space beyond mainstream cinema became the proving ground for voices that spoke to viewers in languages distinct from feature fiction.

Narrative Story-telling

Together with the development of a poetic voice, the period after 1906 also saw the development of an even more dominant narrative voice. This is the second element missing from scientific observation and the "cinema of attractions" that goes into the construction of documentary and its voice. In narrative story telling, style (from individual preferences to common approaches such as expressionism, neo-realism, or surrealism) coupled with the construction of a plot to tell a story that revealed, through the unique combination of style and plot, the voice or perspective of filmmakers on the world they created, and, obliquely, through this imagined world, on the historical world they shared with others.

What mattered most for the development of documentary was the refinement of story-telling techniques for the cinema as such, from the parallel editing of D. W. Griffith to the ways in which an action or event could be told from different perspectives (from the perspective of an omniscient narrator, the perspective of a third-person observer, or the points of view of different characters, for example).

Narrative offered a formal way of telling stories that could be applied to the historical world as well as an imaginary one. History and biography, for example, usually take the form of narratives but in a non-fiction mode. Narratives resolve conflict and achieve order. The problem/solution structure of many documentaries makes use of narrative techniques as well as rhetoric. Narrative perfects the sense of an ending by returning to problems or dilemmas posed at the beginning and resolving them.

Narrative also welcomes forms of suspense, or delay, where complications can mount and anticipation grow. It provides ways of elaborating a sense of character, not only through the performance of actors trained to act for the camera, but through the techniques of lighting, composition, and editing, among others, that can be applied to non-actors as readily as actors. It refined the techniques of continuity editing to give a seamless sense of coherent time and space to the locations in which characters acted. Even when documentaries turned to evidentiary editing and the assembly of material from various times and places, the techniques of continuity editing facilitated the smooth flow of one image to another by matching movement, action, eyeline, or scale from one shot to another. All of these developments found uses in documentary, most vividly, perhaps, in strictly observational films (such as *Primary* or *Salesman*) that looked in on the lives of people and invited the audience to interpret what it saw as if it were a fiction.

Writing in the postwar years in France, André Bazin celebrated the achievements of Italian neo-realism for reasons similar to those later used to celebrate *cinéma vérité* or observational documentary. Although the Italian films were fictional narratives, they demonstrated what Bazin considered a profound respect for reality by finding a narrative "voice" that was humble and modest but hardly silent.

The neo-realists eschewed attempts to evoke the quality of *photogénie* through extremes of stylization favored by the French impressionists. They avoided the expressionist techniques favored by German directors such as Robert Wiene (*The Cabinet of Dr. Caligari*, 1920), F. W. Murnau (*Nosferatu*, 1922), and Fritz Lang (*Metropolis*, 1927) that also modified the look of the image to suggest a distorted, unbalanced world of menacing forces and unstable personalities. The neo-realists shunned the montage techniques favored by Soviet directors such as Sergei Eisenstein (*October*, 1927), Vsevolod Pudovkin (*The End of St. Petersburg*, 1927), and Dziga Vertov (*The Man with a Movie Camera*, 1929) that juxtaposed shots to jar the spectator and produce new insights from the way different shots are brought together. They coupled narrative to the documentary purity of Lumière to achieve a style of enduring significance.

Neo-realists such as Roberto Rossellini (*Rome, Open City*, 1946), Vittorio De Sica (*Bicycle Thief*, 1948), and Luchino Visconti (*La Terra Trema*, 1948) stressed narrative qualities in tune with the photographic realism of the motion picture: a casual, unadorned view of everyday life; a meandering, coincidence-laden series of actions and events; natural lighting and location shooting; a reliance on untrained actors; a rejection of close-ups doting on the faces of stars; and a stress on the problems confronting ordinary people in the present moment rather than the historical past or an imagined future. Here was an important strand of narrative filmmaking that contributed to the continuing development of documentary.

This sense of a photographic realism, of revealing what life has to offer when it is filmed simply and truly, is not, in fact, a truth but a style. It is an effect achieved by using specific but unassuming, definite but self-effacing means. It corresponds to what amounts to one of three important ways in which the term "realism" has significance for documentary film.

> • *Photographic realism* can also be referred to as *physical* or *empirical realism*. It generates a realism of time and place through location photography, straightforward filming, and continuity editing where the distorting and subjective uses of editing favored by the avant-garde are minimized.

VITTORIO DE SICA'S

THE **BICYCLE** THIEF

Lamberto Maggiorani and Enzo Staiola

KINO VIDEO
333 West 39th Street
New York, NY 10018
ph(212)629-6880 fax(212)714-0871
kinoint@infohouse.com

The Bicycle Thief (Vittorio De Sica, 1948)

The genius of Robert Flaherty lay in drawing out stories that felt as if they were intimately tied to a concrete sense of time and place. This type of story-telling skill reverberated throughout the Italian neo-realist film movement, with its use of location photography, non-actors, and stories of everyday life and basic survival.

- *Psychological realism* involves conveying the inner states of characters or social actors in plausible and convincing ways. Anxiety, happiness, anger, ecstasy and so on can be realistically portrayed and conveyed. We consider the representation of such states realistic when we sense that the inner life of a character has been effectively conveyed even if this calls for inventiveness on the part of the director, such as holding a shot longer than usual, adopting a revealing camera angle, adding suggestive music, or juxtaposing one image or sequence with another.

- *Emotional realism* concerns the creation of an appropriate emotional state in the viewer. An outlandish musical number can generate a feeling of exuberance in the audience even though there is little psychological depth provided to the characters and the physical setting is clearly a fabrication. We still recognize a realistic dimension to the experience: it is like other emotional experiences we have had. The emotion itself is familiar and genuinely felt.

All three of these forms of realism hold relevance for documentary film. Neo-realism made use of all three, giving us a vivid sense of the look of post-war Italy, of the hopes and anxieties of ordinary people, and generating a strong sense of empathy, if not humanistic sentimentality, in its audience.

Documentary also frequently relies heavily on a realism of time and place. It depends on finding people, or social actors, who reveal themselves in front of a camera with an openness and lack of self-consciousness similar to what we find in trained professionals. And documentary seeks to impart to viewers a feeling of emotional involvement or engagement with the people and issues portrayed. Neo-realism helped to demonstrate that this form of narrative style provided a common thread between fiction and nonfiction that continues to the present: story telling and giving voice to a view of the historical world need not be seen as polarized alternatives.

RHETORIC AND ORATORY

Showing (in the tradition of the "cinema of attractions"), telling (in the tradition of narrative cinema), and poetic form (in the tradition of the avant-garde) provide three of the legs for documentary film. The fourth is also shared with other genres but remains most distinctive to documentary itself.

The classic voice of oratory sought to speak about the historical world in ways that reveal a particular perspective on the world. It sought to persuade us of the merits of a perspective as well as to predispose us to action or to the adoption of sensibilities and values of one kind or another in relation to the world we actually inhabit. Such a voice was clearly heard in Robert Flaherty's *Nanook of the North* as it had been by a smaller audience for Edward Curtis's 1915 film, *In the Land of the Headhunters* (a film restored and reissued in 1972 as *In the Land of the War Canoes*). These films combined a series of "attractions" with a coherent narrative, the poetic orchestration of scenes, and an oratorical voice that confirmed a perspective on the historical world.

Along with Flaherty's *Moana* (1926), about Polynesian culture, other early works such as Merian Cooper and Ernest Schoedsack's *Grass* (1925), about the nomadic peoples of Turkey and Persia, Victor Turin's *Turksib* (1929), on the construction of an important new rail link between far-flung parts of the Soviet Union, and Jean Vigo's *A Propos de Nice* (1930), a savage look at class differences at this beach resort, affirmed the idea of a documentary voice. This voice adapted showing "attractions," telling stories, and cinematic poetry to speak about the social world in important ways.

These developments took distinctive shape in the Soviet Union, where an earlier, pre-revolutionary period of experimentation in the arts continued to flourish in the early years of the new Soviet state in the forms of constructivist art and Soviet cinema. (The gradual imposition of an "official" state style of art and film, Socialist Realism, eliminated almost all experimentation by the middle of the 1930s.)

In an influential essay, the constructivist painter, designer, and photomontage artist Aleksandr Rodchenko argued against the "synthetic portrait," which would capture a whole personality in a single painting. Instead, he championed an assembled series of documentary photographs, each revealing a different facet of a complex figure. In another essay, "Constructivism in the Cinema" (1928), the Russian artist Alexei Gan called for a new type of cinema, both poetic and demonstrative:

> It is not enough to link, by means of montage, individual moments of episodic phenomena of life, united under a more or less successful title [*Berlin: Symphony of a City* may have been the type of work Gan had in mind]. The most unexpected accidents, occurrences and events are always linked organically with the fundamental root of social reality. While apprehending them with the shell of their outer manifestations, one should be able to expose their inner essence by a series of other scenes. Only on such a basis can one build a vivid film of concrete, active reality—gradually departing from the newsreel, from whose material this new ciné form is developing. ("Constructivism and the Cinema," in Stephen Bann, ed., *The Tradition of Constructivism*, p. 130)

Dziga Vertov also championed an attitude of poetic reconstruction to those records of what the camera saw. Editing and the interval (the effect of the transitions between shots) formed the core of his style of non-fiction cinema called *kino-eye:*

1. Editing during observation—orienting the unaided eye at any place, any time.
2. Editing after observation—mentally organizing what has been seen, according to characteristic features [akin to the functions of invention and memory in classic rhetoric].
3. Editing during filming—orienting the aided eye of the movie camera in the place inspected in step 1.
4. Editing after filming—roughly organizing the footage according to characteristic features. Looking for the montage fragments that are lacking.
5. Gauging by sight (hunting for montage fragments)—instantaneous orienting in any visual environment so as to capture the essential link shots. Exceptional attentiveness. A military rule: gauging by sight, speed, attack.
6. The final editing—reveal minor, concealed themes together with the ma-

The Prince Is Back (Marina Goldovskaya, 1999). Photos courtesy of Marina Goldovskaya.

The Family. This group portrait of the Meschersky family from 1912, in pre-revolutionary Russia, affirms both their kinship and their good standing within the Russian aristocracy.

The Prince Is Back

The Prince. In the 1990s, Prince Meschersky decides to reclaim his family estate from the government and restore it.

jor ones. Reorganizing all the footage into the best sequence. Bringing out the core of the film-object. Coordinating similar elements, and finally, numerically calculating the montage groupings. ("Kino-Eye," 1926, in Annette Michelson, ed., *Kino-Eye: The Writings of Dziga-Vertov,* p. 72)

These writings addressed issues of film form, specifically the assembly of shots into a pattern that both disclosed less visible aspects of the world and affirmed the voice of the filmmaker. This call for montage or assembly moved beyond showing "attractions" or making scientific observations but still summoned cinema to acknowledge its capacity to represent the historical world with photographic fidelity. Soviet theories of constructivist art and cinematic montage harnessed this capacity to the filmmaker's desire to remake the world in the image of a revolutionary new society.

Montage stressed the rearrangement of events into fragments. By juxtaposing shots that did not "naturally" go together, the filmmaker constructed new impressions and insights. Eisenstein likened traditional photographic realism to an imposed ideology:

Absolute realism is by no means the correct form of perception. It is simply the function of a certain form of social structure. Following a state monarchy, a state uniformity of thought is implanted. ("The Cinematographic Principle and the Ideogram," in Jay Leyda, ed., *Film Form and the Film Sense,* p. 35)

What did Eisenstein see as an alternative? Distorting reality to create a radically new vision of it.

The Prince Is Back
The Estate. This model suggests how the prince's palace looked prior to the 1917 Revolution.

The Prince Is Back
The Problem. Eighty-plus years after the Revolution. Can one man and his family restore what's left of the family home? Can a country move forward if its citizens want to go backward? Marina Goldovskaya raises larger issues only implicitly in her intimate portrait of the prince's pursuit of a dream.

Is this not exactly what we of the cinema do . . . when we cause a monstrous disproportion of the parts of a normally flowing event, and suddenly dismember the event into "close-up of clutching hands," "medium shot of the struggle," and "extreme close-up of bulging eyes," in making a montage disintegration of the event in various planes? In making an eye twice as large as a man's full figure! By combining these monstrous incongruities we newly collect the disintegrated event into one whole, but in *our* aspect. According to the treatment of our relation to the event. ("The Cinematographic Principle," p. 34; italics in original)

The Soviet cinema was a vividly rhetorical cinema. In the work of many of its practitioners, from the famous films of Sergei Eisenstein himself (*Strike, Battleship Potemkin, October, The Old and the New,* etc.) to the less well known but pioneering compilation documentaries of Esther Shub (*The Great Road,* 1927; *The Fall of the Romanov Dynasty,* 1927; and *The Russia of Nicholas II and Leo Tolstoy,* 1928) techniques of montage laid the groundwork for the didactic emphasis that John Grierson gave to documentary in the Great Britain of the 1930s.

In the 1920s, the sense that the voice of the filmmaker—and through this voice a government or society—took shape through the ways in which views of the world were recast in shooting and editing held paramount importance. These practices demonstrated that complex films could be constructed from fragments of the historical world rejoined to give expression to a particular viewpoint. Rhetoric in all its forms and all its purposes provides the final, distinguishing element of documentary. The exhibitor of attractions, the teller of stories, and the poet of *photogénie* condense in the figure of the documentary filmmaker as orator, speaking in a voice all his own about a world we all share.

These elements first came together in the Soviet Union through the 1920s as the challenge of constructing a new society took precedence in all the arts. This particular melding of elements took root in other countries in the late 1920s and early 1930s as governments, thanks to advocates like John Grierson, saw the value of using film to promote a sense of participatory citizenship and to support the role in government in confronting the most difficult issues of the day, such as inflation, poverty, and the Depression. Answers to these problems varied widely from democratic Britain to fascist Germany and from a New Deal United States to a Communist Russia, but in each case, the voice of the documentarian contributed significantly to framing a national agenda and proposing courses of action.

Chapter 6

What Types of Documentary Are There?

GROUPING THE MANY VOICES OF DOCUMENTARY

Every documentary has its own distinct voice. Like every speaking voice, every cinematic voice has a style or "grain" all its own that acts like a signature or fingerprint. It attests to the individuality of the filmmaker or director or, sometimes, to the determining power of a sponsor or controlling organization. Television news has a voice of its own just as Fred Wiseman or Chris Marker, Esther Shub or Marina Goldovskaya does.

Individual voices lend themselves to an *auteur* theory of cinema, while shared voices lend themselves to a genre theory of cinema. Genre study considers the qualities that characterize various groupings of filmmakers and films. In documentary film and video, we can identify six modes of representation that function something like sub-genres of the documentary film genre itself: poetic, expository, participatory, observational, reflexive, performative.

These six modes establish a loose framework of affiliation within which individuals may work; they set up conventions that a given film may adopt; and they provide specific expectations viewers anticipate having fulfilled. Each mode possesses examples that we can identify as prototypes or mod-

els: they seem to give exemplary expression to the most distinctive qualities of that mode. They cannot be copied, but they can be emulated as other
filmmakers, in other voices, set out to represent aspects of the historical
world from their own distinct perspectives.

The order of presentation for these six modes corresponds roughly to
the chronology of their introduction. It may therefore seem to provide a history of documentary film, but it does so only imperfectly. A film identified
with a given mode need not be so entirely. A reflexive documentary can
contain sizable portions of observational or participatory footage; an expository documentary can include poetic or performative segments. The
characteristics of a given mode function as a *dominant* in a given film: they
give structure to the overall film, but they do not dictate or determine every
aspect of its organization. Considerable latitude remains possible.

A more recent film need not have a more recent mode as its dominant.
It can revert to an earlier mode while still including elements of later modes.
A performative documentary can exhibit many qualities of a poetic documentary, for example. The modes do not represent an evolutionary chain
in which later modes demonstrate superiority over earlier ones and van-
quish them. Once established through a set of conventions and paradigmatic films, a given mode remains available to all. Expository documentary, for example, goes back to the 1920s but remains highly influential
today. Most television news and reality TV shows depend heavily on its quite
dated conventions, as do almost all science and nature documentaries, biographies such as the *A&E Biography* series, and the majority of large-
scale historical documentaries such as *The Civil War* (1990), *Eyes on the
Prize* (1987, 1990), *The American Cinema* (1994), or *The People's Century*
(1998).

To some extent, each mode of documentary representation arises in
part through a growing sense of dissatisfaction among filmmakers with a
previous mode. In this sense the modes do convey some sense of a documentary history. The observational mode of representation arose, in part,
from the availability of mobile 16mm cameras and magnetic tape recorders
in the 1960s. Poetic documentary suddenly seemed too abstract and expository documentary too didactic when it now proved possible to film everyday events with minimal staging or intervention.

Observation was necessarily limited to the present moment as filmmakers recorded what happened before them. But observation shared a
trait, or convention, with poetic and expository modes of representation:
it, too, camouflaged the actual presence and shaping influence of the filmmaker. Participatory documentary took shape with the realization that filmmakers need not disguise their close relationship with their subjects by

telling stories or observing events that seemed to occur as if they were not there.

Intertitles in *Nanook,* for example, tell us that Nanook and his family face starvation if this great hunter of the north cannot find food, but they do not tell us what Flaherty himself ate or whether he made food available to Nanook. Flaherty asks us to suspend our disbelief in the fictional aspect of his story at the price of a certain dishonesty in what he reveals to us about his actual relation to his subject. With filmmakers like Jean Rouch (*Chronicle of a Summer,* 1960), Nick Broomfield (*The Aileen Wourmos Story,* 1992), Kazuo Hara (*The Emperor's Naked Army Marches On,* 1987), and Jon Silver (*Watsonville on Strike,* 1989) what happens *because of* the filmmaker's presence becomes as crucial as anything that happens *despite* his presence.

The desire to come up with different ways of representing the world contributes to the formation of each mode, as does a changing set of circumstances. New modes arise partly in response to perceived deficiencies in previous ones, but the perception of deficiency comes about partly from a sense of what it takes to represent the historical world from a particular perspective at a given moment in time. The seeming neutrality and "make of it what you will" quality of observational cinema arose at the end of the quiet fifties and during the heyday of descriptive, observation-based forms of sociology. It flourished in part as the embodiment of a presumed "end of ideology" and a fascination with the everyday world, but not necessarily of affinity with the social plight or political anger of those who occupy the margins of society.

Similarly, the emotional intensity and subjective expressiveness of performative documentary took shape in the 1980s and 1990s. It took strongest root among those groups whose sense of commonality had grown during this period as a result of an identity politics that affirmed the relative autonomy and social distinctiveness of marginalized groups. These films rejected techniques such as the voice-of-God commentary not because it lacked humility but because it belonged to an entire epistemology, or way of seeing and knowing the world, no longer deemed acceptable.

We do well to take with a grain of salt any claims that a new mode advances the art of cinema and captures aspects of the world never before possible. What changes is the *mode* of representation, not the quality or ultimate status of the representation. A new mode is not so much better as it is different, even though the idea of "improvement" is frequently touted, especially among champions and practitioners of a new mode. A new mode carries a different set of emphases and implications. It will eventually prove vulnerable, in turn, to criticism for limitations that yet another mode of rep-

The Day after Trinity (Jon Else, 1980). Photo courtesy of Jon Else.

Post-'60s reconsiderations of Cold War rhetoric invited a revision of the postwar record. Filmmakers such as Connie Field in *The Life and Times of Rosie the Riveter* and John Else in *The Day after Trinity* recirculate historical footage in a new context. In this case, Else re-examines Robert J. Oppenheimer's hesitancies and doubts about the development of the atomic bomb as a lost, or suppressed, voice of reason during a period of near-hysteria. Oppenheimer himself was accused of treason.

resentation promises to overcome. New modes signal less a better way to represent the historical world than a new dominant to organize a film, a new ideology to explain our relation to reality, and a new set of issues and desires to preoccupy an audience.

We can now say a bit more about each of the modes in turn.

THE POETIC MODE

As we saw in Chapter 4, poetic documentary shares a common terrain with the modernist avant-garde. The poetic mode sacrifices the conventions of continuity editing and the sense of a very specific location in time and place that follows from it to explore associations and patterns that involve temporal rhythms and spatial juxtapositions. Social actors seldom take on the full-blooded form of characters with psychological complexity and a fixed view of the world. People more typically function on a par with other objects as raw material that filmmakers select and arrange into associations and patterns of their choosing. We get to know none of the social actors in Joris Ivens's *Rain* (1929), for example, but we do come to appreciate the lyric impression Ivens creates of a summer shower pass-ing over Amsterdam.

The poetic mode is particularly adept at opening up the possibility of al-ternative forms of knowledge to the straightforward transfer of information, the prosecution of a particular argument or point of view, or the presenta-tion of reasoned propositions about problems in need of solution. This mode stresses mood, tone, and affect much more than displays of knowledge or acts of persuasion. The rhetorical element remains underdeveloped.

Laszlo Moholy-Nagy's *Play of Light: Black, White, Grey* (1930), for ex-ample, presents various views of one of his own kinetic sculptures to em-phasize the gradations of light passing across the film frame rather than to document the material shape of the sculpture itself. The effect of this play of light on the viewer takes on more importance than the object it refers to in the historical world. Similarly, Jean Mitry's *Pacific 231* (1944) is in part a homage to Abel Gance's *La Roue* and in part a poetic evocation of the power and speed of a steam locomotive as it gradually builds up speed and hur-tles toward its (unspecified) destination. The editing stresses rhythm and form more than it details the actual workings of a locomotive.

The documentary dimension to the poetic mode of representation stems largely from the degree to which modernist films rely on the histori-cal world for their source material. Some avant-garde films such as Oscar Fischinger's *Composition in Blue* (1935) use abstract patterns of form or color or animated figures and have minimal relation to a documentary tra-dition of representing *the* historical world rather than *a* world of the artist's imagining. Poetic documentaries, though, draw on the historical world for their raw material but transform this material in distinctive ways. Francis Thompson's *N.Y., N.Y.* (1957), for example, uses shots of New York City that provide evidence of how New York looked in the mid-1950s but gives greater priority to how these shots can be selected and arranged to pro-duce a poetic impression of the city as a mass of volume, color, and move-ment. Thompson's film continues the tradition of the city symphony film and affirms the poetic potential of documentary to see the historical world anew.

The poetic mode began in tandem with modernism as a way of repre-senting reality in terms of a series of fragments, subjective impressions, in-coherent acts, and loose associations. These qualities were often attributed to the transformations of industrialization generally and the effects of World War I in particular. The modernist event no longer seemed to make sense in traditional narrative, realist terms. Breaking up time and space into mul-tiple perspectives, denying coherence to personalities vulnerable to erup-tions from the unconscious, and refusing to provide solutions to insur-mountable problems had the sense of an honesty about it even as it created

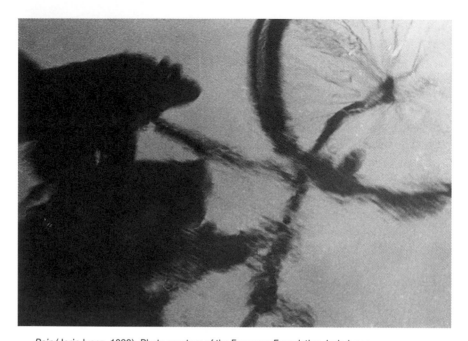

Rain (Joris Ivens, 1929). Photo courtesy of the European Foundation Joris Ivens.

Images such as this convey a feeling or impression of what a rain shower is like rather than convey information or an argument. This is a distinct and distinctly poetic perspective on the historical world. Pursuing such a perspective was a common goal of many who would later identify themselves more specifically as documentary or experimental filmmakers.

works of art that were puzzling or ambiguous in their effect. Although some films explored more classical conceptions of the poetic as a source of order, wholeness, and unity, this stress on fragmentation and ambiguity remains a prominent feature in many poetic documentaries.

Un Chien Andalou (Luis Buñuel and Salvador Dali, 1928) and *L'Age d'or* (Luis Buñuel, 1930), for example, gave the impression of a documentary reality but then populated that reality with characters caught up in uncontrollable urges, abrupt shifts of time and place, and more puzzles than answers. Filmmakers like Kenneth Anger continued aspects of this poetic mode in films like *Scorpio Rising* (1963), a representation of ritual acts performed by members of a motorcycle gang, as did Chris Marker in *San Soleil* (1982), a complex meditation on filmmaking, memory, and post-colonialism. (At the time of their release, works like Anger's seemed firmly rooted in an experimental film tradition, but in retrospect we can see how they combine experimental and documentary elements. How we place them depends heavily on the assumptions we adopt about categories and genres.)

By contrast, work like Basil Wright's *Song of Ceylon* (1934), on the untouched beauty of Ceylon (Sri Lanka) despite the inroads of commerce and colonialism, Bert Haanstra's *Glass* (1958), a tribute to the skill of traditional glass blowers and the beauty of their work, or Les Blank's *Always for Pleasure* (1978), a celebration of Mardi Gras festivities in New Orleans, return to a more classic sense of unity and beauty and discover traces of them in the historical world. The poetic mode has many facets, but they all emphasize the ways in which the filmmaker's voice gives fragments of the historical world a formal, aesthetic integrity peculiar to the film itself.

Péter Forgács's remarkable reworkings of amateur movies into historical documents stresses poetic, associative qualities over transferring information or winning us over to a particular point of view. *Free Fall* (1998), for example, chronicles the fate of European Jews in the 1930s and 40s through the home movies of a successful Jewish businessman, Gyorgy Peto, and *Danube Exodus* (1999) follows the journeys of a Danube cruise ship as it takes Jews from Hungary to the Black Sea on their flight to Palestine and then takes Germans from Bessarabia (the northern part of Romania at the time) as they are driven out by the Russians and evacuated to Germany, only to be relocated in Poland. The historical footage, freeze frames, slow motion, tinted images, selective moments of color, occasional titles to identify time and place, voices that recite diary entries, and haunting music build a tone and mood far more than they explain the war or describe its course of action.

THE EXPOSITORY MODE

This mode assembles fragments of the historical world into a more rhetorical or argumentative frame than an aesthetic or poetic one. The expository mode addresses the viewer directly, with titles or voices that propose a perspective, advance an argument, or recount history. Expository films adopt either a voice-of-God commentary (the speaker is heard but never seen), such as we find in the *Why We Fight* series, *Victory at Sea* (1952–53), *The City* (1939), *Blood of the Beasts* (1949), and *Dead Birds* (1963), or utilize a voice-of-authority commentary (the speaker is heard and also seen), such as we find in television newscasts, *America's Most Wanted, The Selling of the Pentagon* (1971), *16 in Webster Groves* (1966), Robert Hughes's *The Shock of the New* (1980), Kenneth Clark's *Civilization,* or John Berger's *Ways of Seeing* (1974).

The voice-of-God tradition fostered the cultivation of the professionally trained, richly toned male voice of commentary that proved a hallmark of the expository mode even though some of the most impressive films chose

Yosemite: The Fate of Heaven (Jon Else, 1988). Photo courtesy of Jon Else.
    The tension between public access and conservation is the focus of this film. Robert Redford's commentary falls into the category of voice-of-God address inasmuch as we never see Mr. Redford. To the extent that Mr. Redford's long-time advocacy for environmental issues makes him a more informed speaker than an anonymous commentator would be, he also fulfills the function of a voice of authority.

less polished voices precisely for the credibility gained by avoiding too much polish. Joris Ivens's great film urging support for the Republican defenders of Spanish democracy, *The Spanish Earth* (1937), for example, exists in at least three versions. None has a professional commentator. All three have identical image tracks, but the French version uses an ad-libbed commentary by the famous French film director Jean Renoir while the English versions rely on Orson Welles and Ernest Hemingway. Ivens chose Welles first, but his delivery proved a bit too elegant; it bestowed a humanistic compassion on the events where Ivens hoped for a tougher sense of visceral engagement. Hemingway, who had written the commentary, proved the more effective voice. He brought a matter-of-fact but clearly committed tone to a film that wanted to galvanize support more than compassion. (Some prints still credit the voice-over to Welles even though the voice we hear is Hemingway's.)

Expository documentaries rely heavily on an informing logic carried by the spoken word. In a reversal of the traditional emphasis in film, images serve a supporting role. They illustrate, illuminate, evoke, or act in counterpoint to what is said. The commentary is typically presented as distinct from the images of the historical world that accompany it. It serves to organize these images and make sense of them just as a written caption guides our attention and emphasizes some of the many meanings and interpretations of a still image. The commentary is therefore presumed to be of a higher order than the accompanying images. It comes from some place that remains unspecified but associated with objectivity or omniscience. The commentary, in fact, represents the perspective or argument of the film. We take our cue from the commentary and understand the images as evidence or demonstration for what is said. Television news descriptions of famine in Ethiopia as "biblical," for example, seemed proved by wide-angle shots of great masses of starving people clustered together on an open plain.

Editing in the expository mode generally serves less to establish a rhythm or formal pattern, as it does in the poetic mode, than to maintain the continuity of the spoken argument or perspective. We can call this evidentiary editing. Such editing may sacrifice spatial and temporal continuity to rope in images from far-flung places if they help advance the argument. The expository filmmaker often has greater freedom in the selection and arrangement of images than the fiction filmmaker. In *The Plow That Broke the Plains* (1936) shots of arid prairie landscapes came from all over the Midwest, for example, to support the claim of widespread damage to the land.

The expository mode emphasizes the impression of objectivity and well-supported argument. The voice-over commentary seems literally "above" the fray; it has the capacity to judge actions in the historical world without being caught up in them. The professional commentator's official tone, like the authoritative manner of news anchors and reporters, strives to build a sense of credibility from qualities such as distance, neutrality, disinterestedness, or omniscience. These qualities can be adapted to an ironic point of view such as we find in Charles Kuralt's commentary for *16 in Webster Groves* or subverted even more thoroughly in a film such as *Land without Bread,* with its implicit attack on the very notion of objectivity.

Expository documentary facilitates generalization and large-scale argumentation. The images can support the basic claims of a general argument

Triumph of the Will (Leni Riefenstahl, 1935)

The physical gap and hierarchical distinction between leader and followers again comes across clearly in this scene of Hitler's parade through the streets of Nuremberg.

The Spanish Earth (Joris Ivens, 1937)

Ivens supported the Republican cause against the Nazi-backed rebellion of General Franco. He stresses the centrality, and valor, of ordinary citizens. This photograph, shot on location, contrasts sharply with Riefenstahl's stress on setting leaders apart from the people.

Triumph of the Will

The soldier's salute, above, parallels this low-angle view of the German eagle and Nazi swastika. Like Hitler, the eagle serves as a symbol of German power. It presides over the stream of marching troops that pass below it, galvanizing their movement into a tribute to national unity.

The Spanish Earth

In contrast to the pageantry of Riefenstahl's endless parades and speeches, Ivens captures the modest quality of everyday rural life in 1930s Spain. This image of the town, Fuenteduena, situated near the shifting battlefront, suggests how ordinary lives are jeopardized, not galvanized, by the fascist rebellion.

rather than construct a vivid sense of the particularities to a given corner of the world. The mode also affords an economy of analysis since points can be made succinctly and pointedly in words. Expository documentary is an ideal mode for conveying information or mobilizing support within a framework that pre-exists the film. In this case, a film will add to our stockpile of knowledge but not challenge or subvert the categories by which such knowledge gets organized. Common sense makes a perfect basis for this type of representation about the world since common sense, like rhetoric, is less subject to logic than to belief.

Frank Capra could organize much of his argument for why young American men should willingly join the battle during World War II in the *Why We Fight* series, for example, by appealing to a mix of native patriotism, the ideals of American democracy, the atrocities of the Axis war machine, and the malignant evil of Hitler, Mussolini, and Hirohito. In the black and white alternatives of a "free world" versus a "slave world," who would not choose to defend a free world? Common sense made the answer simple—to the predominantly white audience thoroughly imbued with a "melting pot" belief in American values.

Some fifty years later, Capra's appeal seems remarkably naive and overblown in its treatment of patriotic virtue and democratic ideals. Common sense is less an enduring than a historically conditioned set of values and perspectives. For this reason some expository films that seem classic examples of oratorical persuasiveness at one moment will seem quite dated at another. The basic argument may still have merit, but what counts as common sense may change considerably.

THE OBSERVATIONAL MODE

Poetic and expository modes of documentary often sacrificed the specific act of filming people to construct formal patterns or persuasive arguments. The filmmaker gathered the necessary raw materials and then fashioned a meditation, perspective, or argument from them. What if the filmmaker were simply to observe what happens in front of the camera without overt intervention? Would this not be a new, compelling form of documentation?

Developments in Canada, Europe, and the United States in the years after World War II culminated around 1960 in various 16mm cameras such as the Arriflex and Auricon and tape recorders such as the Nagra that could be easily handled by one person. Speech could now be synchronized with images without the use of bulky equipment or cables that tethered recorders and camera together. The camera and tape recorder could move freely about a scene and record what happened as it happened.

Victory at Sea (Henry Solomon and Isaac Kleinerman, 1952–53)

Like *Night and Fog*, *Victory at Sea* returns to the recent past to tell the story of World War II. Made as a television series for CBS, it adopts a commemorative stance. It recalls battles and strategies, setbacks and victories from the perspective of the survivor or veteran. It celebrates naval power and its contribution, giving scant attention to the ground war or the civilian consequences that are at the heart of *Night and Fog*. Both films, however, rely on compilation of footage shot contemporaneously with the events to which the films now return. Compilation films invariably alter the meaning of the footage they incorporate. Here, both films use footage for purposes that are possible only to those who reflect on the meaning of the past rather than report the occurrences of the moment.

All of the forms of control that a poetic or expository filmmaker might exercise over the staging, arrangement, or composition of a scene became sacrificed to observing lived experience spontaneously. Honoring this spirit of observation in post-production editing as well as during shooting resulted in films with no voice-over commentary, no supplementary music or sound effects, no intertitles, no historical reenactments, no behavior repeated for the camera, and not even any interviews. What we saw was what there was, or so it seemed in *Primary* (1960), *High School* (1968), *Les Racquetteurs* (Michel Brault and Gilles Groulx, 1958), about a group of Montrealers enjoying various games in the snow, portions of *Chronicle of a Summer,* which profiles the lives of several individuals in the Paris of 1960, *The Chair* (1962), about the last days of a man condemned to death, *Gimme Shelter* (1970), about the Rolling Stones' infamous concert at Altamont, California, where a man's death at the hands of the Hell's Angels is partially caught on camera, *Don't Look Back* (1967), about Bob Dylan's tour of England in 1965, *Monterey Pop* (1968), about a music festival featuring Otis Redding, Janis Joplin, Jimi Hendrix, the Jefferson Airplane, and others, or *Jane* (1962), profiling Jane Fonda as she prepares for a role in a Broadway play.

The resulting footage often recalled the work of the Italian neo-realists. We look in on life as it is lived. Social actors engage with one another, ignoring the filmmakers. Often the characters are caught up in pressing demands or a crisis of their own. This requires their attention and draws it away from the presence of filmmakers. The scenes tend, like fiction, to reveal aspects of character and individuality. We make inferences and come to conclusions on the basis of behavior we observe or overhear. The filmmaker's retirement to the position of observer calls on the viewer to take a more active role in determining the significance of what is said and done.

The observational mode poses a series of ethical considerations that involve the act of observing others go about their affairs. Is such an act in and of itself voyeuristic? Does it place the viewer in a necessarily less comfortable position than in a fiction film? In fiction, scenes are contrived for us to oversee and overhear entirely, whereas documentary scenes represent the lived experience of actual people that we happen to witness. This position, "at the keyhole," can feel uncomfortable if a pleasure in looking seems to take priority over the chance to acknowledge and interact with the one seen. This discomfort can be even more acute when the person is not an actor who has willingly agreed to be observed playing a part in a fiction.

The impression that the filmmaker is not intruding on the behavior of others also raises the question of unacknowledged or indirect intrusion. Do people conduct themselves in ways that will color our perception of them, for better or worse, in order to satisfy a filmmaker who does not say what it is he wants? Does the filmmaker seek out others to represent because they possess qualities that may fascinate viewers for the wrong reasons? This question often comes up with ethnographic films that observe, in other cultures, behavior that may, without adequate contextualization, seem exotic or bizarre, more part of a "cinema of attractions" than science. Has the filmmaker sought the informed consent of participants and made it possible for such informed consent to be understood and given? To what extent can a filmmaker explain the possible consequences of allowing behavior to be observed and represented to others?

Fred Wiseman, for example, requests consent verbally when he shoots but assumes that when he shoots in public institutions he has a right to record what happens; he never grants participants any control over the final result. Even so, many participants in *High School* found the film fair and representative even though most critics have considered it a harsh indictment of school regimentation and discipline. A radically different approach occurs in *Two Laws* (1981), about Aboriginal land rights, where the filmmakers did not film anything without both the consent and collaboration of the participants. Everything from content to camera lenses was open to discussion and mutual agreement.

Since the observational filmmaker adopts a peculiar mode of presence "on the scene" in which he or she appears to be invisible and non-participatory, the question also arises of when does the filmmaker have a responsibility to intervene? What if something happens that may jeopardize or injure one of the social actors? Should a cameraman film the immolation of a Vietnamese monk who, knowing that there are cameras present to record the event, sets himself on fire to protest the Vietnamese war, or should the cameraman refuse or try to dissuade the monk? Should a filmmaker accept a knife as a gift from a participant in the course of filming a murder trial, and then turn that gift over to the police when blood is found on it (as Joe Berlinger and Bruce Sinofsky do in their film *Paradise Lost* [1996])? This last example moves us toward an unexpected or inadvertent form of participation rather than observation as it also raises broad issues about the filmmaker's relationship with his or her subjects.

Observational films exhibit particular strength in giving a sense of the duration of actual events. They break with the dramatic pace of mainstream fiction films and the sometimes hurried assembly of images that support expository or poetic documentaries. When Fred Wiseman, for example, observes the making of a thirty-second television commercial for some twenty-five minutes of screen time in *Model* (1980), he conveys the sense of having observed everything worth noting about the shooting.

Similarly, when David MacDougall films extended discussions between his principal character, Lorang, and one of his peers about the bride price for Lorang's daughter in *Wedding Camels* (1980), he shifts our attention from what the final agreement is or what new narrative issue arises because of it to the feel and texture of the discussion itself: the body language and eye contact, the intonation and tone of the voices, the pauses and "empty" time that give the encounter the sense of concrete, lived reality.

MacDougall himself describes the fascination of lived experience as something that is most vividly experienced as a difference between rushes (the unedited footage as it was originally shot) and an edited sequence. The rushes seem to have a density and vitality that the edited film lacks. A loss occurs even as structure and perspective are added:

The sense of loss seems to identify positive values perceived in the rushes and intended by the filmmaker at the time of filming but unachieved in the completed film. It is as though the very reasons for making films are somehow contradicted by the making of them. The processes of editing a film from the rushes involve both reducing the length overall and cutting most shots to shorter lengths. Both these processes progressively center particular meanings. Sometimes filmmakers appear to recognize this when they try to preserve some of the qualities of the rushes in their films, or reintroduce those qualities through other means. ("When Less Is Less," *Transcultural Cinema,* p. 215)

The presence of the camera "on the scene" testifies to its presence in the historical world. This affirms a sense of commitment or engagement with the immediate, intimate, and personal as it occurs. This also affirms a sense of fidelity to what occurs that can pass on events to us as if they simply happened when they have, in fact, been constructed to have that very appearance. One modest example is the "masked interview." In this case the filmmaker works in a more participatory way with his subjects to establish the general subject of a scene and then films it in an observational manner. David MacDougall has done this quite effectively in several films. An example is the scene in *Kenya Boran* where, without paying heed to the camera but in accord with the general guidelines established before shooting began, two Kenyan tribesmen discuss their views of the government's introduction of birth control measures.

A more complex example is the event staged to become part of the historical record. Press conferences, for example, may be filmed in a purely observational style, but such events would not exist at all if it were not for the presence of the camera. This is the reverse of the basic premise behind observational films, that what we see is what would have occurred were the camera not there to observe it.

This reversal took on monumental proportions in one of the first "observational" documentaries, Leni Riefenstahl's *Triumph of the Will.* After an introductory set of titles that set the stage for the German National Socialist (Nazi) Party's 1934 Nuremberg rally, Riefenstahl observes events with no further commentary. Events—predominantly parades, reviews of troops, mass assemblies, images of Hitler, and speeches—occur as if the camera simply recorded what would have happened anyway. At two hours running time, the film can give the impression of having recorded historical events all too faithfully and unthinkingly.

And yet, very little would have happened as it did were it not for the express intent of the Nazi Party to make a film of this rally. Riefenstahl had enormous resources placed at her disposal, and events were carefully planned to facilitate their filming, including the repeat filming of portions of

Roy Cohn/Jack Smith (Jill Godmilow, 1994). Photo courtesy of Jill Godmilow.

Godmilow's film, like many documentaries of music concerts, observes a public performance; in this case she records two one-man plays by Ron Vawter. Given that such events are understood to be performances in the first place, they allow the filmmaker to avoid some of the accusations that the presence of the camera altered what would have happened had the camera not been there.

some speeches at another time and place when the original footage proved unusable. (The repeated portions are reenacted so that they blend in with the original speeches, hiding the collaboration that went into their making.)

Triumph of the Will demonstrates the power of the image to represent the historical world at the same moment as it participates in the construction of aspects of the historical world itself. Such participation, especially in the context of Nazi Germany, carries an aura of duplicity. This was the last thing observational filmmakers like Robert Drew, D. A. Pennebaker, Richard Leacock, and Fred Wiseman wanted in their own work. The integrity of their observational stance successfully avoided it, for the most part, and yet the underlying act of being present at an event but filming it as if absent, as if the filmmaker were simply a "fly on the wall," invites debate as to how much of what we see would be the same if the camera were not there or how

Roy Cohn/Jack Smith (Jill Godmilow, 1994). Photo courtesy of Jill Godmilow.

Godmilow makes use of editing to create a distinct perspective on Ron Vawter's performance as gay underground filmmaker Jack Smith and right-wing, anti-Communist (and closeted gay) lawyer Roy Cohn. By intercutting the two separate performances she draws increased attention to the contrasting ways in which the two men dealt with their sexuality during the 1950s.

much would differ if the filmmaker's presence were more readily acknowledged. That such debate is by its very nature undecidable continues to fuel a certain sense of mystery, or disquiet, about observational cinema.

THE PARTICIPATORY MODE

The social sciences have long promoted the study of social groups. Anthropology, for example, remains heavily defined by the practice of field work, where an anthropologist lives among a people for an extended period of time and then writes up what she has learned. Such research usually calls for some form of participant-observation. The researcher goes into the field, participates in the lives of others, gains a corporeal or visceral feel for what life in a given context is like, and then reflects on this experience, using the tools and methods of anthropology or sociology to do so. "Being there" calls for participation; "being here" allows for observation. That is to say, the field worker does not allow herself to "go native," under normal circumstances, but retains a degree of detachment that differentiates her from those about whom she writes. Anthropology has, in fact, consistently depended on this complex act of engagement and separation between two cultures to define itself.

Documentary filmmakers also go into the field; they, too, live among others and speak about or represent what they experience. The practice of participant-observation, however, has not become a paradigm. The methods and practices of social science research have remained subordinate to the more prevalent rhetorical practice of moving and persuading an audience. Observational documentary de-emphasizes persuasion to give us a sense of what it is like to *be* in a given situation but without a sense of what it is like for the filmmaker to be there, too. Participatory documentary gives us a sense of what it is like for the filmmaker to be in a given situation and how that situation alters as a result. The types and degrees of alteration help define variations within the participatory mode of documentary.

When we view participatory documentaries we expect to witness the historical world as represented by someone who actively engages with, rather than unobtrusively observes, poetically reconfigures, or argumentatively assembles that world. The filmmaker steps out from behind the cloak of voice-over commentary, steps away from poetic meditation, steps down from a fly-on-the-wall perch, and becomes a social actor (almost) like any other. (Almost like any other because the filmmaker retains the camera, and with it, a certain degree of potential power and control over events.)

Participatory documentaries like *Chronicle of a Summer, Portrait of Jason,* or *Word Is Out* involve the ethics and politics of encounter. This is the encounter between one who wields a movie camera and one who does not. How do filmmaker and social actor respond to each other? How do they negotiate control and share responsibility? How much can the filmmaker insist on testimony when it is painful to provide it? What responsibility does the filmmaker have for the emotional aftermath of appearing on camera? What ties join filmmaker and subject and what needs divide them?

The sense of bodily presence, rather than absence, locates the filmmaker "on the scene." We expect that what we learn will hinge on the nature and quality of the encounter between filmmaker and subject rather than on generalizations supported by images illuminating a given perspective. We may see as well as hear the filmmaker act and respond on the spot, in the same historical arena as the film's subjects. The possibilities of serving as mentor, critic, interrogator, collaborator, or provocateur arise.

Takeover (David and Judith MacDougall, 1981). Photo courtesy of David MacDougall.
The MacDougalls have evolved a collaborative style of filmmaking with the subjects of their ethnographic films. In a series of films made on Aboriginal issues, of which *Takeover* is a prime example, they have often served as witnesses to the testimonial statements of traditions and beliefs that Aboriginal people offer in their disputes with the government over land rights and other matters. The interaction is highly participatory, although the result can seem, at first, unobtrusive or observational since much of the collaboration occurs prior to the act of filming.

Participatory documentary can stress the actual, lived encounter between filmmaker and subject in the spirit of Dziga Vertov's *The Man with a Movie Camera,* Jean Rouch and Edgar Morin's *Chronicle of a Summer,* Jon Alpert's *Hard Metals Disease* (1987), Jon Silver's *Watsonville on Strike* (1989), or Ross McElwhee's *Sherman's March* (1985). The filmmaker's presence takes on heightened importance, from the physical act of "getting the shot" that figures so prominently in *The Man with a Movie Camera* to the political act of joining forces with one's subjects as Jon Silver does at the start of *Watsonville on Strike* when he asks the farm workers if he can film in the union hall or as Jon Alpert does when he translates into Spanish what the workers he accompanies to Mexico try to say to their counterparts about the dangers of HMD (hard metals disease).

This style of filmmaking is what Rouch and Morin termed *cinéma vérité,* translating into French Dziga Vertov's title for his newsreels of Soviet society, *kinopravda.* As "film truth," the idea emphasizes that this is the truth of an encounter rather than the absolute or untampered truth. We see how the filmmaker and subject negotiate a relationship, how they act toward one another, what forms of power and control come into play, and what levels of revelation or rapport stem from this specific form of encounter.

If there is a truth here it is the truth of a form of interaction that would not exist were it not for the camera. In this sense it is the opposite of the observational premise that what we see is what we would have seen had we been there in lieu of the camera. In participatory documentary, what we see is what we can see only when a camera, or filmmaker, is there instead of ourselves. Jean-Luc Godard once claimed that cinema is truth twenty-four times a second: participatory documentary makes good on Godard's claim.

Chronicle of a Summer, for example, involves scenes that result from the collaborative interactions of filmmakers and their subjects, an eclectic group of individuals living in Paris in the summer of 1960. In one instance Marcelline Loridan, a young woman who later married the Dutch filmmaker Joris Ivens, speaks about her experience as a Jewish deportee from France who is sent to a German concentration camp during World War II. The camera follows her as she walks through the Place de la Concorde and then through the former Parisian market, Les Halles. She offers a quite moving monologue on her experiences, but only because Rouch and Morin had planned the scene with her and given her the tape recorder to carry. If they had waited for the event to occur on its own so they could observe it, it never would have occurred. They pursued this notion of collaboration still further by screening parts of the film to the participants and filming the ensuing discussion. Rouch and Morin also appear on camera, discussing their aim to study "this strange tribe living in Paris" and assessing, at the end of the film, what they have learned.

Similarly, in *Not a Love Story* (1981), Bonnie Klein, the filmmaker, and Linda Lee Tracy, an ex-stripper, discuss their reactions to various forms of pornography as they interview participants in the sex industry. In one scene, Linda Lee poses for a nude photograph and then discusses how the experience made her feel. The two women embark on a journey that is partly exploratory in a spirit similar to Rouch and Morin's and partly confessional/redemptive in an entirely different sense. The act of making the film plays a cathartic, redemptive role in their own lives; it is less the world of their subjects that changes than their own.

In some cases, such as Marcel Ophuls's *The Sorrow and the Pity* (1970), on French collaboration with Germany during World War II, the filmmaker's voice emerges primarily as a perspective on the subject matter of the film.

Crumb (Terry Zwigoff, 1994)

Terry Zwigoff adopts a highly participatory relationship to the cartoon strip artist R. Crumb. Many of the conversations and interactions clearly would not have occurred as they do had Zwigoff not been there with his camera. Crumb takes a more reflective attitude toward himself and a more probing attitude toward his brothers as he collaborates with Zwigoff's desire to examine the complexities and contradictions of his life.

The filmmaker serves as a researcher or investigative reporter. In other cases, the filmmaker's voice emerges from direct, personal involvement in the events that unfold. This can remain within the orbit of the investigative reporter who makes his own personal involvement in the story central to its unfolding. An example is the work of Canadian filmmaker Michael Rubbo, such as his *Sad Song of Yellow Skin* (1970), where he explores the ramifications of the Vietnam War among the civilian population of Vietnam. Another is the work of Nicholas Broomfield, who adopts a brasher, more confrontational—if not arrogant—style in his *Kurt and Courtney* (1998): his exasperation with Courtney Love's elusiveness despite unsubstantiated suspicions of her complicity in Kurt Cobain's death compels Broomfield to film his own, apparently spontaneous denunciation of her at a ceremonial dinner sponsored by the American Civil Liberties Union.

In other cases, we move away from the investigative stance to take up a more responsive and reflective relationship to unfolding events that involve the filmmaker. This latter choice moves us toward the diary and personal testimonial. The first-person voice becomes prominent in the overall

Las Madres de la Plaza de Mayo (Susana Muñoz and Lourdes Portillo, 1985). Photo courtesy of Lourdes Portillo.

These two women filmmakers adopt a highly participatory relationship with the mothers who risked their lives to stage public demonstrations during Argentina's "dirty war." The sons and daughters of these women were among the "disappeared" whom the government abducted, and often killed, without any notice or legal proceedings. Muñoz and Portillo could not shape the public events, but they could draw out the personal stories of the mothers whose courage led them to defy a brutally repressive regime.

structure of the film. It is the filmmaker's participatory engagement with unfolding events that holds our attention.

Nicholas Necroponte's involvement with a woman whom he meets in New York's Central Park, who seems to have a complex but not entirely credible history, becomes central to the overall structure of *Jupiter's Wife* (1995). Similarly, it is Emiko Omori's efforts to retrace the suppressed history of her own family's experience in the Japanese-American relocation camps of World War II that gives form to *Rabbit in the Moon* (1999). Marilu Mallet offers an even more explicitly diary-like structure to her portrait of life as a Chilean exile living in Montreal married to Canadian filmmaker Michael Rubbo in *Unfinished Diary* (1983), as does Kazuo Hara to his chronicle of the complex, emotionally volatile relationship he revives with his former wife as he and his current partner follow her over a period of time in *Extremely Personal Eros: Love Song* (1974). These films make the filmmaker as vivid

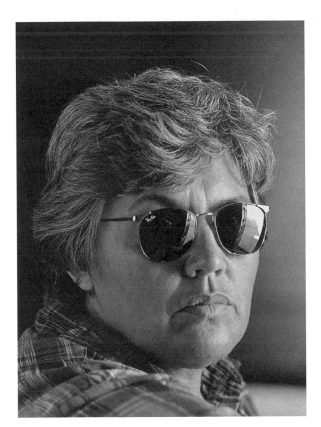

The Devil Never Sleeps [*El Diablo Nunca Duerme*] (Lourdes Portillo, 1995). Photos courtesy of Lourdes Portillo.

Director Lourdes Portillo as a hard-boiled private eye. The film recounts her journey to Mexico to investigate the suspicious death of her uncle. Reflexive and ironic at times, Portillo nonetheless leaves the question of whether her uncle met with foul play, possibly at the hands of a relative, open.

a persona as any other in their films. As testimonial and confession, they often exude a power that is revelatory.

Not all participatory documentaries stress the ongoing, open-ended experience of the filmmaker or the interaction between filmmaker and subjects. The filmmaker may wish to introduce a broader perspective, often one that is historical in nature. How can this be done? The most common answer involves the interview. The interview allows the filmmaker to address people who appear in the film formally rather than address the audience through voice-over commentary. The interview stands as one of the most common forms of encounter between filmmaker and subject in participatory documentary.

Interviews are a distinct form of social encounter. They differ from ordinary conversation and the more coercive process of interrogation by dint of the institutional framework in which they occur and the specific protocols or guidelines that structure them. Interviews occur in anthropological or sociological field work; they go by the name of the "case history" in medicine

The Devil Never Sleeps
   The filmmaker, in the course of an interview, in search of clues, and, ideally, the confession that will solve the mystery. Although she never obtains a confession, the sense that she *might* do so lends an air of narrative, film noir–like suspense to the film.

and social welfare; in psychoanalysis, they take the form of the therapeutic session; in law the interview becomes the pre-trial process of "discovery" and, during trials, testimony; on television, it forms the backbone of talk shows; in journalism, it takes the form of both the interview and the press conference; and in education, it appears as Socratic dialogue. Michel Foucault argues that these forms all involve regulated forms of exchange, with an uneven distribution of power between client and institutional practitioner, and that they have their root in the religious tradition of the confessional.

   Filmmakers make use of the interview to bring different accounts together in a single story. The voice of the filmmaker emerges from the weave of contributing voices and the material brought in to support what they say. This compilation of interviews and supporting material has given us numerous film histories, from *In the Year of the Pig* (1969), on the war in Vietnam, to *Eyes on the Prize,* on the history of the civil rights movement, and from *The Life and Times of Rosie the Riveter,* on women at work during World War II, to *Shoah,* on the aftermath of the Holocaust for those who experienced it.

   Compilation films such as Esther Shub's *The Fall of the Romanov Dy-*

nasty, which relies entirely on archival footage found by Shub and reedited to tell a social history, date back to the beginnings of expository documentary. Participatory documentaries add the active engagement of the filmmaker with her subjects or informants and avoid anonymous voice-over exposition. This situates the film more squarely in a given moment and distinct perspective; it enriches commentary with the grain of individual voices. Some, such as Barbara Kopple's *Harlan County, U.S.A.* (1977), on a coal miner's strike in Kentucky, or Michael Moore's *Roger and Me* (1989), dwell on events in the present to which the filmmmaker is a participant, while adding some historical background. Some, such as Errol Morris's *The Thin Blue Line,* Leon Gasts's *When We Were Kings* (1996), on the 1974 fight between Muhammad Ali and George Foreman, or Ray Mueller's *The Wonderful, Horrible Life of Leni Riefenstahl* (1993), on her controversial career, center on the past and how those with knowledge of it now recount it.

The experience of gays and lesbians in the days before Stonewall, for example, could be recounted as a general social history, with a voice-over commentary and images that illustrate the spoken points. It could also be recounted in the words of those who lived through these times by means of interviews. Jon Adair's *Word Is Out* (1977) opts for the second choice. Adair, like Connie Field for *Rosie the Riveter,* screened scores of possible subjects before settling on the dozen or so who appear in the film. Unlike Field or Emile de Antonio, Adair opts to keep supporting material to a bare minimum; he compiles his history primarily from the "talking heads" of those who can put this chapter of American social history into their own words. Like oral histories that are recorded and written up to serve as one type of primary source material, which this form resembles but also differs from in the careful selection and arrangement of interview material, the articulateness and emotional directness of those who speak gives films of testimony a compelling quality.

Filmmakers who seek to represent their own direct encounter with their surrounding world and those who seek to represent broad social issues and historical perspectives through interviews and compilation footage constitute two large components of the participatory mode. As viewers we have the sense that we are witness to a form of dialogue between filmmaker and subject that stresses situated engagement, negotiated interaction, and emotion-laden encounter. These qualities give the participatory mode of documentary filmmaking considerable appeal as it roams a wide variety of subjects from the most personal to the most historical. Often, in fact, this mode demonstrates how the two intertwine to yield representations of the historical world from specific perspectives that are both contingent and committed.

Cadillac Desert (Jon Else, 1997). Photos courtesy of Jon Else.

    Cadillac Desert is another excellent example of a film that couples archival footage and the tradition of the compilation film with contemporary interviews that add a fresh perspective to historical events without resorting to a voice-over commentary. *Cadillac Desert* retraces the history of water use in California and its devastating impact on the inland valleys of the state.

THE REFLEXIVE MODE

If the historical world provides the meeting place for the processes of negotiation between filmmaker and subject in the participatory mode, the
processes of negotiation between filmmaker and viewer become the focus
of attention for the reflexive mode. Rather than following the filmmaker in
her engagement with other social actors, we now attend to the filmmaker's
engagement with us, speaking not only about the historical world but about
the problems and issues of representing it as well.

Trinh Minh-ha's declaration that she will "speak nearby" rather than
"speak about" Africa, in *Reassemblage* (1982), symbolizes the shift that
reflexivity produces: we now attend to *how* we represent the historical world
as well as to *what* gets represented. Instead of *seeing through* documentaries to the world beyond them, reflexive documentaries ask us to *see documentary* for what it is: a construct or representation. Jean-Luc Godard and
Jean-Pierre Gorin carry this to an extreme in *Letter to Jane* (1972), a 45-
minute "letter" in which they scrutinize in great detail a journalistic photograph of Jane Fonda during her visit to North Vietnam. No aspect of this
apparently factual photo goes unexamined.

Just as the observational mode of documentary depends on the filmmaker's apparent absence from or non-intervention in the events recorded,
the documentary in general depends on the viewer's neglect of his or her
actual situation, in front of a movie screen, interpreting a film, in favor of
imaginary access to the events shown on the screen as if it is only these
events that require interpretation, not the film. The motto that a documentary film is only as good as its content is compelling is what the reflexive
mode of documentary calls into question.

One of the issues brought to the fore in reflexive documentaries is the
one with which we began this book: what to do with people? Some films,
like *Reassemblage, Daughter Rite* (1978), *Bontoc Eulogy* (1995), or *Far from
Poland* (1984), address this question directly by calling the usual means of
representation into question: *Reassemblage* breaks with the realist conventions of ethnography to question the power of the camera's gaze to represent, and misrepresent, others; *Daughter Rite* subverts reliance on social actors by using two actresses to play sisters who reflect on their
relationship to their mother, using insights gathered from interviews with a
wide range of women but withholding the voices of the interviewees themselves; *Bontoc Eulogy* recounts the family history of the filmmaker's own
grandfather, who was taken from the Philippines to appear as part of an exhibit of Filipino life at the St. Louis World Fair in 1904 through staged reenactments and imagined memories that call conventional rules of evidence

Surname Viet Given Name Nam (Trinh T. Minh-ha, 1989). Photos courtesy of Trinh T. Minh-ha. These three successive shots, each an extreme close-up that omits portions of the interviewee's face, correspond to the pre-production storyboard designed by the filmmaker. Their violation of the normal conventions for filming interviews both calls our attention to the formality and conventionality of interviews and signals that this is not a (normal) interview.

into question; *Far from Poland*'s director, Jill Godmilow, addresses us directly to ponder the problems of representing the Solidarity movement in Poland when she has only partial access to the actual events. These films set out to heighten our awareness of the problems of representing others as much as they set out to convince us of the authenticity or truthfulness of representation itself.

Reflexive documentaries also address issues of realism. This is a style that seems to provide unproblematic access to the world; it takes form as physical, psychological, and emotional realism through techniques of evidentiary or continuity editing, character development, and narrative structure. Reflexive documentaries challenge these techniques and conventions. *Surname Viet Given Name Nam* (1989), for example, relies on interviews with women in Vietnam who describe the oppressive conditions they have faced since the end of the war, but then halfway through the film we discover (if various stylistic hints haven't tipped us off) that the interviews were staged in more ways than one: the women who play Vietnamese women in Vietnam are actually immigrants to the United States reciting, on a stage set, accounts transcribed and edited by Trinh from interviews conducted in Vietnam by someone else with other women!

Similarly, in *The Man with a Movie Camera,* Dziga Vertov demonstrates how the impression of reality comes to be constructed by beginning with a scene of the cameraman, Mikhail Kaufman, filming people riding in a horse-drawn carriage from a car that runs alongside the carriage. Vertov then cuts to an editing room, where the editor, Elizaveta Svilova, Vertov's wife, assembles strips of film that represent this event into the sequence we have,

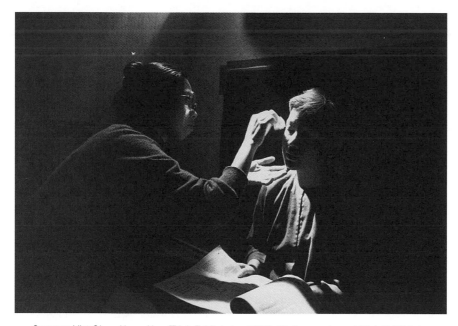

Surname Viet Given Name Nam (Trinh T. Minh-ha, 1989). Photos courtesy of Trinh T. Minh-ha.
Make-up and costume are a more frequent consideration for documentary filmmakers than we might assume. Here filmmaker Trinh T. Minh-ha prepares actress Tran Thi Bich Yen for a scene where she will play an interviewee describing her life in Vietnam. The interview appears to be set in Vietnam but was actually shot in California. Like *Far from Poland,* this film explores the question of how to represent situations not directly available to the filmmaker.

presumably, just seen. The overall result deconstructs the impression of unimpeded access to reality and invites us to reflect on the process by which this impression is itself constructed through editing.

Other films, such as *David Holzman's Diary* (1968), *No Lies* (1973), and *Daughter Rite* (1978), represent themselves, ultimately, as disguised fictions. They rely on trained actors to deliver the performances we initially believe to be the self-presentation of people engaged in everyday life. Our realization of this deception, sometimes through hints and clues during the film, or at the end, when the credits reveal the fabricated nature of the performances we have witnessed, prompts us to question the authenticity of documentary in general: what "truth" do documentaries reveal about the self; how is it different from a staged or scripted performance; what conventions prompt us to believe in the authenticity of documentary performance; and how can this belief be productively subverted?

The reflexive mode is the most self-conscious and self-questioning mode of representation. Realist access to the world, the ability to provide persuasive evidence, the possibility of indisputable proof, the solemn, indexical bond between an indexical image and what it represents—all these notions come under suspicion. That such notions can compel fetishistic belief prompts the reflexive documentary to examine the nature of such belief rather than attest to the validity of what is believed. At its best, reflexive documentary prods the viewer to a heightened form of consciousness about her relation to a documentary and what it represents. Vertov does this in *The Man with a Movie Camera* to demonstrate how we construct our knowledge of the world; Buñuel does this in *Land without Bread* to satirize the presumptions that accompany such knowledge; Trinh does this in *Reassemblage* to question the assumptions that underlie a given body of knowledge or mode of inquiry (ethnography), as Chris Marker does in *Sans Soleil* to question the assumptions that underlie the act of making films of the lives of others in a world divided by racial and political boundaries.

Achieving a heightened form of consciousness involves a shift in levels of awareness. Reflexive documentary sets out to readjust the assumptions and expectations of its audience, not add new knowledge to existing categories. For this reason, documentaries can be reflexive from both formal and political perspectives.

From a formal perspective, reflexivity draws our attention to our assumptions and expectations about documentary form itself. From a political perspective, reflexivity points toward our assumptions and expectations about the world around us. Both perspectives rely on techniques that jar us, that achieve something akin to what Bertolt Brecht described as "alienation effects," or what the Russian formalists termed *ostranenie,* or "making strange." This is similar to the surrealist effort to see the everyday world in unexpected ways. As a formal strategy, making the familiar strange reminds us how documentary works as a film genre whose claims about the world we can receive too unthinkingly; as a political strategy, it reminds us how society works in accord with conventions and codes we may too readily take for granted.

The rise of feminist documentaries in the 1970s provides a vivid example of the works that call social conventions into question. Films such as *The Woman's Film* (1971), *Joyce at Thirty-four* (1972), and *Growing Up Female* (1970) followed most of the conventions of participatory documentary, but they also sought to produce a heightened consciousness about discrimination against women in the contemporary world. They counter the prevailing (stereotypical) images of women with radically different representations and displace the hopes and desires fueled and gratified by advertising and melo-

Wedding Camels (David and Judith MacDougall, 1980). Photo courtesy of David MacDougall.
In this trilogy of films on the Turkana of northern Kenya, David and Judith MacDougall adopt several reflexive strategies to make us aware of the filmmakers' active involvement in shaping the scenes we see. Sometimes it is a question put by the filmmakers that prompts discussion, sometimes it is written titles that remind us of the complex process of representing members of another culture in a form members of an English-speaking culture can understand. Such reflexive acts were rare at the time in ethnographic film. Many such films want to give the impression *Nanook of the North* gave: we witness customs and behavior as they "naturally" occur, not as a result of interaction between filmmaker and subject.

dramas with the experiences and demands of women who have rejected these notions in favor of radically different ones. Such films challenge entrenched notions of the feminine and also serve to give name to what had lain invisible: the oppression, devalorization, and hierarchy that can now be called sexism. Individual experiences combine into common perceptions: a new way of seeing, a distinct perspective on the social order, emerges.

"Alienation" from prevailing assumptions may have a formal or cinematic component, but it is also heavily social or political in its impact. Rather than provoking our awareness primarily of form, politically reflexive documentaries provoke our awareness of social organization and the assumptions

Corpus: A Home Movie for Selena (Lourdes Portillo, 1999). Photo courtesy of Lourdes Portillo.

Director Lourdes Portillo investigates the repercussions that followed from the murder of the popular Tex-Mex singer Selena. Was she a positive role model for young women who learn to channel their energies into becoming popular singers, or was she herself a young woman encouraged to recycle stereotypical images of female sexuality? Portillo does not answer such questions so much as pose them in an engaging way. She does so partly by shooting in video to create a family portrait of Selena and her legacy.

that support it. They tend, therefore, to induce an "aha!" effect, where we grasp a principle or structure at work that helps account for what would otherwise be a representation of more localized experience. Instead we take a deeper look. Politically reflexive documentaries acknowledge the way things are but also invoke the way they might become. Our heightened consciousness opens up a gap between knowledge and desire, between what is and what might be. Politically reflexive documentaries point to *us* as viewers and social actors, not to films, as the agents who can bridge this gap between what exists and the new forms we can make from it.

THE PERFORMATIVE MODE

Like the poetic mode of documentary representation, the performative mode raises questions about what is knowledge. What counts as understanding or comprehension? What besides factual information goes into our understanding of the world? Is knowledge best described as abstract and disembodied, based on generalizations and the typical, in the tradition of Western philosophy? Or is knowledge better described as concrete and embodied, based on the specificities of personal experience, in the tradition of poetry, literature, and rhetoric? Performative documentary endorses the latter position and sets out to demonstrate how embodied knowledge provides entry into an understanding of the more general processes at work in society.

Meaning is clearly a subjective, affect-laden phenomenon. A car or gun, hospital or person will bear different meanings for different people. Experience and memory, emotional involvement, questions of value and belief, commitment and principle all enter into our understanding of those aspects of the world most often addressed by documentary: the institutional framework (governments and churches, families and marriages) and specific social practices (love and war, competition and cooperation) that make up a society (as discussed in Chapter 4). Performative documentary underscores the complexity of our knowledge of the world by emphasizing its subjective and affective dimensions.

Works like Marlon Riggs's *Tongues Untied* (1989), Ngozi Onwurah's *The Body Beautiful* (1991), and Marlon Fuentes's *Bontoc Eulogy* (1995) stress the emotional complexity of experience from the perspective of the filmmaker him-or herself. An autobiographical note enters into these films that bears similarity to the diaristic mode of participatory filmmaking. Performative films give added emphasis to the subjective qualities of experience and memory that depart from factual recounting. Marlon Riggs, for example, makes use of recited poems and enacted scenes that address the intense personal stakes involved in black, gay identity; Onwurah's film builds up to a staged sexual encounter between her own mother and a handsome young man; and Fuentes enacts a fantasy about his grandfather's escape from captivity as an object of display at the 1904 St. Louis World's Fair. Actual occurrences become amplified by imagined ones. The free combination of the actual and the imagined is a common feature of the performative documentary.

What these films and others such as Isaac Julien's *Looking for Langston* (1988), about the life of Langston Hughes, or Julien's *Frantz Fanon: Black Skin/White Mask* (1996), about the life of Frantz Fanon; Larry Andrews's video *Black and Silver Horses* (1992), about issues of race and identity; Robert Gardner's *Forest of Bliss* (1985), about funeral practices in Benares, India; Chris Choy and Renee Tajima's *Who Killed Vincent Chin?* (1988), about the murder of a Chinese American by two out-of-work auto workers who reportedly mistook him for Japanese; Rea Tajiri's *History and Memory* (1991), about her efforts to learn the story of her family's internment in detention camps during World War II; and Pratibha Parmar's *Khush* (1991), about being Asian-British and gay, share is a deflection of documentary emphasis away from a realist representation of the historical world and toward poetic liberties, more unconventional narrative structures, and more subjective forms of representation. The referential quality of documentary that attests to its function as a window onto the world yields to an expressive quality that affirms the highly situated, embodied, and vividly personal perspective of specific subjects, including the filmmaker.

Ever since at least *Turksib* (1929), *Salt for Svanetia* (1930), and, in a satiric vein, *Land without Bread* (1932), documentary has exhibited many performative qualities, but they seldom have served to organize entire films. They were present but not dominant. Some participatory documentaries of the 1980s, such as *Las Madres de la Plaza de Mayo* (1985) and *Roses in December* (1982), include performative moments that draw us into subjective, "as if" renderings of traumatic past events (the "disappearance" of the son of one of the mothers who protested government repression in Argentina and the rape of Jean Donovan and three other women by El Salvadoran military men respectively), but the organizing dominant to the films revolves around a linear history that includes these events. Performative documentaries primarily address us, emotionally and expressively, rather than pointing us to the factual world we hold in common.

These films engage us less with rhetorical commands or imperatives than with a sense of their own vivid responsiveness. The filmmaker's responsiveness seeks to animate our own. We engage with their representation of the historical world but do so obliquely, via the affective charge they apply to it and seek to make our own.

Tongues Untied, for example, begins with a voice-over call that ricochets from left and right, in stereo, "Brother to Brother," "Brother to Brother. . . ," and ends with a declaration, "Black men loving black men is the revolutionary act." The course of the film over a series of declarations, reenactments, poetic recitations, and staged performances that all attest to the complexities of racial and sexual relations within gay subculture strives to animate us to adopt the position of "brother" for ourselves, at least for the duration of the film. We are invited to experience what it is like to occupy the subjective, social position of a black, gay male, such as Marlon Riggs himself.

Just as a feminist aesthetic may strive to move audience members, regardless of their actual gender and sexual orientation, into the subjective position of a feminist character's perspective on the world, performative documentary seeks to move its audience into subjective alignment or affinity with its specific perspective on the world. Like earlier works such as *Listen to Britain* (1941), on resistance to German bombing by the British people

Angela Jendell, from the House of Jendell walking as futuristic
femme queen.

Paris Is Burning (Jenny Livingston, 1991)

   Paris Is Burning enters into a distinct, black, gay sub-culture in which young men cluster into "houses," which compete against each other in various categories of mimicry and drag at "balls." Organized partly to explain this sub-culture to nonparticipants, *Paris Is Burning* also immerses us performatively in the quality and texture of this world to a degree that *16 in Webster Groves* or *Dead Birds* does not.

during World War II, or *Three Songs of Lenin* (1934), on the mourning of Lenin's death by the Soviet people, recent performative documentaries try to give representation to a social subjectivity that joins the general to the particular, the individual to the collective, and the political to the personal. The expressive dimension may be anchored to particular individuals, but it extends to embrace a social, or shared, form of subjective response.

   In recent work this social subjectivity is often that of the underrepresented or misrepresented, of women and ethnic minorities, gays and lesbians. Performative documentary can act as a corrective to those films where "We speak about them to us." They proclaim, instead, that "We speak about ourselves to you," or "We speak about ourselves to us." Performative documentary shares a rebalancing and corrective tendency with auto-ethnography (ethnographically informed work made by members of the communities who are the traditional subjects of Western ethnography, such as the numerous tapes made by the Kayapo people of the Amazon river basin and by the Aboriginal people of Australia). It does not, however, counter error with fact, misinformation with information, but adopts a distinct mode of representation that suggests knowledge and understanding require an entirely different form of engagement.

Like early documentary, before the observational mode placed priority on the direct filming of social encounter, performative documentary freely mixes the expressive techniques that give texture and density to fiction (point-of-view shots, musical scores, renderings of subjective states of mind, flashbacks and freeze frames, etc.) with oratorical techniques for addressing the social issues that neither science nor reason can resolve.

Performative documentary approaches the domain of experimental or avant-garde cinema but gives, finally, less emphasis to the self-contained quality of the film or video than to its expressive dimension *in relation to* representations that refer us back to the historical world for their ultimate meaning. We continue to recognize the historical world by means of familiar people and places (Langston Hughes, Detroit cityscapes, the San Francisco Bay Bridge, and so on), the testimony of others (participants in *Tongues Untied* who describe the experiences of black, gay men; the personal voice-over confidences of Ngozi Onwurah about her relationship to her mother in *The Body Beautiful*); and scenes built around participatory or observational modes of representation (interviews with various people in *Khush* and *I'm British but. . . ;* observed moments of daily life in *Forest of Bliss*).

The world as represented by performative documentaries becomes, however, suffused by evocative tones and expressive shadings that constantly remind us that the world is more than the sum of the visible evidence we derive from it. Another early, partial example of the performative mode, Alain Resnais's *Night and Fog* (1955), about the Holocaust, makes this point vividly. The film's voice-over commentary and images of illustration nominate *Night and Fog* for the expository mode, but the haunting, personal quality of the commentary moves it toward the performative. The film is less about history than memory, less about history from above—what happened when and why—and more about history from below—what one person might experience and what it might feel like to undergo that experience. Through the elliptic, evocative tone of the commentary by Jean Cayrol, a survivor of Auschwitz, *Night and Fog* sets out to represent the unrepresentable:

Night and Fog [*Nuit et brouillard*] (Alain Resnais, 1955)

Much of the footage presented in *Night and Fog* was shot by concentration camp officers, then discovered after the war by the Allies. Alain Resnais compiles this footage into a searing testimony to the horrors of inhumanity. His film offers far more than visual evidence of Nazi atrocities. It urges us to remember, and never forget, what happened long ago in these camps. It links the past to the present and gives to memory the burden of sustaining a moral conscience.

the sheer inconceivability of acts that defy all reason and all narrative order. Visible evidence abounds—of belongings and bodies, of victims and survivors—but the voice of *Night and Fog* extends beyond what evidence confirms: it calls for an emotional responsiveness from us that acknowledges how understanding this event within any pre-established frame of reference is an utter impossibility (even as we may arrive at a judgment of the heinous monstrosity of such genocide).

In a similar spirit, Hungarian filmmaker Péter Forgács has described his goal as not to polemicize, not to explain, not to argue or judge, so much as to evoke a sense of what past experiences were like for those who lived them. His extraordinary documentaries are made from home movies re-organized into performative representations of the social turmoil caused by World War II: *Free Fall* (1998), recounts the life of a successful Jewish businessman in the 1930s, Gyorgy Peto, who is eventually caught up in

Free Fall (Péter Forgács, 1998). Photos courtesy of Péter Forgács.

Péter Forgács relies entirely on found footage, in this case, home movies from the 1930s and 1940s. Such footage reveals life as it was seen and experienced at a given time. Forgács reworks the footage, cropping images, slowing down motion, adding titles and music, to combine a sense of historical perspective with a form of emotional engagement. The result is quite poetic, radically different in tone from the classic World War II documentaries in an expository mode such as the *Why We Fight* series.

Germany's decision, late in the war, to apply their "final solution" to Hungarian Jews; and *Danube Exodus* (1999) tells of the forced migrations of Jews down the Danube en route to Palestine, in the face of British resistance to the arrival of any more refugees, and of Germans who flee upriver from Romania back to Germany when the Soviet army drives them from their land. The film relies primarily on home movies taken by the captain of a Danube cruise ship involved in transporting both of these groups.

Danube Exodus makes no attempt to tell the overall history of World War II. By focusing on these specific events, seen from the viewpoint of a participant rather than a historian, Forgács suggests something, however, about the overall tone of the war: he suggests how, for some participants, the war was primarily an enormous flux of peoples, in and out of various countries, for a wide variety of reasons. Loss occurs, along with dislocation. The war takes its toll not from bombs alone but from these cases of civilian exodus that transformed the face of Europe.

Forgács wants to leave evaluation and judgment to us but also to postpone this kind of reflection while we experience a more directly subjective encounter with these historical events. He invokes affect over effect, emotion over reason, not to reject analysis and judgment but to place them on a different basis. Like Resnais, Vertov, and Kalatozov before him, and like so many of his contemporaries, Forgács sidesteps ready-made positions and prefabricated categories. He invites us, as all great documentarians do, to see the world afresh and to rethink our relation to it. Performative documentary restores a sense of magnitude to the local, specific, and embodied. It animates the personal so that it may become our port of entry to the political.

We can summarize this general sketch of the six modes of documentary representation in the following table. Documentary, like the avant-garde, begins in response to fiction. (The dates in this table signify when a mode becomes a common alternative; each mode has predecessors and each continues to this day.)

Table 6.1

Documentary Modes

Chief Characteristics

—Deficiencies

Hollywood fiction [1910s]: fictional narratives of imaginary worlds
—absence of "reality"

Poetic documentary [1920s]: reassemble fragments of the world poetically
—lack of specificity, too abstract

Expository documentary [1920s]: directly address issues in the historical world
—overly didactic

Observational documentary [1960s]: eschew commentary and reenactment; observe things as they happen
—lack of history, context

Participatory documentary [1960s]: interview or interact with subjects; use archival film to retrieve history
—excessive faith in witnesses, naive history, too intrusive

Reflexive documentary [1980s]: question documentary form, defamiliarize the other modes
—too abstract, lose sight of actual issues

Performative documentary [1980s]: stress subjective aspects of a classically objective discourse
—loss of emphasis on objectivity may relegate such films to the avant-garde; "excessive" use of style.

Chapter 7

How Have Documentaries Addressed Social and Political Issues?

PEOPLE AS VICTIMS OR AGENTS

When we first asked "What to do with people?" in Chapter 1, our discussion fell primarily within an ethical frame. What consequences follow from different forms of response to and engagement with others? How may we represent or speak about others without reducing them to stereotypes, pawns, or victims? These questions allow few easy answers, but they also suggest that the issues are not ethical alone. To act unethically or to misrepresent others involves politics and ideology as well.

In a harsh critique of the documentary tradition, especially as represented by television journalism, Brian Winston argues that 1930s documentary filmmakers in Great Britain took a romantic view of their working-class subjects; they failed to see the worker as an active, self-determining agent of change. Instead, the worker suffered from a "plight" that others, namely government agencies, should do something about.

Housing Problems (1935), for example, gave slum dwellers the opportunity to speak for themselves, in a synchronous sound interview format set within their own homes. The words of actual workers appeared on British screens for the first time, a sensational achievement in the days long before television or reality TV. But they appeared as if they came with hat in hand, to explain their miserable living conditions politely in the hopes that someone else would agree to do something about it. (*Housing Problems* had the Gas Light and Coke Company as a sponsor since government slum clearance, the proposed "solution" to the workers' plight, served the company's own interests of ultimately increasing gas consumption.) There was less militancy than supplication. The stage was set for a politics of charitable benevolence.

As Winston notes, the urge to represent the worker romantically or poetically, within an ethics of social concern and charitable empathy, denied the worker a sense of equal status with the filmmaker. The filmmaker kept control of the act of representation; collaboration was not in the air. A professional corps of filmmakers would go about representing others in accord with their own ethics and their own institutional mandate as government-sponsored propagandists, in the case of John Grierson and his colleagues, and as journalists in the "tradition of the victim" that Winston argues followed from this example. A few years of such films and "The worker would stand revealed as the central subject of the documentary, anonymous and pathetic, and the director of victim documentaries would be as much of an 'artist' as any other filmmaker" ("The Tradition of the Victim in Griersonian Documentary," in Alan Rosenthal, ed., *New Challenges for Documentary*, p. 274).

Parenthetically, we should note that this "tradition," if that is the right word for a form of class prejudice, did not prevail everywhere or with everyone. As we shall see later in the chapter, the 1920s and 1930s Film and Photo Leagues of various nations chose displays of worker resistance such as strikes and protests for their subject matter, and Joris Ivens and Henri Storck made their own clearly partisan and highly activist account of a Belgian coal mine strike, *Misère au Borinage* (1933), as an act of solidarity with the defiant workers. (It is a precursor to Barbara Kopple's Oscar-winning documentary, *Harlan County, U.S.A.*) The target of Winston's ire is more specifically those government- or network-television–sponsored reports that prefer to present workers as docile and helpless but needy.

For Winston one question constitutes a litmus test for the politics of documentary representation: "But if it is the case that housing problems are unaffected by fifty years of documentary effort, what justification can there be for continuing to make such films and tapes?" Winston notes that a failure to achieve social change was not inevitable; it stemmed from the politics of representation put into practice:

> There was nothing, though, in this ambition to be the propagandists for a better and more just society (shared by the entire documentary movement) that would inevitably lead to the constant, repetitive, and ultimately pointless

exposure of the same set of social problems on the televisions of the West night after night. . . . Benchmarks were thereby established for all subsequent work both in film and in television for the entire English-speaking world and beyond. ("Victim," p. 270)

We may take exception to the blanket condemnation of documentary and to the assumption that more radical documentaries alone would solve issues such as housing problems, or, conversely, that the failure to solve pressing issues necessarily demonstrates the impotence of those documentaries that attempt to represent them, without regard to other social and political forces at work in a given historical moment. The degree of activism among workers, the political balance of power in government, the policies and actions of industries implicated in the question of housing, for example, would all have significant bearing—as much as, if not more than, the rhetorical persuasiveness and political efficacy of documentaries on this issue. We can agree, however, that the politics of representation locates documentaries within a larger arena of social debate and contestation. A regard for ethics entails a regard for political, and ideological, consequences as well.

All documentaries have a voice of their own, but not all documentary voices address social and political issues directly. (Poetic documentaries may seem far removed from social issues; this may be a political choice on one level, but it shifts our primary attention to other considerations.) We will look here at some of those documentaries that do address the political directly. These are films such as *Housing Problems, Coal Face,* and *Smoke Menace,* among the British documentaries of the 1930s, for example, that enter into the ongoing debates of the day about social values and beliefs more than about accepted facts or poetic visions.

CONSTRUCTING NATIONAL IDENTITY

Among the many specific debates that documentaries have addressed over their history, we will focus on questions of the nation-state: the construction of nationality and nationalism, and the relation of documentary filmmaking to the interests of governments in power and the interests of the dispossessed, of whom Karl Marx once said, "they cannot represent themselves; they must be represented," a statement to which much documentary film and video production by those who have been the presumed "victims" of the documentary tradition—women, ethnic minorities, gays and lesbians, Third World peoples—gives the lie.

The construction of national identities involves the construction of a sense of community. "Community" invokes feelings of common interest and mutual respect, of reciprocal relationships closer to family ties than contractual obligations. Shared values and beliefs are vital to a sense of community, whereas contractual relationships can be carried out despite differences of value and belief. A sense of community often seems like an "organic" quality that binds people together when they share a tradition, culture, or common goal. As such it may seem far removed from issues of ideology, where competing beliefs struggle to win our hearts and minds.

On the other hand, the most insidious forms of ideology may be precisely the ones that make community seem natural, or organic. We seldom pause to give careful consideration to such questions as: Who do we chose to emulate or identify with and why? Who do we chose as objects of sexual desire, or love, and why? Who do we chose to join with as members of a community, and why? The need for role models, loved ones, and social belonging seems profoundly human. These forms of interdependence "just happen," or so it seems.

And yet, within different societies, at different points in time, individuals enter into very different forms of relationships with one another. Whatever basic drives or needs are involved, they take a variety of concrete forms, and these forms seem, at least in modern times, susceptible to social construction. Be it a Bill of Rights or a Five Year Plan, a benign despotism or a competitive spirit, ideologies come into play to provide stories, images, and myths that promote one set of values over others. The sense of community always comes at the price of alternative values and beliefs deemed deviant, subversive, or illegal. The politics of documentary film and video addresses the ways in which documentary helps give tangible expression to the values and beliefs that build, or contest, specific forms of social belonging, or community, at a given time and place.

Take the Soviet cinema of the 1920s, for example. All filmmaking depended on state support after the Russian Revolution of 1917. Like the Soviet art movement known as constructivism, Soviet cinema explored how film could serve the revolutionary aspirations of the moment: how could it represent the "new man" of communist society; how could it construct a distinct culture freed from bourgeois tradition; how could it transcend old class divisions in the cities, near-feudal relations in the country, and parochial loyalties in the various republics to foster a sense of community revolving around the *union* of Soviet socialist republics and the leadership of the Communist Party?

Answers varied but, on the whole, Soviet cinema adopted a strongly rhetorical means of expression. Persuasive styles and forms predominated, and few were more persuasive in their advocacy of specific strategies than Sergei Eisenstein and Dziga Vertov. Eisenstein's theory of montage insisted on the necessity for the filmmaker to juxtapose images, or shots, in ways that jarred the viewer into achieving new insights. Fragments of what is, of what could be, put before the camera, combined into a vision of the new, of what the filmmaker, like the members of a new society, could fashion in the moment. Although Eisenstein made use of scripts and sometimes actors, he may well have been surprised to find himself considered a fiction filmmaker by later generations: like early documentarians in other countries, Eisenstein's films, such as *Strike, Battleship Potemkin, October,* and *The Old and the New,* set out to give tangible expression to a sense of community in the process of construction, construction that, in this case, revolves around masses of actual people joining together to achieve goals unattainable by any other means. There was little in basic intent to separate him from more avowedly pure documentarists like Dziga Vertov.

Vertov, like the observational filmmakers of the 1960s, eschewed all forms of scripting, staging, acting, or reenacting. He wanted to catch life raw-handed and then to assemble from it a vision of the new society in the process of emergence. His own term for the cinema, *kinopravda* (film-truth), insisted on a radical break with all forms of theatrical, literary structure for film: these forms depended on narrative structures that crippled the potential of cinema to help construct a new visual reality and, with it, a new social reality. His forty-three weekly newsreels made in 1918–1919 on current events, his *Kinopravda* series of reports on life in the post-revolutionary Soviet Union (1923–25), his first feature-length film, *Kinoglaz* [*Kino-Eye* or *Life Caught Unawares*] (1925), and his best-known film, *The Man with a Movie Camera* (1929) all attest to his belief that the cinema could *see* a world invisible to the human eye and help bring such a world into existence.

Cinema and revolution go hand in hand. As Vertov himself put it,

> I am kino-eye, I create a man more perfect than Adam, I create thousands of different people in accordance with preliminary blue-prints and diagrams of different kinds.
> I am kino-eye.
> From one person I take the hands, the strongest and most dexterous, from another I take the legs, the swiftest and most shapely; from a third, the most beautiful and expressive head—and through montage I create a new, perfect man. ("Kinoks: A Revolution" [1923], in Annette Michelson, ed., *Kino-Eye: The Writings of Dziga Vertov*, p. 17)

Kino-eye is understood as "that which the eye doesn't see,"

> as the microscope and telescope of time . . .
> [as] "life caught unawares," etc. etc.

All these different formulations were mutually complementary, since implied in kino-eye were:

all cinematic means,
all cinematic inventions,
all methods and means that might serve to reveal and show the truth.
Not kino-eye for its own sake, but truth through the means and possibilities of film-eye, i.e., *kinopravda* ["film truth"].
Not "filming life unawares," for the sake of the "unaware," but in order to show people without masks, without makeup, to catch them through the eye of the camera in a moment when they are not acting, to read their thoughts, laid bare by the camera.
Kino-eye as the possibility of making the invisible visible, the unclear clear, the hidden manifest, the disguised overt, the acted nonacted, making falsehood into truth.
Kino-eye as the union of science with newsreel to further the battle for the communist decoding of the world, as an attempt to show the truth on the screen—Film-truth. ("The Birth of Kino-Eye" [1923], in Michelson, pp. 41–42)

For Vertov *all true cinema* fell under the banner of kino-eye and *kinopravda*; all other cinema remained an appendage of novels and plays. Vertov did not need to coin a word like "documentary," since, for him, his films embodied the essence of cinema, not the traits of a genre. Ironically, the term *kinopravda* would return to use through the homage paid to Vertov by Jean Rouch and Edgar Morin when they named their new form of documentary filmmaking *cinéma vérité* (French for *kinopravda*), as a *type* (or mode) of documentary, rather than as an all-inclusive category. A term that had begun with Vertov as the definition of all true cinema became associated not only with the more delimited area of one genre, documentary, but also with the further delimited sub-genre of participatory documentary!

Kino-eye contributed to the construction of a new society by demonstrating how the raw materials of everyday life as caught by the camera could be synthetically reconstructed into a new order. Vertov did not return to the historical past since that demanded reenactment with costumes, scripts, and performances. He favored the compilation films of Esther Shub to the reconstructions of historical events by Eisenstein, Dovzhenko, Pudovkin, and others, but he favored even more shooting situations and events from life in the present that could be refashioned to reveal the shape of the future.

Vertov, like many artists of the early twentieth century, held great reverence for technologies of the machine and for radical experimentation with traditional forms. In his hands, a reverence for the perfection of the kino-eye facilitated the construction of a Soviet community that gave priority to collectivity over individuality, change over stasis, and unity as one nationality, with one central leader (Lenin, then Stalin). His dedication to formal innovation, though, would cause him, and most of the other leading figures of Soviet cinema and constructivist art, increasing difficulty in the late 1920s and early 1930s as the State began to impose a more accessible, and formulaic, style of representation that came to be known as "socialist realism" (a return to linear narratives, recognizable characters with familiar psychological profiles, and themes of heightened consciousness that prompt heroes to dedicate themselves to "the people" and the State). By 1939, Vertov lacked the State sponsorship that was necessary to make a film. As he recorded in his diary of that year,

> I feel as if I'm way at the bottom. Facing the first step of a long, steep staircase. My violin lies at the very top, on the landing. I move the bow. . . on air. I ask to be allowed to get my violin. I climb onto the first step. But the person in charge of the step pushes me aside and asks: "Where are you going?"
>
> I point to my bow and explain that my violin's up there. "But what do you plan to play on the violin? Tell us, describe it to us. We'll discuss it; we'll correct it; we'll add to it; we'll coordinate it with the other steps; we'll reject or confirm it."
>
> I say that I'm a composer. And I write not with words, but with sounds.
>
> Then they ask me not to worry.
>
> And take away my bow.

Perhaps the bow was passed to John Grierson. Grierson, along with Flaherty, is often called the father of documentary (a term he is credited with coining in a review of Flaherty's *Moana;* Vertov had little need for such a word since his theory encompassed all of cinema). He persuaded the British government to do with film in 1930 what the Soviet government had done since 1918: make use of an art form to foster a sense of national identity and shared community commensurate with its own political agenda. By establishing a film unit at the Empire Marketing Board from 1930 to 1933 and then at the Government Post Office (G.P.O.) from 1933, Grierson gave the documentary film an institutional base, cultivated a community of practitioners, championed selected forms of documentary convention, and encouraged a specific set of audience expectations.

Grierson extended his example first to Canada, where he became the first film commissioner of the National Film Board of Canada in 1939, and then to the United Nations, where he served as coordinator of mass media for UNESCO in 1947. The model of government sponsorship for documentary film spread to numerous other countries, including the United States, initially through the single-minded determination of Pare Lorentz, who produced *The Plow That Broke the Plains* (1936) and *The River* (1937) for different government agencies, and later, thanks to World War II, through the efforts of converted Hollywood filmmakers like Frank Capra (the *Why We Fight* series), John Ford (*The Battle of Midway*), and John Huston (*Report from the Aleutians, The Battle of San Pietro*).

The River (Pare Lorentz, 1937). Photo courtesy of the National Archives.

The power of the river is matched by the power of the voice-over. Soon, we are told, the turbulent violence of floods will yield to the harnessing power of dams, thanks to federal sponsorship of the Tennessee Valley Authority.

John Grierson, like Pare Lorentz, shied away from the formal or poetic innovation of Dziga Vertov or the European avant-garde generally to stress the role of the documentary filmmaker as orator. These were films designed to enter into the arena of social policy and to orient or predispose public opinion to preferred solutions. From slum clearance in *Housing Problems* to combat in *Prelude to War* (1941), the first of the seven-part *Why We Fight* series, these films strove to orient the viewer toward a particular perspective on the world that called for national consensus on the values and beliefs advanced by the film. The government of the nation-state served the common good, and the common man should therefore serve the government with diligence and good faith. Such efforts affirmed a sense of national identity and inclusive community. Individuals joined in common cause to uphold treasured ideals, as specific films attest, such as *Coal Face,* made by Alberto Cavalcanti in 1935 for the G.P.O. film unit under Grierson as a respectful homage to the working-class men who mine the coal that un-

The River (Pare Lorentz, 1937). Photo courtesy of the National Archive.

"A year's income" hangs in the balance. The soft, dry, hard-to-gather cotton contrasts with the wild fury of the river. *The River* personalizes the issue of conservation by profiling the "little guy" rather than the larger business interests that also seek the benefits of flood control. And, as in *The City,* the "little guy" cannot do for himself what the government must do for him. *Why We Fight,* seeking to motivate men to go to war, will restore a sense of populist initiative that these films in support of the New Deal opted to de-emphasize.

derpins Britain's industrial power, and *The River,* made by Pare Lorentz in 1937 for the Farm Security Administration with its promotion of the Tennessee Valley Administration as the solution to the problem of destructive flooding and a desperate need for rural electrical power.

John Grierson often defined his position in contrast to the romantic idealism of Robert Flaherty. He addressed the issues of the contemporary world and promoted a commonsensical approach to nationalism and community rather than a reverence for the qualities of a bygone world and a mythical vision of kinship and affinity. We can understand Grierson's contribution to documentary not only as a more practical, hard-headed approach to social issues but also as a more conservative version of the Soviet cinema's aesthetics. Rather than fostering the revolutionary potential of the workers and peasants of the world, Grierson promoted the ameliorative potential of parliamentary democracy and government intervention to ease the most pressing issues and most serious abuses of a social system that remained fundamentally unquestioned. This ameliorative impulse no doubt contributes to the "tradition of the victim" described by Brian Winston.

John Grierson also disparaged but left unchallenged the economic dominance of feature fiction filmmaking; documentary was an alternative, morally superior practice for filmmakers of public virtue and social conscience: not quite as entertaining, but definitely better for us. Made-up stories and poetic experimentation had their place, but on a lower rung of a culture's totem-pole. Grierson aligned his concept of documentary with social purpose and public policy, eliminating Vertov's more inclusive claim for kino-eye as *the* essential element to *all* true cinema, not just documentary.

The expansiveness and power of Soviet film theory narrowed into a set of issues surrounding a more limited sense of what documentary as a nonfiction genre could mean or do. The construction of a sense of community and national identity revolved around the coordination of individual aspiration with government policies and priorities by means of a documentary form stripped of its boldest ambitions. John Grierson gave us our prototypical vision of the documentary film that, handled with the invention and sensitivity of an Alberto Cavalcanti, Basil Wright, or Humphrey Jennings, could be a thing of beauty but more often became, in the hands of government and corporate-sponsored hacks, a thing of tedious didacticism.

CONTESTING THE NATION-STATE

John Grierson gave his vision of documentary film form a level of prominence and respectability but at a cost not all filmmakers were willing to pay. Other filmmakers proposed a sense of community based on actions, and changes, that governments seemed unprepared to accept, or make. Their films took up positions that opposed the policies of governments and industries. These filmmakers constituted the political avant-garde of documentary filmmaking.

In the United States such activity traces back to the efforts of the Workers' Film and Photo Leagues of the 1920s and 1930s, which produced information about strikes and other topical issues from the perspective of the working class. Aligned with the Communist Party, similar Leagues arose in Britain, Japan, the Netherlands, and France. They adopted a participatory mode of filmmaking, consistently identifying and collaborating with their worker-subjects, thus avoiding the risk of portraying them as powerless victims. This was a cinema of empowerment that sought to contribute to the radical social movements of the 1930s and to build community from a grass-roots, oppositional level rather than from a top-down, governmentally orchestrated one.

Individuals who had their beginnings in the Film and Photo League broke away in the mid-1930s to form other organizations dedicated to producing films of greater ambition than the sometimes perfunctory newsreels of the League. Figures from writers like Lillian Hellman and Clifford Odets to filmmakers like Leo Hurwitz and Joris Ivens lent their support to this effort. Frontier Films, for example, produced *Heart of Spain* (1937), to garner support for the Republican cause in the Spanish Civil War, while Contemporary Historians, a more ad hoc group of supporters from John Dos Passos to Ernest Hemingway, sponsored the production of Joris Ivens's powerful documentary *The Spanish Earth* (1937) for the same cause.

Joris Ivens can, in fact, be regarded as another one of the multiple "fathers" of documentary, alongside Louis Lumière, Esther Shub, Dziga Vertov, John Grierson, and Robert Flaherty, but his career, which began illustriously with the poetic, experimental films *The Bridge* (1928) and *Rain* (1929), almost disappeared from sight after World War II, when his political beliefs took him to the other side of the Iron Curtain. Ivens made numerous films in Russia (*Komosol,* 1933), East Germany (*Song of the Rivers,* 1954), North Vietnam (*The Seventeenth Parallel,* 1968), and the People's Republic of China (*Before Spring,* 1958; *How Yukong Moved the Mountains,* 1976; *The Tale of the Wind,* 1988). They form little or no part of standard documentary histories in the West.

For Ivens, collaboration proved an essential ingredient to his filmmaking practice. Those forms of rehearsal, reenactment, or staging that might disconcert Vertov were of real value to Ivens if they enhanced the sense of collective effort and common cause forged in the heat of social conflict. (It was not until *after* the advent of observational filmmaking in the 1960s that these practices became subject to intense criticism; reflexive and performative documentaries have restored them to the filmmaker's repertoire.) In making *Misère au Borinage* (1934), in collaboration with Belgian filmmaker Henri Storck, for example, about a massive coal-mine strike in the Borinage region of Belgium, Ivens came to realize that capturing "life unawares" was not enough: one also had to guard against the artistic norms that might color a filmmaker's perspective and diminish his political voice. As Ivens notes in his book, *The Camera and I,*

> When the clean-cut shadow of the barracks window fell on the dirty rags and dishes of a table the pleasant effect of the shadow actually destroyed the effect of dirtiness we wanted, so we broke the edges of the shadow. Our aim was to prevent agreeable photographic effects distracting the audience from

the unpleasant truths we were showing. . . .There have also been cases in the history of documentary when photographers became so fascinated by dirt that the result was the dirt looked interesting and strange, not something repellent to the cinema audience. The filmmaker must be indignant and angry about the waste of people before he can find the right camera angle on the dirt and on the truth. (p. 87)

This gritty realism culminates in the final scene of the film, when the workers reenact a protest march that had taken place before Ivens and Storck arrived. Not only did the workers collaborate by determining the exact nature of the march, they found themselves reexperiencing the sense of community or solidarity they had experienced in the original march! The participatory *act* of filming helped occasion the very sense of community that Ivens sought to represent.

Unlike Leni Riefenstahl's collaboration with the Nazi Party to film the Nuremberg rally of 1934, Ivens and Storck collaborated not with the government, or the police, but with the very people whose misery no government had yet addressed, let alone eliminated. Their participatory involvement helped generate the very qualities they sought to document, not as spectacle to fascinate aesthetically and subdue politically but as activism to engage aesthetically and transform politically. A cinema of oratory made in collaboration with the "wretched of the earth" claimed a solid foundation that would go on to support numerous other examples of politically engaged filmmaking from the other side of the barricades.

Constructing consensus along the lines of national identity, be it in affirmation of or in opposition to established governments, played a defining role in the first few decades of documentary. Many early ethnographic filmmaking efforts partook of a similar perspective in relation to other cultures. Individual actions became subordinated to commentaries that identified such behavior as representative or typical and thereby turned our attention to the characteristics of the culture as a whole. *Trance and Dance in Bali* (1936/1952), *Les Maîtres Fous* (1955), *Dead Birds,* and *Four Families* (1959), for example, follow the example of *Nanook* in treating the individual as gateway to a unified, homogenized sense of community and culture. Along with "national identity" comes "national character" as a reductive, melting-pot idea; ethnography suffered from it as much as state-sponsored documentaries did.

But an alternative conception of individuals and the community to which they belong stands in opposition to this reductionism and the stereotyping to which it is susceptible. Communities do not align themselves perfectly with nation-states; differences remain and distinguish the one from the many,

Borinage (aka *Misère au Borinage,* Joris Ivens and Henri Storck, 1934). Photo courtesy of the European Foundation Joris Ivens.

In contrast to Jill Godmilow in *Far from Poland,* Joris Ivens was able to be there, on location, during a coal mine strike. But he, too, opts for reenactment, in this case to shoot a strikers' march that had already occurred. Ivens has no desire to be reflexive and draw attention to the problems of representation. On the contrary, that the workers regained their sense of militant spirit during the reenactment added a level of authenticity to the filming that Ivens fully endorsed. The intensity of emotion during the reenactment itself blurs the distinction between history and recreation, document and representation, in ways that point to the formative power of the documentary filmmaker.

subcultures from the dominant culture, minorities from the majority. The melting pot remains only partially blended; communities of descent—ethnic identities inherited from generation to generation despite diaspora and exile, and communities of consent—collective identities formed by an active choice to adopt and defend the practices and values of a given group, also gain representation. They serve as evidence of the mythic dimension to claims of full equality and the assumptions of a nationalism that knows no differences of race, class, or color.

The work of these filmmakers challenged the ideology of equal opportunity and justice for all; it sought more radical change than mere amelioration. Luis Buñuel's *Land without Bread,* for example, identified a region of misery outside the norms acceptable to the Spanish government (they banned the film for many years); Leo Hurwitz's *Strange Victory* (1948) questioned the victorious postwar mood of triumph over fascism when class conflict and racial discrimination remained an entrenched fact of American life, and Joris Ivens's *Indonesia Calling* (1946) supported the Indonesian independence movement against the colonial rule of the Netherlands (the film made him unwelcome in his native land for years afterward).

The 1960s and '70s brought this tendency to represent "history from below"—from the point of view of those who remained marginalized and dispossessed—to even sharper focus. The most notable example of collective filmmaking, for example, which avoids the promotion of the documentary filmmaker as an individual artist "free" to find in life what others find in fiction, is the American filmmaking group called Newsreel. With highly active filmmaking centers in New York and San Francisco and distribution support in several other cities, Newsreel made or distributed dozens of films from 1967 onward that reported on the war in Vietnam, draft resistance, college strikes (at Columbia University and San Francisco State), national liberation movements around the world, and the women's movement.

Newsreel films identified themselves with a logo composed of a flickering machine gun with the word "Newsreel" emblazoned on its side. There was no doubt that these were agit-prop films, like the early newsreels of Dziga Vertov in 1918–1919, designed to foster political resistance to government actions and policies. The films bore no individual credits. The effort was a collective one, and the idea of an individual artistic vision came second to the commitment of the group to a radical political position. San Francisco Newsreel went so far as to set up a rotating work plan, where members would take jobs for a period of time and pool their earnings to support the group and its filmmaking initiatives. Distributing their own films and showing them on campuses, in community centers, and on the walls of buildings, Newsreel contributed to the grass-roots political activism of the 1960s and early '70s.

San Francisco Newsreel's film *The Woman's Film* (1971), for example, represented the perspective of a range of working-class women on how their everyday experience gave rise to an awareness of oppression. *The Woman's Film,* made primarily by women members of the group, stood out as one of the first feminist documentaries of the postwar era. Its series of interviews coupled with scenes of each participant's everyday life confirmed women as *filmmakers* and as political activists as well as the proper subjects of documentary representation.

BEYOND NATIONALISM:
NEW FORMS OF IDENTITY

"We speak about us to them" took on a new inflection that rippled into a wide range of neglected corners to social life, from the experience of women to that of African Americans, Asian Americans, and Native Americans, Latinos and Latinas, gays and lesbians. Associated with the rise of a "politics of identity" that celebrated the pride and integrity of marginalized or ostracized groups, the voice of documentary gave memorable form to cultures and histories that had remained ignored or suppressed beneath the dominant values and beliefs of society. Standing in support of or in opposition to government policies became secondary to the more localized (and sometimes insular) task of retrieving histories and proclaiming identities that myths, or ideologies, of national unity denied.

This process of giving form, name, and visibility to an identity that had never known one was most vividly displayed in relation to issues of sexuality and gender, although work by African Americans and a wide variety of Fourth World people (individuals with roots in the Third World but living in the industrialized world) demonstrates a comparable vividness. *The Woman's Film* began the process, but other films arrived to buttress the women's movement with work that explored experiences of oppression, recovered lost histories, and profiled currents of change. Geri Ashur's *Janie's Janie* (1971), like *The Woman's Film,* linked oppression with exploitation, sexism with economic deprivation. Like *Housing Problems* (1935) long before, these two films gave voice to working-class experience but in a sustained, participatory mode that refused to turn the disadvantaged into victims awaiting charitable assistance. Women commanded the camera's attention rather than having their voices subsumed within an argument or perspective belonging solely to the filmmaker.

By contrast, Julia Reichert and Jim Klein's *Growing Up Female* (1974) and Joyce Chopra and Claudia Weill's *Joyce at 34* (1972) de-emphasized economics to present middle-class views of sexism as a primarily psychological experience that is nonetheless shared by large numbers of women. Yvonne Rainer's *A Film about a Woman Who . . .* (1974) and Chantal Ackerman's *Jeanne Dielmann, 23 Quai du Commerce, 1080 Bruxelles* (1975) pushed this aspect of feminism yet further. Their works came close to fiction in the invention of characters and situations but brought autobiographical and essayist qualities to bear, including a highly performative, Brechtian form of representation in Rainer's case and an intensely ethnographic, hyperrealist style in Ackerman's. The result in each instance was to open a window on feminist perspectives on romance and housework, objectification and self-determination that had never been seen before.

Julia Reichert, Jim Klein, and Miles Mogelescu's *Union Maids* (1976) and Loraine Grey, Lynn Goldfarb, and Anne Bohlen's *With Babies and Banners* (1977) adopted a participatory, compilation film approach through the use of interviews and archival footage to tell the stories of labor organizing and mass strikes during the 1930s from a women's point of view. They pick up the thread of an earlier suffragette movement and carry it forward, providing valuable historical context to the story of wartime work opportunities and their postwar disappearance told in Connie Field's *The Life and Times of Rosie the Riveter* (1980). These works of retrieval remind us of the subjects and perspectives that documentaries from the 1930s had not addressed in their emphasis on the unifying rhetoric of nation-building or male-dominated forms of working-class resistance.

Documentaries of the early women's movement have their parallel in documentaries of the early gay and lesbian movement. Here, too, we find work that explores the experience of oppression, recovers lost histories, and profiles currents of change. The collectively made *Word Is Out* (Mariposa, 1977) built around a series of interviews with a wide range of gays and lesbians who recount their personal experience of discovering their sexuality and social resistance to it. Potential subjects were selected through an extended series of preliminary interviews that included videotaped discussions; this material then served to assist in fund-raising efforts as well as to give preliminary structure to the film. The experiences take place in the pre-Stonewall days of closeted existence, before a gay and lesbian movement claimed a public space of its own. (Stonewall was a gay bar in New York City; a "routine" police raid turned into a battle with enraged gay customers. This confrontation is used to mark the beginning of a militant gay and lesbian movement.)

Word Is Out chooses its subjects with care and collaborates with them extensively to produce representations of personal histories that reverberate with the broader issues of sexual politics from the 1940s to the 1970s. An assimilationist tone of respectability and normalcy, apart from a different choice of love object, pervades the film. More militant gay activists found this tone too timid, but the very mildness of *Word Is Out* effectively countered many of the more hysterically conceived notions of homosexual desire. Leather bars and dykes on bikes remained on the horizon, but the voices of the gays and lesbians who spoke nonetheless resonated vividly with the experience of others.

A more fundamentally historical perspective on homosexual experience dominates Greta Schiller and Robert Rosenberg's *Before Stonewall: The Making of a Gay and Lesbian Community* (1984). Here interviewees not only refer to personal experience but also adopt the voice of witnesses and

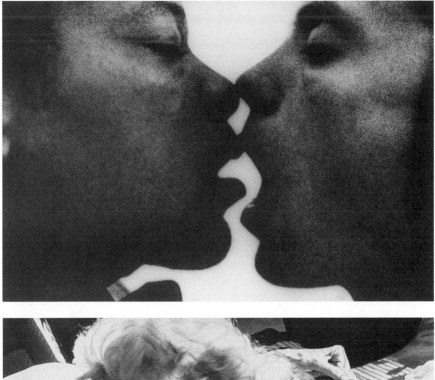

Nitrate Kisses (Barbara Hammer, 1992)

    Nitrate Kisses uses experimental film technique to explore the history of the representation of gay and lesbian culture in cinema. Hammer also explores dimensions of sexuality routinely suppressed, such as sexual intimacy between those who have passed beyond the "body beautiful" phase of the human life cycle. The advertising and entertainment industries would have us believe that sexual relations rarely occur before the age of 15 or after the age of 50.

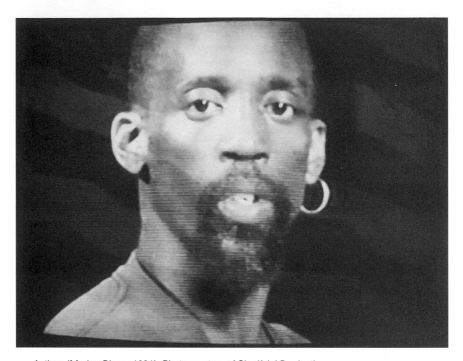

Anthem (Marlon Riggs, 1991). Photo courtesy of Signifyin' Productions.

Marlon Riggs's *Anthem* continues, in a post-Stonewall context, what *Word Is Out* began. A stirring celebration of gay pride, *Anthem* exemplifies the affective, emotion-laden quality of performative documentary. As in *Tongues Untied*, Riggs incorporates the direct, powerful poetry of Essex Hemphill, above.

experts to make perceptible the highly invisible experience of closeted gay life. The subjects are themselves members of the community they describe. They provide an insider's perspective. *Before Stonewall*, like most other films engaged with identity politics, eschews the commentary of outside experts and authorities in the classic model of sociology and journalism to turn to the self-perceptions and self-descriptions by members *of* the community that forms the film's subject.

Similarly, Barbara Hammer's *Nitrate Kisses* (1992) recovers the history of doubly suppressed homosexual experiences such as that of older lesbians and of interracial couples. It also departs from the standardized interview format. Hammer adopts experimental film techniques along with some graphic sexual enactments to represent the texture and subjectivity of such experience as well as its historical outlines. Less a linear narrative of the struggle to build a community, *Nitrate Kisses* sketches out, in evocative, performative terms, the qualities and texture of what the community

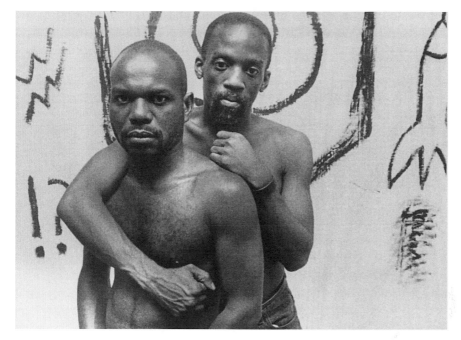

Tongues Untied (Marlon Riggs, 1989). Photo courtesy of Signifyin' Productions.

Neither Marlon Riggs's previous work on stereotypical images of African-Americans in popular culture (*Ethnic Notions*, 1986) nor his follow-up documentary on the representation of race on television (*Color Adjustment*, 1991) prepares viewers for *Tongues Untied*. Highly personal, poetic and polemical, Riggs's video fractured the myth of a gay identity blind to race. With a frank acknowledgment of the impact of AIDS, on gays in general and on himself in particular, Riggs, pictured here with poet Essex Hemphill, established a visual form of testimonial statement comparable in impact to Rigoberta Menchú's written testimonial of her experience as a Guatemalan Indian, *I, Rigoberta*.

its subjects constructed is like. The result is closer to Péter Forgács's *Free Fall* than to the Mariposa Collective's *Word Is Out*.

As gay film critic Tom Waugh has pointed out, it is within a performative mode of representation that gay and lesbian documentary has primarily flourished. Performance itself has been central to an understanding of gendered identity. Most thoroughly, and radically, articulated in Judith Butler's book *Gender Trouble,* the performative dimension of sexuality not simply implies a choice of drag or camp as a parody of sexual norms but also insists on the construction of any sexual identity, straight or gay, as a performative act in which sexual identity can only be established by what one *does* rather than what one presumably *is* or *says.*

Jan Oxenberg's pioneering lesbian film, *A Comedy in Six Unnatural Acts*

(1975), for example, relies primarily on a performative mode of representation to shatter stereotypes and myths about lesbians, much to the consternation of some early viewers. Later films such as Marlon Riggs's *Tongues Untied* (1989) and *Anthem* (1991) utilize staged performance, reenactment, poetry, and confessional commentary as well as, in *Anthem,* a music video editing style to affirm the active construction of homoerotic desire and black gay identity.

Jennie Livingston's *Paris Is Burning* (1990) uses a mix of the observational and participatory modes to describe the rich subculture of black and Latino "houses" of gay men who share a life that revolves around the mimicry and, often, elaborate parody of fashion, dress, and everyday "straight" behavior. Livingston enters into a subculture within the gay community that has the potential for exotic representation, with its staged balls and vogueing contests. Whether she successfully avoids this potential has stimulated considerable debate. The sense of participatory collaboration between filmmaker and subjects that characterizes *Tongues Untied* or *The Times of Harvey Milk* (1986), on the San Francisco city supervisor who was among the first openly gay politicians, seems more muted here since Livingston's own sexual orientation remains unacknowledged and performance functions more to draw attention *to* the subject than to the relation *between* camera and subject. (The same concern has surfaced regarding *Hoop Dreams* [1994] where the act of filming two young, black, inner-city youths over several years is not itself acknowledged as a possible influence on the young men's behavior or decisions. Like Flaherty, the filmmakers appear to discover the events they report rather than collaborate, perhaps unwittingly, in their creation.)

These performative films on gender and sexuality step away from a specific political agenda, issues of social policy, or the construction of a national identity to enlarge our sense of the subjective dimension to "forbidden" lives and loves. At their best they generate a feeling of tension between the film as a representation and the world that stands beyond it. They give us a sense of incommensurate magnitudes: a film represents the world in ways that always leave more unsaid than said, that confess to a failure to exhaust a topic through the mere act of representing it. The world is of a greater order of magnitude than any representation, but a representation can heighten our sense of this discrepancy. Experience does not boil down to explanations. It always exceeds them. We understand this intuitively. Documentaries that remain open to a difference in orders of magnitude between their own representations and what they represent allow us to remain open to the real, historical process of forging a society and culture, with values and beliefs, that are never reducible to a single mold or a fixed system.

William Gates, 22, (l) and Arthur Agee, 22 (r), from the award-winning documentary film **"Hoop Dreams,"** shared a common goal of aspiring to play professional basketball in the NBA. Their stories chronicle the trials of coming of age, facing family struggles, and balancing academics with athletics. **"Hoop Dreams"** makes its television premiere on Wednesday, November 15, 1995, at 8PM (ET) on PBS.

Hoop Dreams (Steve James, Fred Marx, Peter Gilbert, 1994). Photo courtesy of Fine Line Features.

A publicity still for the "stars" of *Hoop Dreams*. Although pitched as a familiar, suspenseful narrative of "Will they or won't they succeed?" *Hoop Dreams* is also an extraordinary example of the filmmakers' commitment to the gradual unfolding of individual lives. Many films are shot during a few months of production, but *Hoop Dreams* was shot over a period of six years.

The political dimension to documentaries on issues of sexuality and gender, or other topics, joins an emphatically performative mode of documentary representation to the very issues of personal experience and desire that lead outward, by implication, to broader issues of difference, equality, and non-discrimination. Like many other works, they contribute to the social construction of a common identity among members of a given community. They give social visibility to experiences once treated as exclusively or primarily personal; they attest to a commonality of experience and to the forms of struggle necessary to overcome stereotyping, discrimination, and bigotry. The political voice of these documentaries embodies the perspectives and visions of communities that share a history of exclusion and a goal of social transformation.

REDEFINING THE POLITICS OF IDENTITY

To the extent that an important political voice of documentary has become implicated with a politics of identity, it has also had to address the question of alliances and affinities among various subcultures, groups, and movements. This represents another shift from the earlier construction of national identities to the recognition of partial or hybrid identities that seldom settle into a single, permanent category. Such categories, with their elusive, variable nature, even call into question the adequacy of any notion of community that can be permanently identified and fixed. Such identification aids in the creation of group identity, and pride, but it also risks producing a false sense of security or permanence. As a result, an emphasis on hybridity and diaspora, exile and displacement exists in tension with the more sharply defined contours of an identity politics.

Gay men and lesbian women, for example, also live their lives in relation to class and ethnic identities; Jews live their ethnic identity in relation to superimposed national, class, and gender identities. The model of a fundamental identity that can then be multiplied and complicated is also put into question by the upheavals and transformations of modern history that suggest that all identities are provisional in their construction and political in their implications. To take on the primary identity of a Jew or a Bosnian, a black male or an Asian female has a contingent, political dimension to it, pegged to a specific historical context, that runs counter to any notion of a fixed or essentialized group identity. This sense of fluid, liminal boundaries that defy categories and blur identities has itself become the subject of documentary representation.

In a cinematically reflexive vein, Chris Marker examines the experience of dislocation and displacement in his stunningly complex film *Sans Soleil*

(1982). A female voice reads letters written by an itinerant filmmaker, San-dor Krasna, whose experience seems an uncanny parallel for Marker's own. Images flow between Africa, Greenland, and Japan as "Krasna" tries to make some sense of the global interrelationships among nations and people and of his own fragmented encounters over many years and many films. The film refuses to identify a concrete thesis, let alone "add up" to a con-clusion. Instead it works to convey the subjective experiences of cruelty and innocence, place and displacement, memory and time that characterize our passage through the landscape of modern events.

Trinh Minh-ha's *Surname Viet Given Name Nam* (1989) adopts a simi-lar thesis about the instability of categories. Its complex mix of fact and fiction, of staged and unstaged scenes, of interviews that are acted and in-terviews that are, apparently, spontaneous, prompts us to rethink the use-fulness of any notion of documentary as a form that conveys information, or truth, naturally, without problem. The film also prompts us to rethink what it means to understand another person's life, in this case the lives of Viet-namese women in Vietnam and in the United States.

Trinh, like Marker, wants us to remember that any claim to knowledge that we take away with us comes thoroughly filtered through the *form* in which that knowledge reaches us. The style of the acted interviews with women in Vietnam gives a sense of a controlled or stage-managed perfor-mance through the careful lighting and composition, the superimposition of printed versions of what the women say over their images, and the slow, deliberate way in which they appear to speak, or recite, their comments. The style of the interviews with the same women in their "real" roles as women living in San Jose, California, exhibits the spontaneity of interaction found in classic participatory documentaries like *Chronicle of a Summer* or *Roger and Me* through the dependence on available light, less formal, more catch-as-catch-can framing, the lack of superimposed versions of what is said, and the more rapid, unguarded manner in which the women speak.

The result, though, is less to confirm the San Jose scenes as "true" and the staged Vietnam scenes as "false" than to put on display two different forms of representation as our means of access to the historical world. Cat-egories and concepts are our own social creation—sometimes useful, sometimes a bane. People, social actors, migrate through these abstrac-tions, including concepts of personal and collective identity, in ways that at-tempts to pin categories down to dictionary definitions oversimplify. That the women in *Surname Viet Given Name Nam* are from Vietnam but now be-long to an immigrant community that is itself part of a war-induced dis-placement, or diaspora, of people is no coincidence: hybrid identities, pro-visional alliances, and a tension between past and present realities render

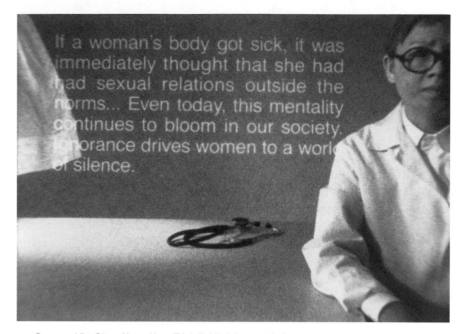

Surname Viet Given Name Nam (Trinh T. Minh-ha, 1989). Photo courtesy of Trinh T. Minh-ha. Another use of "sub-titles." Trinh superimposes a version of the words spoken by the interviewee simultaneously with her speech. This produces a split in our attention. This split may also heighten our awareness of the staged quality to interviews: scenes seem less "natural" when filmmakers alter the conventions to which we have grown accustomed.

most categories less a reassuring source of knowledge than a disturbing form of incompleteness. Trinh tries to lead us to *understand* this without falling into the trap of providing yet another category to *explain* it.

In a similar but more familiarly personal vein, Marilu Mallet's *Unfinished Diary* (1983) stresses the experience of exile from her native Chile, which she fled after the defeat of the Allende government and the installation of a dictatorship under General Pinochet. She must learn French and adapt to Quebec customs. She must also learn English and use it in her relationship with her Australian-born husband, Canadian filmmaker Michael Rubbo. Mallet experiences daily issues of loss and exile that separate her from a feminism that assumes the stability of national identity in order to address the issues of gender hierarchy. (She is not simply a Canadian woman any more than the Vietnamese women in *Surname Viet Given Name Nam* are simply American women.) A sense of hybrid identity and diasporic experience that does not fit comfortably within the existing categories of social identity arises. A gap, or order of magnitude, separates Mallet from those who locate themselves within other social categories. Identity, it seems, must be negotiated *across* categories as much as, if not more than, within them.

This sketch of some of the ways in which documentary reveals a political voice has focused on the issue of community. It touched on (1) the construction of national identity in terms of a melting-pot homogeneity, (2) the challenges to this construct associated with political confrontation (worker militancy, anti-war protests), (3) the emergence of an identity politics that gave voice to suppressed minorities, and, finally, (4) the acknowledgment of the hazards of categories and identities themselves in a time of catastrophic events, trauma, exile, and diaspora.

Although far too much a sketch to serve as a comprehensive history of political representation in documentary, it contains the germ of an historical account. It also suggests how the choices of modes of representation and topics for representation change not from internal pressures alone but in relation to a larger historical context. Nationalism, identity politics, diaspora, and exile do not originate with documentary. Documentary filmmakers strive to find the means to represent these issues in ways that retain a sense of their magnitude in the lives of the people who must confront them.

SOCIAL ISSUES AND PERSONAL PORTRAITURE

We can conclude by looking at two emphases that characterize the political voice of many of the films discussed in this chapter. These emphases present a spectrum of possibilities more than an either/or choice, and they can be found at work in all six modes of documentary representation. We can call them an emphasis on social issues and an emphasis on personal portraiture.

Social issue documentary might seem to go with the expository mode and an earlier moment in documentary, whereas personal portraiture might seem to go with observational or participatory modes and contemporary debates about the politics of identity. Even though there is a grain of truth to this generalization, there is, in fact, a greater degree of diffusion of both these emphases across the full range of documentary representation. The prevalence of one or the other emphasis at a given moment in time is less indicative of any innate capacity or tendency in documentary than of the interrelationship between documentary and the larger historical world to which it belongs.

Social issue documentaries take up public issues from a social perspective. Individuals recruited to the film illustrate or provide perspective on the issue. *Why We Fight,* for example, relies on the unseen voice of Walter

Huston to guide us through the complexities of World War II, while the individuals we see tend to exemplify what Huston states. *In the Year of the Pig* (1969), by contrast, relies on the interview-based testimony of numerous individuals plus the implicit arguments made by Emile de Antonio through his editing and the juxtaposition of sound and image, to develop a critical perspective on those aspects of American foreign policy that drew the nation into what de Antonio presents as a civil war in Vietnam.

Personal portrait documentaries take up social issues from a personal perspective. Individuals recruited to the film attest to or implicitly live out the underlying issue without even necessarily identifying it. *Nanook of the North,* for example, relies on the portrait Flaherty constructs of Nanook and his family to give us a sense of the everyday realities of Eskimo culture as enacted by a member of that culture. Similarly, *Wedding Camels* relies on its portraits of the interactions between Lorang and his daughter's suitor as they negotiate the bride price owed Lorang for his daughter to give us a sense of the values and practices of Turkana culture.

Shirley Clark's *Portrait of Jason* (1967) allows us to unravel layers of performance and negotiation between Ms. Clark and her subject, Jason, a black gay hustler filmed over the course of a single, protracted encounter. Her interactions with Jason and Jason's frank disclosures introduce issues of race, gender, and the filmmaker's complicity in what takes place before the camera in ways that many observational films ignore. Ms. Clark confirmed what Jean Rouch and Edgar Morin had shown in *Chronicle of a Summer:* the relation between filmmaker and subject is a vital part of the act of representation.

Twenty-five years later, through its touching self-portrait of Mark Massi and Tom Joslin in what began as a home movie by Tom Joslin, *Silverlake Life: The View from Here* (1992) gives us a sense of the devastation wrought upon millions of people by the HIV virus. When Mr. Joslin dies from AIDS the project is brought to completion by Mark Massi and a friend, Peter Friedman. Joslin's subject, Mark Massi, becomes the filmmaker, and the filmmaker, Tom Joslin, becomes the subject. This reversal reveals dimensions to both individuals that the usual separation of responsibilities masks.

These films place their focus on the individual rather than the social issue. At their best they reveal the one by means of the other. (Some personal portraits, or biographies, will repress the political in favor of a concept of the subject as a self-contained, self-determining entity.) The films described here demonstrate an intimate connection between the personal and the political, whereas most social issue documentaries tend to assume that public issues command our attention on their own merits: the personal domain remains private or out of bounds as long as we turn our public self to the issue at hand. Works such as Péter Forgács's *Free Fall*, Marlon Riggs's *Tongues Untied*, or Steve James, Fred Marx, and Peter Gilbert's *Hoop Dreams* occupy a border zone between the extremes of either emphasis: they clearly build outward from central characters to larger issues but also flesh out their characters with considerable care.

The differences between these two emphases is represented in table 7.1. These two emphases remind us of the oratorical efforts of documentary to enlist our response. The task of documentaries to move us toward a predisposition or point of view regarding some aspect of the world revolves around credible, convincing, and compelling representations. Among the possible ways of achieving these ends, two prevalent alternatives are drawing our attention to the issues that unite and divide us as a people and profiling individuals who attest to the ways such issues take form in relation to their own lives. Each poses different ethical issues for the filmmaker regarding the question "What to do with people?" and each approaches the realm of political engagement from a distinct angle. Together they remind us that whether we approach a question from the perspective of the individual or from that of society as a whole, it is in the interrelationship between the individual and society where questions of power and hierarchy, ideology and politics reveal themselves most forcefully.

CODA

Some documentaries set out to *explain* aspects of the world to us. They analyze problems and propose solutions. They try to account for aspects of the historical world by means of their representations. They seek to mobilize our support for one position instead of another. Other documentaries invite us to *understand* aspects of the world more fully. They observe, describe, or poetically evoke situations and interactions. They try to enrich our understanding of aspects of the historical world by means of their representations. They complicate our adherence to positions by undercutting certainty with complexity or doubt.

We need explanations, with their concepts and categories, to get things done. If we know what causes poverty or sexual abuse, pollution or war we can then take measures to address the issue. We need understanding, with its requirements of empathy and insight, to grasp the implications and consequences of what we do. Actions rely on values, and values are subject to question. Lives, as well as concepts and categories, are at stake. Understanding, like critical perspective, leavens explanations, policies, solutions. Social actors are not pawns but people.

Documentary film and video constitutes a tradition that has addressed

Table 7.1. Two Emphases in Documentary

Social Issue Documentary	Personal Portrait Documentary
Voice of filmmaker or agency as authority, plus voice of witnesses and experts to corroborate. Filmmaker interacts when it pertains to the social issue. May rely heavily on rhetoric.	Voice of social actors (people) who speak for themselves, or filmmaker interacts with others, often to negotiate their relationship. May rely heavily on style.
Discourse of sobriety. Style is second to content; content is what counts—the real world as found or existing.	Poetic or subjective discourse. Style counts as much as content; form is what counts—the reality of seeing the world from a distinct perspective.
Stress objectivity, knowledge, enduring importance of historical events.	Stress subjectivity, experience, enduring worth to specific moments.
Public Issues.	Private Moments.
—Right to know guides a quest for knowledge.	—Right to privacy is a conscious consideration.
—Minimal psychological depth to characters compared to concepts or issues.	—Psychological depth to characters becomes a goal; larger issues are implied.

—Individuals represented as:
 	
    typical or representative
 	
    victim
	—Individuals represented as:
	
	    unique or distinctive
	
	    mythic

Maximum attention to issue, problem, or topic, presented directly and expressly named: sexism, unemployment, AIDS, etc.	Underlying issue or problem is raised indirectly, evoked, or implied but seldom expressly named.
Stress filmmaker's mission or social purpose over style or expressiveness.	Stress filmmaker's style or expressiveness over social purpose.

Filmmaker exists in an omniscient or transcendent realm apart from subjects.	Filmmaker exists in same social historical realm as subjects.
Often has problem/solution structure; may offer explanations.	Often presents problem or situation without clear solution; may invite understanding.
Stress drama of finding a solution.	Stress drama of experiencing a problem or situation.
Common problems and solutions recur: poverty, welfare, sexism, violence, injustice, etc.	Familiar dramatic form to specific problems recurs: crisis, intense experience, maturation, catharsis, insight.
Examples: TV news, *Consuming Hunger, Ways of Seeing, Eyes on the Prize, The Man with a Movie Camera, Why We Fight, Before Stonewall, In the Year of the Pig, The Life and Times of Rosie the Riveter, Ethnic Notions, Color Adjustment, Land without Bread* (ironic pov).	Examples: *Nanook of the North, Bontoc Eulogy, Portrait of Jason, Surname Viet Given Name Nam, Silverlake Life: The View from Here, Roses in December, Antonia: Portrait of a Woman, Sink or Swim, Juggling Gender, Hotel Terminus: The Life and Times of Klaus Barbie, Roger and Me* (mock heroic pov).

exactly this point, sometimes imperfectly, sometimes eloquently. It moves forward in relation to all the work that has gone before, addressing issues, exploring situations, engaging viewers in ways that will continue to instruct and please, move and compel. Its history belongs to the future and to those efforts yet to come that will enlarge an existing tradition as they strive to effect the world we have yet to create.

Chapter 8

How Can We Write Effectively about Documentary?

Several books offer useful information and suggestions about writing film criticism. This chapter assumes some of this knowledge and emphasizes writing about documentary specifically. Let's begin with a hypothetical essay question:

Documentary *represents* the historical world by shaping its photographic record of some aspect of the world *from a distinct perspective or point of view.* Identify the point of view adopted by Robert Flaherty in *Nanook of the North* and consider some of its implications. Research is encouraged but not required. Length: 500–750 words.

The first step is preparation. Seeing *Nanook* is the most obvious preparation, but seeing it more than once is also important. On first viewing we become immersed in the viewing experience. We may ask ourselves some questions about what we are seeing, but on second viewing this process of asking and thinking about what we see becomes more central. We might ask, for example, Why does Flaherty begin the way he does? What does this set up for the rest of the film? Why does he end as he does? How does this relate to the beginning? What kind of relationship is there between Flaherty, or the camera, and Nanook? How are scenes edited? How is one

Nanook of the North (Robert Flaherty, 1922)

Nanook bites a record. Is this an act of playful hamming for the camera, or is this Flaherty's way of demonstrating the backwardness of his subject? The two sample essays that follow take different paths in interpreting this classic documentary film.

scene joined to another? What does the narrative structure of the film revolve around? How does Flaherty represent people? How does he characterize them or convey a sense of their individuality?

These questions might be guided by a specific idea we already have for a paper or be preliminary: they may serve to give us ideas about Flaherty's distinct approach. Note taking becomes quite valuable at this point. Some viewers like to make notes on the first viewing of a film; others find it distracting. But on repeat viewing notes can help provide the raw material that will later support critical writing about the film. Notes can track the chronology of scenes (what comes first, second, and so on); the types of camera shots (wide angle, telephoto, tracking shots, zooms, composition within the frame, etc.); editing techniques (continuity editing, point of view shots, unusual juxtapositions or jumps in time and space); speech (dialogue, commentary) or written words (titles, subtitles, intertitles); rhetorical technique (how the film makes itself seem credible, convincing, and compelling, or not); mode (how the film relies on a documentary mode of representation to organize itself, what other modes make an appearance), and other distinctive qualities such as the degree of acknowledged presence of the filmmaker on the scene and the political perspective, if any, that the film conveys.

Taking notes is a selective business. We can attend to only so many aspects of a film. We may chose to focus on the camera style or poetic editing, on the filmmaker's own presence or the development of social actors as complex characters, but we cannot concentrate on everything at once. Notes provide a record of some of our own preoccupations and interests. When done in relation to an essay, they provide source material for the points we plan to make in our commentary.

Let's assume that two hypothetical students, Robert and Roberta, have seen *Nanook* once and have formed an initial opinion. Let's talk through the process of moving forward toward a finished essay.

Robert: *What did you think of Nanook?*

Roberta: *I hated it.*

Robert: *Oh, I loved it.*

As an essay this type of comment would not even register as a half-hearted attempt. It does provide a valuable starting place for *thinking about* the film, however. Each viewer has a strong response, and that response can motivate the process of writing an essay. To do so, the initial, emotional response has to be shaped into a critical analysis that has substantive support for its points.

At this point two paths diverge. One leads to a review and one to criticism. A useful distinction is that a reviewer writes for those who have not seen the film, as a kind of consumer guide. A critic writes for those who have, as part of a critical dialogue. Although some professional reviewers also pose issues that contribute to a critical dialogue among those who have seen the film, classroom essays seldom serve as reviews: the professor has already seen the film. We can therefore turn our attention to a critical analysis of the film. One important consequence: *there will be little reason to summarize the plot.*

Once an essay begins to summarize or describe a scene, it is very tempting to continue the summary for other scenes. This reverses priorities. For criticism, it is more vital to make a point and then provide supporting evidence through references to what happens in the film than to refer to the film through a plot summary and then append critical comments to the summary. Developing arguments has the highest priority. For this reason, we must also take care to avoid delivering opinions that lack supporting evidence. This is why the initial statements of love and hate do not yet qualify as criticism. Let's take them a bit further.

Robert: I loved the way Flaherty showed me things about Eskimo culture I hadn't seen before.

Roberta: I hated the way Flaherty made Nanook act like a typical primitive who knew all about nature but couldn't figure out a phonograph record.

This at least gets the ball rolling. Each student has given us some sense of *why* they love or hate the film. Some justification and specificity has been added. Robert has begun to put his finger on the quality he admires about Flaherty. From here he could begin to think about *what* does Flaherty show him and *how* does Flaherty show him these things; what about the representation seems to deserve admiration. Roberta has begun to link Flaherty with a set of misrepresentations in which traditional cultures appear like earlier, or more infantile, versions of our own. From here she could begin to think about *what* Flaherty does to give her this feeling and *how* Flaherty's style contributes to it.

Robert and Roberta may now make some preliminary notes or an outline for their papers and review the film again, looking for scenes and moments that will support their theses. Let's see what they come up with next.

Robert: I loved the way Flaherty adopts the perspective of a single family as a way to understand Eskimo culture. This gives us a convenient handle since we are already familiar with family roles but not familiar with the specific problems and tasks facing this family. Flaherty involves us mainly with Nanook but also shows how the kids begin to learn Eskimo ways and how Nyla, Nanook's wife, contributes to the success of the group. Flaherty has a way of letting scenes linger; they don't rush to a conclusion. This is a really harsh environment, and men must be very determined and skilled to survive.

Roberta: I hated Flaherty's hackneyed attempt to make us love Eskimos by making us love Nanook. This is a trite way of saying that we should admire other cultures because the people are cute and colorful, the sort of thing I see in travel brochures for exotic locales all the time. Nanook acts like a ham when Flaherty gives him a chance to respond to the camera, especially at the trading post. He's more in his element when hunting seals, but that's where we expect him to be most at ease. Is this Flaherty's way *of keeping him in his place? Nanook seems like Eskimo brawn to the white man's brain.*

This is better. These drafts might get a four (out of ten). They are short and jump around a bit. They also throw in opinions, and Roberta uses an anachronistic judgement: she finds Flaherty wanting because he reminds her of travel brochures she's seen. These brochures, though, would most likely come some eighty years after the film. A much more telling point would be to see if this type of travel brochure existed in the 1910s or 1920s so that Roberta could then argue they may have actually influenced Flaherty's approach. Both essays still lack adequate substantiation, but the points where such support is needed are also becoming clear.

Robert and Roberta may now strengthen their outlines, review their notes again, do some research on issues they want to clarify or substantiate, see the film, or parts of the film, again, and prepare a complete draft. They will revise what they've written, looking for ways to make their points in an essay format. The conversational, colloquial tone needs to be converted into a more expository tone.

The opening sentences of each student, for example, begin with "I loved" and "I hated." These bald statements of likes and dislikes can be dropped entirely as the emphasis shifts from what *the author* likes or dislikes to what *the film or filmmaker* is doing. (A less usual but conceivable alternative would be for Robert or Roberta to explore *their story,* as discussed in Chapter 4, and what aspects of their past experience color or inflect the way they see this film by Flaherty.) We could rewrite Robert's sentence as "Flaherty adopts the perspective of a single family as a way to understand Eskimo culture." This becomes a more forceful assertion about the film itself and could even serve as a statement of the essay's thesis. It marks the beginning of a critical perspective. What's lacking is further clarification of the thesis, substantiation, and a stronger overall organization.

Robert: *Flaherty adopts the perspective of a single Eskimo family as our entry into the entirety of Eskimo culture. This strategy may be one reason for the film's enormous popularity. Another may be the way Flaherty succeeds in giving us the impression that he draws his insights from what Nanook and his family naturally do. Apart from his introduction of the family all piling out of a kayak and some hamming it up at the trading post, Flaherty respectfully observes Nanook's family as they go about the difficult business of survival in the forbidding north.*

Nanook's family has a strongly representative quality. His wife complements his own skills and clearly has skills of her own, such as tending the children and preparing their food. Nanook gradually earns our respect as a hunter. If he seems a bit of a buffoon in the early scenes, this may be Flaherty's way of letting us feel somewhat superior to this "savage," but it is not a feeling he lets us indulge for long.

Nanook may foolishly bite into a phonograph record as if this could help him find the sound, for example, but if biting and tasting things is an essential part of survival in the wilderness, who is more foolish, Nanook for doing it or us for laughing at him? Flaherty goes on to demonstrate how Nanook's ability to provide for his family through his hunting prowess deserves our full respect. Nanook's biting episode may not fit into the etiquette of a trading post, and of the civilized world the post stands for, but it is part and parcel of his own world. The later scene of Nanook and his family chewing their leather boots to soften them functions like a proof of Nanook's ultimate wisdom. Flaherty's inclusion of this scene serves to remind us of our own folly in judging too quickly.

Not only are we admonished not to judge too quickly, we are urged to exercise patience in coming to an understanding of what we see. Several times Flaherty introduces us to a scene without fully explaining what is going on. This puts us in a state of suspense. The suspense is not the highly charged tension of a shoot-out but it does involve life and death in terms of whether Nanook can survive and how actions we don't immediately understand help him do so.

For example, when Nanook builds an igloo a title tells us that one more thing remains to be done. What, we ask ourselves? Instead of telling us, Flaherty just watches as Nanook finds a piece of clear ice and cuts it free. When he plunks it onto the side of the igloo we may figure out what is going on, or it may take us another minute or so, as Nanook cleans and buffs the ice, to realize that he has made a window for the igloo!

This shooting style is one of Flaherty's great contributions to documentary. He lets his camera follow actions so that they unfold at their own rhythm. We discover the meaning of events by observing them rather than having a meaning imposed by comments, titles, or editing. The scene when Nanook finds a hole in the ice, suspends a thread across it, and then waits, and waits, is another great example. We are not at all sure what he's doing, but when he finally hurls his spear into the hole because he's seen the thread quiver, we realize just how skillful a hunter Nanook really is, even if it takes a little longer to learn that there's a seal on the end of the line.

Professor Edmund Carpenter has written that Flaherty's method was highly appropriate to Eskimo culture. Carpenter says that an Eskimo carver doesn't set out to carve a seal from ivory. He examines the ivory, mulls it over, and begins to carve aimlessly, trying to find the form already inside it.

"Then he brings it out; Seal, hidden, emerges. It was always there: he didn't create it; he released it; he helped it step forth."[1]

Flaherty lets us also mull and view suspensefully, trying to find the meaning of a culture we do not know. When we realize what Nanook is doing in scenes like the window making or the seal hunting we suddenly discover what his world is like. It was always there; Flaherty just helps it step forth.

[762 words]

1. *Edmund Carpenter, "Notes on Eskimo Art Film," cited in Arthur Calder Marshall, The Innocent Eye. Based on research material by Paul Rotha and Basil Wright. (Baltimore, Maryland: Penguin Books, 1970), p. 70.*

Robert has developed a very solid essay. He has presented a clear thesis: Flaherty involves us in Eskimo culture through the familiar figure of the family but then urges us to discover what this culture is like by observing events and inferring meaning for ourselves, in a spirit similar to the way Eskimos approach their own art. He has also provided good substantiation through reference to specific scenes. The writing is clear and the paragraphs well organized. Opinion is present, but more as a motivation for critical argument than as an end in itself. A provocative, clear theme developed in relation to specific cinematic qualities allows an *interpretation* of the film to emerge that acknowledges both the actual form of the film and Robert's experience of it.

Now let's see what Roberta's essay looks like.

Roberta: Robert Flaherty can be considered the first filmmaker to make use of the participant-observation style of documentary and a pioneer in ethnographic filmmaking, but if this is so, it may demonstrate more about the problems with ethnography than the virtues of Flaherty.

For example, in an early scene Nanook comes to the trading post to trade his furs for commodities. This is the only reference to Western goods in the film. Why doesn't Nanook acquire supplies that will help him the most, like a rifle for hunting? Why doesn't the film identify the post with Revillon Frères, the film's sponsor? By making the trader a benevolent patriarch who doles out treats for the kids and amusements for Nanook, Flaherty makes this an implicit ad for how well Revillon treats the natives. Nanook is as easily distracted by gadgets as his kids are by biscuits and lard. The phonograph scene presents Nanook as a clown. Technology poses no threat; it's just a curiosity. Nanook and his family go away happy. Everyone benefits, or so it seems.

Flaherty observes more than he participates, at least on camera. Behind the scenes, Flaherty participates more than he admits. Why, if the family gets treated to a feast at the trading post, are they soon in danger of star-

vation? Is Flaherty prepared to film Nanook starving to death? It is more likely that this is what is called a "hook" in fiction films: it's a way to involve us in a drama by finding a dramatic angle. Will Nanook find food? Stay tuned and we'll see. This is Flaherty actively working, off camera, to set the stage for the drama to come. The trick is that he then presents this drama as if he just happened to be there to record it.

For example, in the scene where Nanook and other men (where did they come from, Central Casting?) spear a walrus, Flaherty is nearby, filming. According to Flaherty's own account, the men begged him to use his rifle to kill the walrus, but Flaherty pretended not to hear them. This forced them to risk their lives unnecessarily, but it also allowed Flaherty to "observe" an "authentic" hunt as if he wasn't there.[2]

Flaherty's whole effort is a form of fraud. He wants to give us an infantalized image of a culture populated by innocents. He wants to act as if that culture had no contact with our own when Flaherty himself, and the trading post, is proof that it does. Flaherty doesn't want to explore the consequences of these relationships, at least in the film. He is willing to take money from Revillon to make the film, and he is willing to treat Nanook as a friend, at least as long as it takes to make the film.

According to our class discussion, this kind of effort apparently fits a model of "salvage ethnography," where ethnographers describe other cultures as they were before contact with the Western world in an attempt to salvage a record of what will soon be lost. This served a valuable purpose in giving us a record of cultures before they disappeared. But it also denied the reality of ethnographers, or filmmakers, interacting with the same cultures they described as having no contact with whites. Where did that leave the filmmaker? It's the filmmaker who disappears, along with all the bargaining and negotiation that happens so that he can get his information.

Fatimah Tobing Rony describes a film made in 1988, Nanook Revisited, that clarifies how much Flaherty hid. An Inuit man tells how the polar bear skin clothing, the igloo set (half exposed to the weather), and the seal hunt were all distortions. He also explains that the man who "played" Nanook, Allakariallak, couldn't help laughing much of the time because what Flaherty asked him to do was so hopelessly funny. Flaherty clearly enlisted Allakariallak and other Inuits to help him make his film, but as the film hero's impish laughter suggests, it may be because, for them, this was a fictional comedy far more than an ethnographic document.

[755 words]

2. Erik Barnouw quotes Flaherty's own diary, where he wrote that the men were afraid they would be dragged into the sea. Barnouw hesitates to pass judgment on Flaherty. Flaherty's refusal may seem justifiable to Barnouw since it enables Fla-

*herty to film the Eskimo's "traditional ways," despite the risk and despite interven-
ing to set up the scene in the first place. Barnouw,* Documentary *(New York: Oxford
University Press, 1993), p. 37.*

Roberta has also developed a solid, coherent thesis with ample supporting material. Her research has given her valuable information that could not
be derived from the film alone (precisely because Flaherty masked what
she reveals). There is a strongly accusatory tone that may not do justice to
the complexity of Flaherty's achievement, or to the reasons for its having
been considered such a great film despite the failings she identifies. (The
reference to "central casting," for example, is somewhat gratuitous, and
"fraud" is probably too strong a word for Flaherty's mixture of concealment
and reenactment.)

A longer paper might examine why this revision of Flaherty's reputation
and achievement has been so slow in coming rather than adopt a tone of
indignation that Flaherty has gotten away with something. Clearly, another
challenge would be to see if we can understand Flaherty's film in a way that
would take account of both Robert and Roberta's arguments. Robert's thesis, in fact, parallels the view of Flaherty that prevailed until the early 1980s
or so, while Roberta's has more in common with recent revisions of the "Flaherty myth." This does not invalidate either one but helps to locate them
within a larger historical context.

Both papers, though, fulfill the assignment: they move away from opinion and toward analysis. They identify a distinct perspective belonging to
Flaherty and examine some of its implications or consequences successfully. They also demonstrate how it is possible for the specific facts and
events present in a film to lead to more than one interpretation. The apparent authenticity or indexicality of the image, the location shooting, and
the long takes do not clinch the case for a single argument or conclusion
any more than the forensic evidence put before a jury automatically clinches
the case for guilt or innocence. An interpretative or explanatory frame must
be introduced. The one proposed by the filmmaker will clearly be one of
them, but it will also clearly not be the only one.

In their move away from opinion, the essays focus on the story of the
film, and the filmmaker, and de-emphasize the story of the critic. In another
context we might want to return to the story of the critic, to the particular
perspective the critic brings to the viewing experience. It may not be entirely coincidental, for example, that Robert as a male seems to identify with
Flaherty as explorer, whose efforts prove beneficial for the insights they provide into another culture, and that Roberta as a female takes exception to
the ways in which a male explorer chooses to speak about, or represent,
others different from himself.

If our interest were in the authors of these accounts as such we would want to pursue their stories, too, and see how their particular points of view stem from their own experience and historical context. Clearly, Flaherty's film can be read in many ways. Part of the challenge of film history is understanding how analyses vary with time and place as different viewers, with different perspectives, bring their critical skills to bear on a given film. But in terms of film criticism, both of these essays give us a better idea of how basic techniques of film analysis can be applied to the study of documentary film and video.

Notes on Source Material

Discussion about documentary has increased exponentially since the beginning of the 1990s. Before that, documentary film occupied a clearly secondary place in the film literature with just a few staples, usually centered around key figures like John Grierson and Robert Flaherty. Since then the field has blossomed remarkably as scholars and critics have realized that documentary identifies a tendency within the broader arena of film that poses as rich and perplexing an array of questions as any other.

A number of works offer an overview of important aspects of documentary. I will highlight only books here, since most books include bibliographies and footnotes that help point to the periodical literature. There are many resources available for finding books and other materials. The various research indexes for film, such as the FIAF CD-ROM index (from the International Federation of Film Archives), which complements the *International Index to Film Periodicals,* the *Film Literature Index,* and Dissertation Abstracts are all valuable resources. The University of California's Digital Library, accessed through their Melyvl database at www.dbs.cdlib.org/, gives information about film and video holdings as well as books and periodicals. The Pacific Film Archive, at www.bampfa .berkeley.edu/main.html, offers access to program notes and clipping files that pertain to the vast array of films screened at the PFA over the years. Other more commercial Web sites, such as docos.com or the Internet Movie Database, imdb.com/, have some information for the student or scholar and even more for the filmmaker or fan.

Among the books that offer a broad overview are three standard histories of the form: Eric Barnouw, *Documentary,* 2nd ed. (New York: Oxford University Press, 1993); John Ellis, *The Documentary Idea* (Englewood Cliffs, N.J.: Prentice-Hall, 1989); and Richard Meran Barsam, *Nonfiction Film* (New York: Dutton, 1973). Ellis's book borrows some of its organization from Paul Rotha's much earlier and still pertinent history, *Documentary Film* (New York: Norton, 1939). Among more recent books, my *Representing Reality: Issues and Concepts in Documentary* (Bloomington: Indiana University Press, 1991), has provided a foundation and stimulus for much of the work that has followed since. More advanced than this text, it offers aspects that will be noted at various points in the Appendix where they are particularly relevant.

Other books that offer a valuable overview and that, like *Representing Reality,* are more conceptual than historical, include Michael Renov's *Theorizing Documentary* (New York: Routledge, 1993), and Michael Renov and Jane Gaines, eds., *Collecting Visible Evidence* (Minneapolis: University of Minnesota Press, 1999). *Collecting Visible Evidence* ends with a review of the state of documentary filmmaking and criticism by Michael Renov: it is part of the Visible Evidence series published by the University of Minnesota. Brian Winston, *Claiming the Real* (London: British Film Institute, 1995), challenges much of the received wisdom about John Grierson to argue that his efforts in the 1930s turned documentary away from active social engagement. John Corner, *The Art of Record: Critical Introduction to the Documentary* (Manchester: University of Manchester Press, 1996), provides an intelligent, well-researched overview, while John Izod, *An Introduction to Television Documentary* (New York: St. Martin's Press, 1997), gives us an informative account of TV documentary in Great Britain. A. William Bluem's *Documentary in American Television* (New York: Hastings House, 1965), although older, offers a broad perspective on the rise of documentary and its place in television history.

Of considerable value to the newcomer to documentary is Barry Grant and Jeannette Sloniowski, eds., *Documenting the Documentary* (Detroit: Wayne State University Press, 1998), a collection of essays each of which is devoted to a particular documentary film. William Rothman, *Documentary Film Classics* (New York: Cambridge University Press, 1997), covers similar ground from a more personal point of view. Alan Rosenthal, ed., *New Challenges for Documentary* (Berkeley: University of California Press, 1988), collects a large number of very useful essays; Rosenthal's earlier *The New Documentary in Action* (Berkeley: University of California Press, 1971), provides a revealing set of interviews with documentary filmmakers. Lewis Jacob's *The Documentary Tradition,* 2nd ed. (New York: Norton, 1979), is a valuable collection of older essays that gives a good sense of the development of both documentary film and discussions about it.

Timothy Druckery, ed., *Electronic Culture: Technology and Visual Representation* (New York: Aperture, 1996), provides both a conceptual and a historical guide to the implications of digital technology for visual representation generally, while Winston's *Claiming the Real* takes this issue up in passing and his *Technologies of Seeing* (London: British Film

Institute, 1996) offers a useful historical perspective on technology and representation.

Three books of interest to those who want to know more about how to make a documentary film are Ilisa Barbash and Lucien Taylor, *Cross-Cultural Filmmaking* (Berkeley: University of California Press, 1997); Michael Rabiger, *Directing the Documentary* (Boston and London: Focal Press, 1987); and Alan Rosenthal, *Writing, Directing, and Producing Documentary Films* (Carbondale: Southern Illinois University Press, 1990). Dai Vaughn, *For Documentary* (Berkeley: University of California Press, 1999), is a wonderful set of observations by one of the most respected editors of documentary film.

For questions of ethics in documentary film and video, the single most useful text is Larry Gross, John Stuart Katz, and Jay Ruby, eds., *Image Ethics* (New York: Oxford University Press, 1988). *Representing Reality* includes a chapter devoted to ethical considerations in relation to documentary film form and style. *New Challenges for Documentary* includes Brian Winston's essay "The Tradition of the Victim in Griersonian Documentary," which is a scathing attack on the tendency to treat people as victims, especially in television news and special reports. Books that gather together interviews with filmmakers, such as *The Documentary Conscience,* or that include essays by filmmakers, such as Kevin Mac-Donald and Mark Cousins, eds., *Imagined Reality* (London: Faber and Faber, 1996), inevitably touch on ethical considerations.

Another useful reference is the code of ethics developed by the American Sociological Association and the similar code developed by the American Anthropological Association. These codes address many of the issues that arise when researchers enter into the lives of people markedly different from themselves. Jane Gaines, *Contested Culture: The Image, the Voice and the Law* (Chapel Hill: University of North Carolina Press, 1991), sketches out many of the legal issues involved in the commodification of speech and image, issues that clearly have an ethical dimension as well.

Issues of the relationship between speaker and recipient and the role of pronouns and other markers in establishing such relationships is addressed by the linguist Emile Benveniste in his *Problems in General Linguistics* (Coral Gables, Fla.: University of Miami Press, 1971), while Christian Metz explores some of the implications for film study in his *The Imaginary Signifier: Psychoanalysis and the Cinema* (Bloomington: Indiana University Press, 1982).

Going further in an exploration of how to define or conceptualize documentary is best done through works that are devoted specifically to documentary film and video. Some caution is advisable when referring to standard introductory film textbooks and basic film history textbooks. These books invariably place their emphasis on narrative fiction and often overlook documentary, provide idiosyncratic or dated definitions, and lack subtleness in their discussion of documentary definitions, history, or form.

Defining documentary as a form, genre, or particular type of social practice is taken up by *Representing Reality* in some detail. The issues involved in a definition of documentary as a "fuzzy" genre are explored quite helpfully in Carl R. Plantinga, *Rhetoric and Representation in Nonfiction Film* (New York: Cambridge University Press, 1997). Edward Brannigan, *Narrative Comprehension and Film* (New York: Routledge Press, 1992), is a formal and technical book, but it devotes a chapter to Chris Marker's *San Soleil* and the question of how narrative structure is understood in documentary differently from how it is understood in fiction.

The question of film genres in a more general sense is well addressed in Charles Altman, *Film/Genre* (London: British Film Institute, 1999). It is also taken up by Barry Grant, ed., *Film Genre: Theory and Criticism* (Metuchen, N.J.: Scarecrow Press, 1977), and by Stephen Neale, *Genre* (London: British Film Institute, 1980). The background to and definitions for observational documentaries are well addressed in Steven Mamber, *Cinema Verite in America: Studies in Uncontrolled Documentary* (Cambridge, Mass.: MIT Press, 1974). The specific case of docudrama as a form or genre is addressed by Derek Paget, *No Other Way to Tell It* (Manchester and New York: Manchester University Press, and New York: St. Martin's Press, 1998), while the overlap and interrelationship of the genres of ethnographic and experimental film is a central concern of Catherine Russell, *Experimental Ethnography* (Durham, N.C.: Duke University Press, 1999).

The larger array of documentary practices that arise in a given period and include a film component is illuminatingly discussed in William Stott, *Documentary Expression in Thirties America* (New York: Oxford University Press, 1973), and in Paula Rabinowitz, *They Must Be Represented* (New York: Verso, 1994), a book that also focuses on the 1930s.

Considerations of voice in documentary, in the sense discussed in Chapter 3, occur in *Representing Reality.* Voice in the more literal sense of spoken words is itself an important concept that has been well explored, particularly from a feminist perspective. Kaja Silverman, *The Acoustic Mirror* (Bloomington: Indiana University Press, 1988), and Sara Kozloff, *Invisible Storytellers: Voice-over Narration in American Fiction Film* (Berkeley: University of California Press, 1988), are the most directly relevant. On sound and voice more generally, Charles Altman has edited a special issue of *Yale French Studies* on "Cinema/Sound" (no. 60, 1980); John Belton and Elisabeth Weis have edited *Film Sound: Theory and Practice* (New York: Columbia University Press, 1985); and Michel Chion has written an influential book, *Le Son au cinéma* (Paris: Editions de L'Etoile, 1992).

Discussions of rhetoric are abundant since it has remained a source of lively debate since ancient times. Of particular use for the treatment of rhetoric here are Cicero, *De Oratore* (English and Latin), 2 vols. (Cambridge, Mass.: Harvard University Press, 1967–68); Quintillian, *Instituto Oratorio,* 4 vols. (Cambridge, Mass.: Harvard University Press, 1953); and Aristotle, *The "Art" of Rhetoric* (Cambridge, Mass.: Harvard University Press, 1975). A contemporary and very insightful rethinking of rhetorical terms and categories occurs in Richard Lanham, *A Handlist of Rhetorical Terms,* 2nd ed. (Berkeley: University of California Press, 1991).

The idea that a sense of voice can be collective as well as individual receives examination from the point of view of collective, or common, expression in Chris Holmlund and Cynthia Fuchs, eds., *Between the Sheets, in the Streets: Queer, Lesbian and Gay Documentary* (Minneapolis: University of Minnesota Press, 1997), and in Diane Waldman and Janet Walker, eds., *Feminism and Documentary* (Minneapolis: University of Minnesota Press, 1999). The idea of an individual "voice" as used here also slides toward the idea of personal "vision" or individual style (although the terms are not entirely identical). There are numerous studies of individual filmmakers in documentary. These can be found by searching a library database using the filmmaker's name as a subject heading. The lists of bibliographic material on documentary filmmakers, contemporary and historical, found at www.lib.berkeley.edu /MRC/documentary.bib.html provide a useful starting point.

General film histories such as Kristen Thompson and David Bordwell, *Film History: An Introduction* (New York: McGraw-Hill, 1994), David Cook, *History of the Narrative Film* (New York: Norton, 1996), and Gerald Mast and Bruce Kawin, *A Short History of the Movies* (New York: Allan and Bacon, 2000), have the same flaws as general introductory textbooks, although they do give some passing sense of how documentary film history relates to a larger history of narrative fiction film.

All of the standard histories of documentary provide a sense of the form's beginnings and subsequent development, although the argument advanced here differs from the emphasis in these books on early cinema (1895–1906) as the beginnings of the documentary genre. André

Bazin, *What Is Cinema?* vol. 1 (Berkeley: University of California Press, 1967), traces the origins of cinema generally to a desire to preserve or embalm that has strong implications for documentary film. (His entire aesthetic is very sympathetic to documentary qualities in narrative cinema generally.) The 1920s avant-garde film movement in Europe and the constructive art and Soviet cinema initiatives in the USSR, the arenas from which documentary film takes shape in the account given here, are covered in a number of books. Among them are Richard Abel, *French Film Theory and Criticism,* 1907–1939, 2 vols. (Princeton: Princeton University Press, 1988); Stephen C. Foster, ed., *Hans Richter: Activism, Modernism and the Avant-Garde* (Cambridge, Mass.: MIT Press, 1998); Thomas Waugh, "Joris Ivens and the Evolution of the Radical Documentary, 1926–1946" (Ph.D. dissertation, Columbia University, 1981, University Microfilms); Kees Bakker, ed., *Joris Ivens and the Documentary Context* (Amsterdam: Amsterdam University Press, 1999); Alan Lovell, *Anarchist Cinema* (on Jean Vigo, Georges Franju, and Luis Buñuel) (London: Peace Press, 1967); Stephen Bann, ed., *The Tradition of Constructivism* (New York: Viking, 1974); Amos Vogel, *Film as a Subversive Art* (New York: Random House, 1974); and Jay Leyda, *Kino: A History of the Russian and Soviet Film* (New York: Macmillan, 1960). Siegfried Kracauer, *From Caligari to Hitler* (New York: Noonday Press, 1959), contains an informative appendix, "Propaganda and the Nazi War Film." Joris Ivens's autobiographical account, *The Camera and I* (New York: International Publishers, 1969), gives a first-hand account of the social and aesthetic issues he faced during this period. Roger Odin edited *L'Age D'Or du Documentaire* (Paris: Editions L'Harmatten, 1998), a well-selected set of essays on European documentary filmmaking in the 1950s.

Italian neo-realism is one of the film movements that sits on the boundary of documentary and fiction. André Bazin discusses it informatively in *What Is Cinema?* and Robert Kolker, *The Altering Eye* (New York: Oxford University Press, 1983), gives a more critical but still appreciative account of this movement. David MacDougall, *Transcultural Cinema* (Princeton: Princeton University Press, 1998), a collection of the filmmaker's most important essays, makes several valuable references to Italian neo-realism and its influence.

The broader issue of realism itself is helpfully addressed in most introductory film textbooks as well as in John Hill and Pamela Church Gibson, eds., *The Oxford Guide to Film Studies* (New York: Oxford University Press, 1998); Linda Nochlin, *Realism* (Baltimore, Md.: Penguin, 1976); Jacques Aumont et al., *Aesthetics of Film* (Austin: University of Texas Press, 1992), and Ien Ang, *Watching Dallas* (New York: Methuen, 1985), which convincingly discusses psychological and emotional realism.

The role of narrative in film, both fiction and documentary, can be better understood when studied in the context of several works. Among them are Hayden White, *The Content of the Form* (Baltimore, Md.: Johns Hopkins University Press, 1987); Tom Gunning, *D. W. Griffith and the Origins of American Narrative Film* (Urbana and Chicago: University of Illinois Press, 1991); Gunning's important essay on the early "cinema of attractions" in Thomas Elsaesser and Adam Barker, eds., *Early Cinema: Space, Frame, Narrative* (London: British Film Institute, 1990); David Bordwell, *Narration in the Fiction Film* (Madison: University of Wisconsin Press, 1985), and two of Christian Metz's books, *Film Language: A Semiotics of Cinema* (New York: Oxford University Press, 1974) and *The Imaginary Signifier: Psychoanalysis and the Cinema* (Bloomington: Indiana University Press, 1982).

Various ways exist to divide up documentary film and video into different clusters, movements, or modes. Four of the modes discussed here (expository, observation, participatory [previously called interactive], and reflexive) are treated further in *Representing Reality,* while the performative mode receives a separate chapter in Bill Nichols, *Blurred Boundaries: Questions of Meaning in Contemporary Culture* (Bloomington: Indiana University Press, 1994). Carl Plantinga takes up this issue in *Rhetoric and Representation in Nonfiction Film,* and Michael Renov advances an alternative set of divisions in his edited volume, *Theorizing Documentary.*

The poetic mode can be placed in a broader context through reference to readings devoted to the avant-garde and experimental film mentioned above. Laszlo Moholy-Nagy, *Painting, Photography, Film* (Cambridge, Mass.: MIT Press, 1969), is a stimulating survey of the potential of each of these media. Richard Abel, *French Film Theory and Criticism* contains many essays by filmmakers and early theorists on the poetic possibilities of cinema. P. Adams Sitney has contributed two useful books on experimental cinema that can also be read with documentary film in mind: *Visionary Film: The American Avant-Garde,* 2nd ed. (New York: Oxford University Press, 1979), and the edited volume *The Avant-Garde Film: A Reader of Theory and Criticism* (New York: New York University Press, 1978).

Expository documentary receives discussion in Thomas Waugh, ed., *"Show Us Life!": Toward a History and Aesthetic of the Committed Documentary* (Metuchen, N.J.: Scarecrow Press, 1984), and in Jay Leyda,

Film Begets Film (New York: Hill and Wang, 1964), although Leyda's book does not use that term for the structure of the compilation film. Additional discussion occurs in Bill Nichols, *Ideology and the Image* (Bloomington: Indiana University Press, 1988).

Observational cinema is well covered by Steven Mamber, *Cinema Verite in America,* and by portions of David MacDougall, *Transcultural Cinema.* Gary Evans, *In the National Interest: A Chronicle of the NFB of Canada from 1949–1989* (Toronto: University of Toronto Press, 1991), gives insight into the Canadian contribution to this mode. Barry Grant, *Voyage of Discovery: The Films of Frederick Wiseman* (Urbana: University of Illinois Press, 1992), examines the films of one of this mode's purest practitioners. Paul Hockings, ed., *Principles of Visual Anthropology,* 2nd ed. (Berlin and New York: Mouton, 1995), includes several essays that discuss the implications of observational modes of film for ethnography and visual anthropology.

Although sometimes mistakenly thought of as expository because of its propagandistic uses, *Triumph of the Will* is one of the early examples of observational documentary, one that raises rich questions about the line between observing and staging. Additional discussion of this film takes place in Brian Winston, *Claiming the Real;* Linda Deutschman, *Triumph of the Will: The Image of the Third Reich* (Wakefield, N.H.: Longwood Press, 1991); David Hinton, *The Films of Leni Riefenstahl* (Metuchen, N.J.: Scarecrow Press, 1991); while Richard M. Barsam has provided a useful bibliographic reference, *Filmguide to Triumph of the Will* (Bloomington: Indiana University Press, 1975).

Important references for the participatory mode of documentary include, at the general level of the interview and confession, Michel Foucault, *The History of Sexuality,* vol. 1 (New York: Vintage, 1980); Jack Douglas, *Creative Interviewing* (Beverly Hills: Sage, 1985); and Philip Bell and Theo Van Leeuven, *The Media Interview: Confession, Contest, Conversation* (Kensington, NSW: University of New South Wales Press, 1994). Paul Hockings, ed., *Principles of Visual Anthropology,* addresses some of the issues involved with field work, a process that has appreciable analogy with many types of documentary filmmaking practice. A more critical look at ethnography and the issues of representing others in appropriate written forms occurs in James Clifford and George Marcus, eds., *Writing Culture: Poetics and Politics of Ethnography* (Berkeley: University of California Press, 1986); it has relevance for documentary and ethnographic film but lacks a counterpart devoted specifically to these forms. Mick Eaton, *Anthropology, Reality, Cinema: The Films of Jean Rouch* (London: British Film Institute, 1979), explores issues of participatory filmmaking as they arise in relation to the work of one of the founders of this mode.

Reflexive documentary work receives frequent consideration in the collected interviews with Trinh T. Minh-ha: *Framer Framed* (New York: Routledge Press, 1992), and *Cinema Interval* (New York: Routledge, 1999); these books include scripts and sketches from her films, which reveal the high degree of conscious fabrication she employs. Annette Michelson, *Kino-Eye: The Writings of Dziga Vertov* (Berkeley: University of California Press, 1984), gives us the original essays and manifestos by this pioneering Soviet filmmaker who is often cited as a precursor to reflexive documentary. Valuable contextual readings include Bertolt Brecht's theories of theater as presented in John Willet, ed., *Brecht on Theatre* (New York: Hill and Wang, 1992), and Victor Shklovsky's theories of estrangement or *ostranenie* in literature, especially in his essay "Art as Technique," found in Lee Lemon and Marion Reis, eds., *Russian Formalist Criticism: Four Essays* (Lincoln: University of Nebraska Press, 1965).

Contextual readings for performative documentary include two books by Judith Butler, *Gender Trouble* (New York: Routledge, 1990) and *Excitable Speech* (New York: Routledge, 1997). A chapter in Bill Nichols, *Blurred Boundaries* (Bloomington: Indiana University Press, 1994), discusses performative documentary in some detail. Aspects of Michael Renov and Erika Suderberg, eds., *Resolution: Contemporary Video Practice* (Minneapolis: University of Minnesota Press, 1996), take up issues of performativity, as well as reflexivity. Ilan Avisar's sensitive reading of *Night and Fog* in *Screening the Holocaust: Cinema's Image of the Unimaginable* (Bloomington: Indiana University Press, 1988), suggests ways in which this landmark film could be considered performative even though Avisar does not use that term specifically.

The question of what is documentary about in a general sense invites reflection on the basic forms of social organization and the types of visible phenomena that accompany them. Further reading useful to this topic can be found in Peter Berger and Thomas Luckman, *The Social Construction of Reality* (New York: Anchor, 1990); George Lakoff and Mark Johnson, *Metaphors We Live By* (Chicago: University of Chicago Press, 1980); Irving Goffman, *Interaction Ritual: Essays on Face to Face Behaviour* (Chicago: Aldine, 1967), and his *Presentation of Self in Everyday Life* (New York: Doubleday, 1959); Sol Worth, *Through Navajo Eyes: An Exploration in Film Communication and Anthropology* (Bloomington: Indiana University Press, 1973), and his *Studying Visual Communication,* edited by Larry Gross (Philadelphia: University of

Pennsylvania Press, 1981); and in W. J. T. Mitchell, *Iconology: Image, Text, Ideology* (Chicago: University of Chicago Press, 1986), and his *Picture Theory: Essays on Verbal and Visual Representation* (Chicago: University of Chicago Press, 1994).

David MacDougall, *Transcultural Cinema,* has pursued some of the implications of the concept of tacit knowledge as a form of knowledge quite different from verbal or written knowledge that can be potentially generated by cinema, while Richard Lanham's *Handlist of Rhetorical Terms* demonstrates how rhetoric arises to address situations and issues that cannot be resolved by scientific investigation or pure logic.

Many books address the question of the political dimension to film and to documentary in particular. Brian Winston, *Claiming the Real,* is one important revision of documentary history based on an assessment of the political impact of the form. Paula Rabinowitz, *They Must Be Represented,* gives a broad overview to the political issues surrounding documentary representation in the 1930s. William Alexander, *Films on the Left: American Documentary Film: 1931–1942* (Princeton: Princeton University Press, 1981), recounts the struggles to build a leftist filmmaking community in the United States, while Bill Nichols, *Newsreel: Documentary Filmmaking on the American Left, 1969–1974* (New York: Arno Press, 1980), picks up the story with the attempt by Newsreel to be the filmmaking arm of the New Left. Peter Steven's *Brink of Reality: New Canadian Documentary Film and Video* (Toronto: Between the Lines, 1993) examines the impact of video in a country with an exceptionally rich documentary film tradition that has been historically tied to government patronage. Benedict Anderson, *Imagined Community: Reflections on the Origin and Spread of Nationalism* (New York: Verso, 1991), has stirred controversy with its argument that nation-states are constructs heavily beholden to the work of symbolic representation by such media as journalism, film, and television. Patricia Zimmerman, *States of Emergency: Documentaries, Wars and Democracies* (Minneapolis: University of Minnesota Press, 2000), brings issues of the nation-state and film into the era of the global economy and cybernetic systems.

The consequences of a shifting political climate for an individual artist's career receives illuminating discussion in Thomas Waugh, "Joris Ivens and the Evolution of the Radical Documentary, 1926–1946"; in Annette Michelson, ed., *Kino-Eye: The Writings of Dziga Vertov;* and in the catalogue for the MOMA exhibition edited by Magdalena Dabrowski, *Aleksandr Rodchenko* (New York: MOMA, 1998), devoted to the work of this early Soviet artist, designer, and photographer who was a contemporary of Dziga Vertov.

The shift from national politics to a more personal sense of politics and of the ramifications of identity politics receives exploration in Chris Holmlund and Cynthia Fuchs, eds., *Between the Sheets, In the Streets;* Patricia Zimmerman, *Reel Families: A Social History of Amateur Film* (Bloomington: Indiana University Press, 1995); and Diane Waldman and Janet Walker, *Feminism and Documentary.* An earlier but helpful discussion of feminist film theory and documentary occurs in E. Ann Kaplan, *Women and Film: Both Sides of the Camera* (New York: Methuen, 1983). Her later book, *Looking for the Other: Feminism, Film and the Imperial Gaze* (New York: Routledge, 1997), extends into issues of cross-cultural representation in fiction and non-fiction. Thomas Waugh has given us an excellent history of gay erotica in *Hard to Imagine: Gay Male Eroticism in Photography and Film from Their Beginnings to Stonewall* (New York: Cambridge University Press, 1996); his collected writings, *The Fruit Machine: Twenty Years of Writing on Queer Cinema* (Durham, N.C.: Duke University Press, 2000), focus more pointedly on documentary and fiction film.

Chon A. Noriega, *Shot in America: Television, the State and the Rise of Chicano Cinema* (Minneapolis: University of Minnesota Press, 2000), and Phyllis R. Klotman and Janet K. Cutler, eds., *Struggles for Representation: African American Documentary Film and Video* (Bloomington: Indiana University Press, 1999), both give thoughtful consideration to documentary film as a means of personal but also collective expression in relation to the Chicano and African-American communities.

For guidance in writing about documentary, several basic reference works are useful. These include *The Chicago Manual of Style,* 13th ed. (Chicago: University of Chicago Press, 1982); Joseph Gibaldi, *MLA Style Manual and Guide to Scholarly Publishing,* 2nd ed. (New York: MLA, 1998); and Kate Turabian, *A Manual for Writers of Term Papers, Theses and Dissertations,* 6th ed. (Chicago: University of Chicago Press, 1996). Timothy Corrigan, *A Short Guide to Writing about Film,* 3rd ed. (New York: Longman, 1998), gives many film-specific examples and tips.

Although Robert Flaherty is one of the more frequently written about figures in documentary, reviews, articles, and books can be found that pertain to most established documentary filmmakers. The Web site previously listed, www.lib.berkeley.edu/MRC/documentary.bib.html, is one starting point for researching individual filmmakers.

For further information on Robert Flaherty specifically, consult Flaherty's own *My Eskimo Friends, "Nanook of the North,"* in collaboration with Francis Hubbard Flaherty (Garden City, N.Y.: Doubleday, 1924); William T. Murphy, *Robert Flaherty: A Guide to References and Re-*

sources (Boston: G. K. Hall, 1978); Arthur Calder Marshall, *The Innocent Eye* (Baltimore, Md.: Penguin, 1970); Paul Rotha, *Robert J. Flaherty: A Biography,* ed. Jay Ruby (Philadelphia: University of Pennsylvania, 1983); Richard M. Barsam, *The Vision of Robert Flaherty: The Artist as Myth and Filmmaker* (Bloomington: Indiana University Press, 1988); and Fatimah Tobing Rony, *The Third Eye: Race, Cinema and Ethnographic Spectacle* (Durham, N.C.: Duke University Press, 1996). Peter Wintonik's film *Cinéma Vérité: Defining the Moment* (Montreal: National Film Board of Canada, 1999), is one of many films that include illustrative clips from *Nanook of the North. Nanook* itself is available as a film from the Museum of Modern Art and as a videotape, in a remastered version, from Kino Video.

Filmography

This filmography gives basic information primarily about documentaries discussed in this book. Other films mentioned in the text are omitted if they are readily found in other works. The country of origin is the United States unless otherwise stated. Listings for films shot in one country but originating elsewhere give the country of origin last.

16 in Webster Groves, Arthur Barron, CBS Special, 46 min., 1966

Abortion Stories: North and South, Gail Singer, National Film Board of Canada: Ireland, Japan, Thailand, Peru, Columbia/Canada, 55 min., 1984

Act of Seeing with One's Own Eyes, The, Stan Brakhage, 32 min., 1971

Aileen Wuornos: The Selling of a Serial Killer, Nick Broomfield, 87 min., 1992

Always for Pleasure, Les Blank, 58 min., 1978

American Cinema, The, New York Center for Visual History/Public Broadcasting System (PBS), 10 one-hour episodes, 1994

American Family, An, Craig Gilbert, National Educational Television (NET), 12 one-hour episodes, 1972

Andalusian Dog, An. See *Un Chien andalou*

Anderson Platoon, The (Section Anderson, La), Pierre Schoendorffer, Vietnam/France, French Broadcasting System, France, 65 min., 1966

Anemic Cinema (Anémic cinéma), Marcel Duchamp, France, 5 min., 1926

Anthem, Marlon Riggs, 9 min., 1991

Arrival of a Train (Arrivée d'un train), August and Louis Lumière, France, 1 min., 1895

Ax Flight, The, Timothy Asch and Napoleon Chagnon, Yanomamö series, Venezuela/United States, 30 min., 1971

Ballet Mécanique, Fernand Léger, France, 14 min., 1924

Battle of San Pietro, The, John Huston, 33 min., 1945

Battleship Potemkin (Bronenosets Potyomkin), Sergei M. Eisenstein, Soviet Union, 75 min., 1925

Before Spring, Joris Ivens, China, 38 min., 1958

Before Stonewall: The Making of a Gay and Lesbian Community, Greta Shiller and Robert Rosenberg, 87 min., 1984

Berlin: Symphony of a Great City, Walter Ruttmann, Germany, 53 min., 1927

Bicycle Thief, The (Ladri di Biciclette), Vittorio De Sica, Italy, 93 min., 1948

Big One, The, Michael Moore, 90 min., 1997

Black and Silver Horses, Larry Andrews, 28 min., 1992

Blair Witch Project, The, Daniel Myrick and Eduardo Sánchez, 80 min., 1999

Blood of the Beasts (La Sang des bêtes), Georges Franju, France, 22 min., 1949

Body Beautiful, The, Ngozi Onwurah, 20 min., 1991

Bontoc Eulogy, Marlon Fuentes, Philippines/United States, 50 min., 1995

Bridge, The, Joris Ivens, 11 min., 1928

Cane Toads: An Unnatural History, Mark Lewis, Australia, 46 min., 1987

Cannibal Tours, Dennis O'Rourke, Papua New Guinea/Australia, 70 min., 1988

Chair, The, Drew Associates, Gregory Shukur, Richard Leacock, D.A. Pennebaker, 60 min., 1962

Chronicle of a Summer (Chronique d'un eté), Jean Rouch and Edgar Morin, France, 90 min., 1960

City, The, Ralph Steiner and Willard Van Dyke, 43 min., 1939

Civil War, The, Ken Burns, Public Broadcasting System, 9 parts, 680 min., 1990

Coal Face, Alberto Cavalcanti, Great Britain, 10 min., 1935

Complaints of a Dutiful Daughter, Deborah Hoffmann, 44 min., 1994

Composition in Blue (Komposition in Blau), Oskar Fischinger, Germany, 4 min., 1935

Contempt (Le Mépris), Jean-Luc Godard, Italy/France, 105 min., 1963

Crumb, Terry Zwigoff, 119 min., 1994

Daisy: The Story of a Facelift, Michael Rubbo, National Film Board of Canada, 57 min., 1982

Danube Exodus, Péter Forgács, Hungary, 60 min., 1998

Daughter Rite, Michelle Citron, 55 min., 1978

David Holzman's Diary, Jim McBride and L. M. Kit Carson, 71 min., 1968

Dead Birds, Robert Gardner, West New Guinea/United States, 83 min., 1963

Diagonal Symphony (Symphonie diagonale), Viking Eggeling, Germany, 5 min., 1924

Don't Look Back, D. A. Pennebaker, Great Britain/United States, 96 min., 1967

Emperor's Naked Army Marches On, The (Yuki Yukite shingun), Kazuo Hara, Japan, 123 min., 1987

End of St. Petersburg, The (Konyets Sankt-Peterburga), Vsevolod Pudovkin, Soviet Union, 69 min., 1927

Enthusiasm (Simfoniya Donbassa), Dziga Vertov, Soviet Union, 69 min., 1930

Every Day except Christmas, Lindsay Anderson, Great Britain, 41 min., 1957

Extremely Personal Eros: Love Song, Kazuo Hara, Japan, 92 min., 1974

Eyes on the Prize, Henry Hampton, Public Broadcasting System, 14 one-hour segments, series I: 1987, series II: 1990

Fall of the Romanov Dynasty, The (Padeniye dinastii Romanovykh), Esther Shub, Soviet Union, 90 min., 1927

Family Business, Tom Cohen, Middletown series, Public Broadcasting System, Peter Davis, Producer, 90 min., 1982

Far from Poland, Jill Godmilow, 106 min., 1984

Fast, Cheap, and Out of Control, Errol Morris, 80 min., 1997

Feeding the Baby (Repas de bébé), Louis Lumière, France, 1 min., 1895

Fiévre, Louis Delluc, France, 30 min., 1921

Film about a Woman Who . . . , A, Yvonne Ranier, 105 min., 1972/4

Finding Christa, Camille Billops and James Hatch, 55 min., 1991

First Contact, Robin Anderson and Bob Connelly, Papua New Guinea/Australia, 54 min., 1984

Forest of Bliss, Robert Gardner, India/United States, 91 min., 1985

Four Families, Fali Billimoira et al., National Film Board of Canada, 58 min., 1959

Frank: A Vietnam Veteran, Fred Simon and Vince Canzoneri, 52 min., 1984

Frantz Fanon: Black Skin, White Mask, Isaac Julien, France, Martinique/Great Britain, 70 min., 1996

Free Fall (Az Örvény), Péter Forgács, Hungary, 75 min., 1996

Gardener, The (Waterer Watered, The) (L'Arroseur arrosé), Louis Lumière, 1 min., 1895

Gimme Shelter, David Maysles, Albert Maysles, and Charlotte Zwerin, 91 min., 1970

Grass: A Nation's Battle for Life, Merian C. Cooper and Ernest B. Schoedsack, 70 min., 1925

Growing Up Female: As Six Becomes One, Julia Reichert and Jim Klein, 60 min., 1970

Hard Metals Disease, Jon Alpert, 57 min., 1987

Harlan County, U.S.A., Barbara Kopple, 103 min., 1977

Harvest of Shame, Edward R. Murrow, CBS News, 60 min., 1960

Heart of Spain, Herbert Kline and Geza Karpathi, Frontier Films, Spain/United States, 30 min., 1937

Herb Schiller Reads the New York Times, Herb Schiller, Paper Tiger Television, 28 min., 1982

High School, Frederick Wiseman, 75 min., 1968

History and Memory, Rea Tajiri, 33 min., 1991

Hoop Dreams, Steve James, Frederick Marx, and Peter Gilbert, 170 min., 1994

Hospital, Frederick Wiseman, 84 min., 1970

Hour of the Furnaces, The (La Hora de los hornos), Octavio Getino and Fernando E. Solanas, Argentina, 260 min., 1968

Housing Problems, Edgar Anstey and Arthur Elton, United Kingdom, 30 min., 1935

How Yukong Moved the Mountains (Comment Yukong déplaça les montagnes), Joris Ivens and Marceline Loridan, France/China, 12 one-hour segments, 1976

I'm British but . . . , Gurinder Chadha, United Kingdom, 30 min., 1989

In the Land of the Head Hunters, Edward S. Curtis, 47 min., 1914

In the Year of the Pig, Emile de Antonio, 101 min., 1969

Indonesia Calling, Joris Ivens, Australia, 15 min., 1946

Intimate Stranger, Alan Berliner, 60 min., 1992

It's Elementary: Talking about Gay Issues in School, Debra Chasnoff and Helen Cohen, 77 min., 1996

Janie's Janie, Geri Ashur and Peter Barton, 25 min., 1971

Jeanne Dielman, 23 Quai du Commerce, 1080 Bruxelles, Chantal Ackerman, Belgium, 201 min., 1975

Journal Inachevé. See *Unfinished Diary*

Joyce at Thirty-four, Joyce Chopra and Claudia Weill, 28 min., 1972

Jupiter's Wife, Michel Negroponte, 87 min., 1995

Kenya Boran, parts 1 and 2, David McDougall and James Blue, Faces of Change series, 33 min. each, 1974

Khush, Pratibha Parmar, Great Britain, 24 min., 1991

Kino Glaz (Kino-Eye, or Life Caught Unawares), Dziga Vertov, Soviet Union, 74 min., 1924

Kinopravda (Cinema Truth), Dziga Vertov, Soviet Union, 81 min., 1925

Komosol (Komsomolsk) (Song of Heroes), Joris Ivens, Soviet Union, 50 min., 1932

Koyaanisqatsi, Godfrey Reggio, 87 min., 1983

Kurt and Courtney, Nick Broomfield, 95 min., 1998

L'Affiche (The Poster), Jean Epstein, France, 73 min., 1924

L'Age d'or (The Golden Age), Luis Buñuel, France, 60 min., 1930

L'Etoile de Mer, Man Ray, France, 15 min., 1928

La Roue (The Wheel), Abel Gance, France, 130 min., 1923

La Terra Trema (The Earth Trembles), Luchino Visconti, Italy, 160 min., 1948

Land without Bread (Terre sans Pain or Las Hurdes), Luis Buñuel, Spain, 27 min., 1932

Las Madres de la Plaza de Mayo, Susana Muñoz and Lourdes Portillo, Argentina/United States, 64 min., 1985

Last Days, The, James Moll, Hungary/United States, 87 min., 1998

Le Retour à la Raison (Return to Reason), Man Ray, France, 3 min., 1923

Les Maîtres Fous, Jean Rouch, France, 30 min., 1923

Les Racquetteurs, Gilles Groulx and Michel Brault, National Film Board of Canada, 15 min., 1958

Letter to Jane, Jean-Luc Godard and Jean-Pierre Gorin, France, 45 min., 1972

Letter without Words, Lisa Lewenz, 62 min., 1998

Letters from China. See *Before Spring*

Life and Times of Rosie the Riveter, The, Connie Field, 60 min., 1980

Listen to Britain, Humphrey Jennings, Great Britain, 21 min., 1941

Loneliness of the Long-Distance Runner, The, Tony Richardson, Great Britain, 104 min., 1962

Lonely Boy, Roman Kroiter and Wolf Koenig, National Film Board of Canada, 27 min., 1962

Looking for Langston, Isaac Julien, Great Britain, 55 min., 1988

Louisiana Story, Robert Flaherty, 75 min., 1948

Man with a Movie Camera, The (Chelovek s kinoapparatom), Dziga Vertov, Soviet Union, 103 min., 1929

Married Couple, A, Allan King, Canada, 90 min., 1970

Meat, Frederick Wiseman, 112 min., 1976

Memorandum, Beryl Fox, National Film Board of Canada, 58 min., 1965

Ménilmontant, Dimitri Kirsanoff, France, 1926

Misère au Borinage, Joris Ivens and Henri Storck, Belgium, 36 min., 1934

Moana, Robert J. Flaherty, Samoa/United States, 26 min., 1927

Model, Frederick Wiseman, 129 min., 1980

Momma Don't Allow, Karel Reis and Tony Richardson, Great Britain, 22 min., 1956

Mondo Cane (It's a Dog's World), Gualtiero Jacopetti and Franco E. Prosperi, Italy, 105 min., 1963

Monterey Pop, D. A. Pennebaker, 82 min., 1967

N!ai: The Story of a !Kung Woman, John Marshall, Odyssey series/PBS, Kalahari Desert (Nambia, Angolia)/United States, 58 min., 1980

Nanook of the North, Robert Flaherty, Canada/United States, 55 min., 1922

Netsilk Eskimo series, Asen Balikci and Guy Mary-Rousseliere, Education Development Corporation and National Film Board of Canada, Canada, 18 episodes, approximately 10 hours running time, 1967–68

Night and Fog (Nuit et brouillard), Alain Resnais, Poland/France, 31 min., 1955

Night Mail, Harry Watt and Basil Wright, 30 min., 1936

Nitrate Kisses, Barbara Hammer, 67 min., 1996

No Lies, Mitchell Block, 25 min., 1973

Nobody's Business, Alan Berliner, 60 min., 1996

Not a Love Story: A Film about Pornography, Bonnie Klein, National Film Board of Canada, Canada, 68 min., 1981

Nuer, The, Hilary Harris, George Breidenbach, and Robert Gardner, Ethiopia/United States, 75 min., 1970

N.Y., N.Y., Francis Thompson, 15 min., 1957

Obedience, Stanley Milgram, 45 min., 1965

October (Ten Days That Shook the World), Sergei M. Eisenstein, Soviet Union, 104 min., 1927

Old and the New, The (The General Line), Sergei M. Eisenstein, Soviet Union, 70 min., 1929

Operation Abolition, House Un-American Activities Committee with Washington Video Productions, 45 min., 1960

Operation Correction, American Civil Liberties Union, 47 min., 1961

Pacific 231, Jean Mitry, 10 min., 1948

Paradise Lost: The Child Murders at Robin Hood Hills, Joe Berlinger and Bruce Sinofsky, 150 min., 1996

Paris Is Burning, Jennie Livingston, 71 min., 1990

Paris qui dort (The Crazy Ray), René Clair, France, 36 min., 1924

People's Century, The, WGBH-Boston/PBS, 26 one-hour episodes, 1998

People's War, The, N.Y. Newsreel, 40 min., 1969

Pets or Meat: The Return to Flint, Michael Moore, 23 min., 1992

Play of Light: Black, White, Grey (Zeigt ein Lichtspiel: Schwarz, weiss, grau), Laszlo Moholy-Nagy, 6 min., 1930

Plow That Broke the Plains, The, Pare Lorentz, U.S. Resettlement Administration, 25 min., 1936

Portrait of Jason, Shirley Clarke, 105 min., 1967

Primary, Drew Associates, D. A. Pennebaker and Richard Leacock, with Terence Macartney-Filgate and Albert Maysles, 60 min., 1960

Propos de Nice, À, Jean Vigo, France, 18 min., 1930

Rabbit in the Moon, Emiko Omori, 85 min., 1999

Race Symphony (Rennsymphonie), Hans Richter, Germany, 7 min., 1929

Rain, Joris Ivens, Holland, 14 min., 1931

Reassemblage, Trinh T. Minh-ha, Senegal/United States, 40 min., 1982

Report from the Aleutians, John Huston, U.S. Army Signal Corps, 47 min., 1943

Rhythmus 21, Hans Richter, Germany, 15 min., 1921

Rhythmus 23, Hans Richter, Germany, 4 min., 1923

Rien que les Heures, Alberto Cavalcanti, France, 1926

River, The, Pare Lorentz, Farm Security Administration, 31 min., 1937

Roger and Me, Michael Moore, 87 min., 1989

Rome, Open City (*Roma, città aperta*), Roberto Rossellini, Italy, 100 min., 1946

Roses in December, Ana Carringan and Bernard Stone, El Salvador/United States, 56 min., 1982

Roy Cohn/Jack Smith, Jill Godmilow, 90 min., 1994

Russia of Nicolas II and Leo Tolstoy, The, Esther Shub, Soviet Union, 60 min., 1928

Sad Song of Yellow Skin, Michael Rubbo, National Film Board of Canada, South Vietnam/Canada, 58 min., 1970

Salesman, Albert Maysles, David Maysles, and Charlotte Zwerin, 90 min., 1969

Salt for Svanetia (*Sol Svanetii*), Mikhail Kalatozov, Soviet Union, 53 min., 1930

Sans Soleil, Chris Marker, France, 100 min., 1982

Scorpio Rising, Kenneth Anger, 30 min., 1964

Selling of the Pentagon, The, Peter Davis, CBS News, 52 min., 1971

Seventeenth Parallel, The, Joris Ivens, Vietnam/France, 113 min., 1968

Shadows, John Cassavetes, 87 min., 1961

Sherman's March, Ross McElwee, 155 min., 1985

Shoah, Claude Lanzman, Poland/France, part 1, 273 min.; part 2, 290 min., 1985

Shock of the New, The, Robert Hughes, 7 one-hour episodes, BBC-TV and Time-Life Television, 1980

Silverlake Life: The View from Here, Tom Joslin, Mark Massi, and Peter Friedman, 99 min., 1993

Smiling Madame Beudet, The (*La souriante Madame Beudet*), Germaine Dulac, France, 54 min., 1922

Smoke Menace, John Taylor, Great Britain, 14 min., 1937

Soldier Girls, Joan Churchill and Nicolas Broomfield, 87 min., 1980

Solovky Power (*Solovetsky vlast*), Marina Goldovskaya, Soviet Union, 90 min., 1988

Song of Ceylon, Basil Wright, Ceylon/Great Britain, 40 min., 1934

Song of the Rivers (*Des Lied der Ströme*), Joris Ivens and Joop Huisken, East Germany, 100 min., 1954

Sorrow and the Pity, The (*La Chagrin et le Pitié*), Marcel Ophuls, France, 260 min., 1970

Sous les toits de Paris (*Under the Roofs of Paris*), René Clair, France, 96 min., 1930

Spanish Earth, The, Joris Ivens, 52 min., 1937

Speak Body, Kay Armitage, Canada, 20 min., 1987

Strange Victory, Leo Hurwuitz, 80 min., 1948

Strike, Sergei M. Eisenstein, Soviet Union, 82 min., 1925

Surname Viet Given Name Nam, Trinh T. Minh-ha, 108 min., 1989

Takeover, David and Judith MacDougall, 90 min., Australia, 1981

Tale of the Wind (*Une histoire de vent*), Joris Ivens, France, 80 min., 1988

Terre sans Pain. See *Land without Bread*

Thin Blue Line, The, Errol Morris, American Playhouse/PBS, 115 min., 1987

Things I Cannot Change, The, Tanya Ballantyne, National Film Board of Canada, 58 min., 1966

This Is Spinal Tap, Rob Reiner, 82 min., 1984

Three Songs of Lenin (*Tri pesni o Lenine*), Dziga Vertov, Soviet Union, 62 min., 1934

Ties That Bind, The, Su Friedrich, 55 min., 1984

Times of Harvey Milk, The, Robert Epstein and Richard Schmiechen, 87 min., 1989

Tongues Untied, Marlon Riggs, 45 min., 1989

Trance and Dance in Bali, Gregory Bateson and Margaret Mead, Character Formation in Different Culture series, Bali/United States, 20 min., based on fieldwork in 1936–38, released in 1952

Trip to the Moon, A (*Voyage dans la lune*), Georges Méliès, France, 14 min., 1902

Triumph of the Will, Leni Riefenstahl, Germany, 107 min., 1934

Turksib, Victor A. Turin, Soviet Union, 57 min., 1929

TV Nation, Michael Moor, TV series, 1994

Two Laws, Carolyn Strachan and Alessandro Cavadini with the Borrolola community, 130 min., 1981

Two or Three Things I Know about Her (*Deux ou trois choses que je sais d'elle*), Jean-Luc Godard, France, 90 min., 1967

Un Chien andalou (*An Andalusian Dog*), Luis Buñuel and Salvador Dali, France, 16 min., 1929

Unfinished Diary (*Journal Inachevé*), Marilu Mallet, Canada, 55 min., 1983

Union Maids, Jim Klein, Miles Mogulescu, and Julia Reichert, 51 min., 1976

Vent d'est (*Wind from the East*), Jean-Luc Goddard, France, 95 min., 1970

Victory at Sea, Henry Salomon and Isaac Kleinerman, NBC Television, 26 thirty-minute episodes, 1952–53

War Comes to America, Frank Capra and Anatole Litvak, U.S. War Dept., part 7 of the Why We Fight series, 70 min., 1945

War Game, The, Peter Watkins, Great Britain, 45 min., 1966

Watsonville on Strike, Jon Silver, 70 min., 1989

Ways of Seeing, parts 1–4, with John Berger, BBC, Great Britain, 4 thirty-minute episodes, 1974

We Are the Lambeth Boys, Karel Reisz, Great Britain, 52 min., 1958

Wedding Camels, David and Judith MacDougall, Turkana Conversations Trilogy, Kenya/Australia, 108 min., 1980

Wheel, The. See *La Roue.*

When We Were Kings, Leon Gast, 87 min., 1996

Who Killed Vincent Chin?, Renee Tajima and Christine Choy, 87 min., 1988

Why Vietnam?, U.S. Department of Defense, Vietnam/United States, 32 min., 1965

Why We Fight series, Frank Capra and Anatole Litvak, U.S. War Dept., seven films of varying length, 1942–45

Wind from the East. See *Vent d'est*

With Babies and Banners: The Story of the Women's Emergency Brigade, Lorraine Gray, Anne Bohlen, and Lynn Goldfard, 45 min., 1977

Woman's Film, The, S.F. Newsreel women's caucus, 40 min., 1971

Wonder Ring, The, Stan Brakhage, 6 min., 1955

Wonderful, Horrible Life of Leni Riefenstahl, The, Ray Müller, Germany, 180 min., 1993

Word Is Out, Mariposa collective, Nancy Adair, Peter Adair, Andrew Brown, Robert Epstein, Lucy Massie Phenix, Veronica Silver, 130 min., 1977

Workers Leaving the Lumière Factory (*La Sortie des usines Lumière*), Louis Lumière, France, 1 min., 1895

Yanomamö series. See *The Ax-Fight*

Yidl in the Middle: Growing Up Jewish in Iowa, Marlene Booth, 58 min., 1998

Yuki Yikite shingun. See *The Emperor's Naked Army Marches On*

Zvenigora, Aleksandr Dovzhenko, Soviet Union, 90 min., 1928

List of Distributors

Note: A regularly updated version of this list is available at
http://iupress.indiana.edu/nichols/

Bullfrog Films
P.O. Box 149
Oley, PA 19547
Phone: 610-779-8226
Web site: www.bullfrogfilms.com
Contact: video@bullfrogfilms.com

Bullfrog Films carries more than 500 titles on such topics as globalization, environmental contamination, women's issues, health, and human rights. Examples of recent titles include *Drumbeat for Mother Earth; The Golf War; Rising Waters;* and *Secrets of Silicon Valley.*

California Newsreel
149 Ninth Street, Suite 420
San Francisco, CA 94103
Phone: 415-621-6196
Fax: 415-621-6522
Web site: www.newsreel.org
Contact: contact@newsreel.org

California Newsreel carries some of the classic Newsreel titles such as *Black Panther* and *San Francisco State: On Strike,* many more recent films on Africa, and both fiction and documentary. Their documentary titles include *Black Is, Black Ain't; The Strange Demise of Jim Crow; Long Nights Journey into Day; Legacy; KPFA on the Air;* and *Nuyorican Dream.*

Cambridge Documentary
Box 390385
Cambridge, MA 02139-0004
Phone: 617-354-3677
Fax 617-484-0754
Web site: www.cambridgedocumentaryfilms.org
Contact: cdf@shore.net

This distributor specializes in social issue documentaries and carries titles such as *Beyond Killing Us Softly: The Strength to Resist; Defending Our Lives; Pink Triangles;* and *Choosing Children.*

Canadian Film Distribution Center
Canadian Studies Resources Specialist
Feinberg Library
SUNY at Plattsburgh
Plattsburgh, NY 12901-2697
518-564-2396
Web site: canada-acsus.plattsburgh.edu/video/video.htm
Contact: mathew.smith@plattsburgh.edu

The nonprofit Center distributes many National Film Board of Canada films but also other Canadian films such as *Acid Rain: Requiem or Recovery* for nominal fees to educational institutions.

Canyon Cinema
2325 Third Street, Suite 338
San Francisco, CA 94107
415-626-2255
Web site: www.canyoncinema.com
Contact: film@canyoncinema.com

Canyon Cinema began as a filmmaker's co-op to distribute the work of West Coast experimental filmmakers. It is still the best source for such work, but it also represents the work of filmmakers from around the world. The emphasis is on experimental film, but many of these films have a documentary import. Its list runs from the complete works of Kenneth Anger and Bruce Conner to radical '60s Newsreel titles like *Off the Pig* and *People's Park,* as well as newer work by independent filmmakers.

Carousel Film and Video
250 Fifth Avenue, Suite 204
New York, NY 10001
Phone: 800-683-1660
Phone: 212-683-1660
Fax: 212-683-1662

Carousel carries a wide variety of documentaries with a special focus on black history (*A Poet's Voice; Middle Passage En Route*) and gay/lesbian topics (*The Real Ellen Story; Maid of Honor; When Shirley Met Florence*).

Cinema Guild
130 Madison Avenue, Second Floor
New York, NY 10016
Phone: 800-723-5522
Phone: 212-685-6242
Fax: 212-685-4717
Web site: www.cinemaguild.com
Contact: thecinemag@aol.com

The Cinema Guild carries a wide array of contemporary documentaries, particularly films with an emphasis on social change such as *From Swastika to Jim*

Crow; Witness: Voices from the Holocaust; Stripped and Teased: Tales from Las Vegas Women; and *By Any Means Necessary.* Its collection also includes a large number of Latin American, Caribbean, Middle Eastern, and African titles, such as *Maquila: A Tale of Two Mexicos; Lanfanmi Selavi; Hanan Ashrawi: A Woman of Her Time;* and *The Man Who Drove Mandela.*

Direct Cinema Limited
P.O. Box 10003
Santa Monica, CA 90410-1003
Phone: 310-636-8200
Fax: 310-636-8228
Web site: www.directcinema.com
Contact: dclvideo@aol.com

Direct Cinema Limited has been distributing high-quality documentary films since 1974, and has compiled a collection containing many Oscar and Emmy Award–winning films. It carries both short and feature-length documentaries in subject areas such as the Holocaust (*Angels of Vengeance; The Hunt for Adolf Eichman*), Jewish life and culture (*Half the Kingdom; Intermarriage: When Love Meets Tradition*), history (*Primary; Vietnam Requiem; Four Little Girls*), dance and opera (*Sing Faster: The Stagehand's Ring Cycle; Suzanne Farrell: Elusive Muse*), and anthropology (*The Amish and Us; Cannibal Tours*).

Documentary Educational Resources
101 Morse Street
Watertown, MA 02172
617-926-0491
Web site: www.der.org
Contact: docued@der.org

DER specializes in ethnographic films. The Yanomamo and Bushmen series are represented, as well as such newer works as *Opra Roma: The Gypsies of Canada* and *Seeking the Spirit: Plains Indians in Russia.*

Downtown Community Television Center
87 Lafayette Street
New York, NY 10013
Phone: 212-966-4510
Fax: 212-219-0248
Web site: www.dctvny.org
Contact: jonny@dctvny.org

DCTV distributes social issue documentaries. Its titles include *A Cinderella Season: The Lady Vols Fight Back; High on Crack Street; Lock Up: The Prisoners of Rikers Island; Atomic Horse Milk; Hard Metal Disease;* and *Chiapas: The Fight for Land and Liberty.*

Electronic Arts Intermix
542 W. 22nd Street, Third Floor
New York, NY 10011

Phone: 212-337-0680
Fax: 212-337-0679
Web site: www.eai.org
Contact: info@eai.org

Founded in 1971, Electronic Arts Intermix (EAI) is a leading resource for artists' video and new media. EAI distributes more than 2,500 titles by 175 artists to educational, cultural, arts, and television markets across the United States and around the world. Its collection ranges from historical works of the 1960s to new works by emerging media artists of the 1990s. All titles can be ordered from its Web site. EAI carries the work of Chris Marker, George Kuchar, Beth B, Chip Lord, Alexander Klug, Jean Luc Godard, Péter Forgács, Karen Finley, Sophie Calle, and John Cage, among others.

Em Gee
6924 Canby Avenue, Suite 103
Reseda, CA 91335
818-881-8110
Web site: http://emgee.freeyellow.com
Contact: mglass@worldnet.att.net

Em Gee specializes in early cinema, with more than 6,000 American and international titles in distribution. Some titles of interest include *Rescued by Rover* and *La jetée.*

Facets Multimedia, Inc.
1517 W. Fullerton Avenue
Chicago, IL 60614
Phone: 800-331-6197
Fax: 773-929-5437
Web site: www.facets.org

Facets carries an unusually diverse array of quality films on videotape and DVD that can be purchased from their Web site. Documentaries carried include *Nanook of the North; The Battle of San Pietro; Forever Activists: Stories from the Abraham Lincoln Brigade; Shoah;* and *Mr. Death: The Rise and Fall of Fred A. Leuchter, Jr.*

Fanlight Productions
4196 Washington Street, Suite 2
Boston, MA 02131
800-937-4113
617-469-4999
Web site: www.fanlight.com
Contact: fanlight@fanlight.com

Fanlight specializes in medical and mental health issues and carries titles such as *Dress Him While He Walks; How I Coped When Mommy Died; Narcolepsy; Shadows and Lies;* and *Remembering Tom.*

Filmakers Library
124 East 40th Street
New York, NY 10016
800-555-9815
212-808-4980
Web site: www.filmakers.com
Contact: info@filmakers.com

Filmakers Library offers a very strong selection of documentary titles on topics such as labor (*In the Land of Plenty; Women Unionize the Catfish Industry*), health and disability (*Sound and Fury; A Dyslexic Family Diary*), race relations (*Crickett outta Compton; Roy Smith*), environment (*Lavender Lake; Ships of Shame*), gender studies (*Call to Witness; 99% Woman*) and AIDS (*Living Positive*).

Film-Makers' Cooperative
c/o Clocktower Gallery
108 Leonard Street, 13th Floor
New York, NY 10013
Phone: 212-267-5665
Fax: 212-267-5666
Web site: www.film-makerscoop.com
Contact: film6000@aol.com

The Film-Makers' Cooperative began in 1962 and currently has more than 5,000 films and videotapes in its collection. It is the world's largest archive and distributor of independent and avant-garde films. The Co-op carries the work of Maya Deren, George Kuchar, Stan Brakhage, Michael Snow, Emily Breer, Nestor Almendros, and Gary Edelstein, among others.

Films for the Humanities and Sciences
P.O. Box 2053
Princeton, NJ 08543-2053
800-257-5126
Web site: www.films.com

This distributor carries more than 8,000 titles. Its subject areas include psychology and mental health (*Broken Child: Case Studies of Child Abuse; Patrick's Story: Attempted Suicide; Attempting Life*), multicultural studies (*Chinese Americans: Living in Two Worlds; The Fateful Decade: From Little Rock to the Civil Rights Bill*), women's studies (*Safe: Inside a Battered Women's Shelter; Beyond Borders: Arab Feminists Talk about Their Lives*), and philosophy and ethics (*Rethink the Death Penalty; The Roots of Belief: Animism to Abraham, Moses, and Buddha*).

First Run/Icarus Films
32 Court Street, 21st Floor
Brooklyn, NY 11201
718-488-8900

800-876-1710
Web site: www.frif.com
Contact: info@frif.com

First Run/Icarus Films distributes more than 750 high-quality documentary films and videos, including such titles as *Blood in the Face; Born in Flames; Paulina; States of Terror;* and *One Day in the Life of Andrei Aresenevich.* It also carries a large number of Latin American (*The Comrade: Life of Luiz Carlos Prestes; Chile; Obstinate Memory*), Asian (*Sun Rise over Tiananmen Square; From Opium to Chrysanthemums*), and African titles (*Chronicle of a Genocide Foretold*).

Flower Films
10341 San Pablo Avenue
El Cerrito, CA 94530
Phone: 510-525-0942
Fax: 510-525-1204
Web site: www.lesblank.com
Contact: Blankfilm@aol.com

Les Blank's distribution company carries all his own films and some others; includes *Garlic Is As Good As Ten Mothers; Werner Herzog Eats His Shoe;* and *Burden of Dreams.*

Frameline
346 Ninth Street
San Francisco, CA 94103
415-703-8650
Web site: www.frameline.org
Contact: info@frameline.org

Frameline specializes in films and videos on gay/lesbian themes. It carries titles such as *Two Encounters; Gay Cuba; Surviving Friendly Fire; Lone Star Hate;* and *Tongues Untied.*

Insight Media
2162 Broadway
New York, NY 10024-0621
Phone: 800-233-9910
Fax: 212-799-5309
Web site: www.insight-media.com
Contact: cs@insight-media.com

Insight Media distributes films and videos to the educational market. Its subject areas include communication and film studies (*Classified X; Changing Voices: De-Colonizing the Screen*), Africa (*Fighting for Survival: The Pastoralist Land Rights Movement of Northern Tanzania; Iindawo Zikathixo: In God's Place*), and criminal justice and legal studies (*When a Child Kills; Kolokouris: What's the Verdict?*).

Kino International

333 W. 39th Street, Suite 503
New York, NY 10018
Phone: 212-629-6880
Fax: 212-714-0871
Web site: www.kino.com

Kino distributes high-quality contemporary world cinema, American independents, and documentaries. It also distributes many classic films in their original 35mm formats as well as offering them for sale on video. Its documentary titles include films of the British Documentary Movement (*Desert Victory; England in the Thirties,* etc.), as well as contemporary films released theatrically (*The Specialist* and *The Wonderful Horrible Life of Leni Reifenstahl*).

Ladyslipper

3205 Hillsborough Road
Durham, NC 27705
Phone: 800-634-6044
Fax: 800-577-7892
Web site: www.ladyslipper.org
Contact: info@ladyslipper.org

Ladyslipper carries videos on lesbian and women's issues. Its collection contains fiction films and, to a lesser extent, documentaries. Some documentaries of interest include *All God's Children; Not For Ourselves Alone; Paris Was a Woman;* and *Intimate Portrait: Bella Abzug.*

Maysles Films

250 W. 54th Street
New York, NY 10019
212-582-5050
Web site: www.mayslesfilms.com
Contact: info@maysles.com

Maysles Films sells some of the work of the Maysles brothers to the home video market, including *Salesman; Running Fence;* and *Grey Gardens.*

Movies Unlimited

3015 Darnell Road
Philadelphia, PA 19115
215-722-8398
800-4-MOVIES
Web site: www.moviesunlimited.com
Contact: movies@moviesunlimited.com

This company sells videotapes of films for the home video market. Its catalogue is enormous and includes documentaries such as the Jacques Cousteau Series, the National Geographic Series, the March of Times Series, as well as the films of such notable documentary filmmakers as Robert Flaherty, Charles and Ray Eames, Errol Morris, Barbara Kopple, and Alan Berliner. It also carries a large selection of films on gay/lesbian issues, including *After Stonewall; The Brandon Teena Story;* and *Living with Pride: Ruth Ellis at 100.*

The Museum of Modern Art
Circulating Film and Video Library
11 W. 53rd Street
New York, NY 10019
212-708-9530
Web site: www.moma.org
Contact: circfilm@moma.org

MoMA has a selective repertoire of classic documentary titles, including many Lumière films, 1930s British documentaries, National Film Board of Canada films, the Why We Fight Series, the March of Time Series, both Film and Photo League and Frontier Films productions, and the Navajo Film Themselves Series.

NAATA Distribution
346 Ninth Street, Second Floor
San Francisco, CA 94103
Phone: 415-552-9550
Fax: 415-863-7428
Web site: www.naatanet.org

NAATA distributes a large number of videos on Asian-American issues, such as *Passing Through; Not Black or White; Citizen Hong Kong; First Person Plural; Regret to Inform; Unwanted Soldier;* and *We Served With Pride: The Chinese American Experience in WWII.*

National Film Board of Canada
350 Fifth Avenue, Suite 4820
New York, NY 10118
Phone: 212-629-8890
Phone: 800-542-2164
Fax: 212-629-8502
Web site: www.nfb.ca
Contact: NewYork@nfb.com

National Film Board of Canada (NFB) is a public agency that was created in 1939 to produce and distribute Canadian films. The NFB distributes more than 10,000 films. It carries most of the well-known NFB titles, such as *City of Gold; N-Zone;* and *Sad Song of Yellow Skin.*

New Day Films
22-D Hollywood Avenue
Hohokus, NJ 07432
Phone: 888-367-9154
Fax: 201-652-1973
Web site: www.newday.com

New Day Films is a documentary filmmaker's cooperative with a diverse range of social issue titles such as *El Corrido de Cecilia Rios; Yidl in the Middle: Growing Up Jewish in Iowa; In Whose Honor: American Indian Mascots in Sports; Scout's Honor; Bionic Beauty Salon; Father Roy: Inside the School of Assassins;* and *Yield to Total Elation: The Life and Art of Achilles Rizzoli.*

New Dimensions Media
611 E. State Street
Jacksonville, IL 62650
Phone: 800-288-4456
Fax: 800-242-2288
Web site: www.btsb.com
Contact: ndm@btsb.com

New Dimensions distributes educational films. Its collection includes the titles *East Timor: Free at Last?; Harriet Tubman and the Underground Railroad; Changing Mother Nature: Genetics in Food;* and *All About Eve.*

New Yorker Films
16 W. 61st Street
New York, NY 10023
Phone: 212-247-6110
Fax: 212-307-7855
Web site: www.newyorkerfilms.com

New Yorker distributes a number of important foreign feature films and also high-quality documentaries such as *Paragraph 175; One Day in September; A Place Called Chiapas;* and *American Movie.*

NTIS National Audiovisual Center (NAC)
U.S. Department of Commerce
Technology Administration
Springfield, VA 22161
703-605-6000
Web site: www.ntis.gov/nac

NAC is a clearinghouse for federally developed audiovisual materials. It carries films made under the auspices of government agencies, from *The Plow That Broke the Plains* and the Why We Fight Series to *Red Nightmare* and *Why Vietnam.* The center offers online ordering, distributing materials both in the U.S. and internationally.

Paper Tiger Television
339 Lafayette Street
New York, NY 10012
Phone: 212-420-9045
Fax: 212-420-8196
Web site: www.papertiger.org
Contact: info@papertiger.org

Paper Tiger is a volunteer collective. It is the maverick of satellite transmission, airing material for community access channels and educational institutions. Its programs are also available as videotapes and include *Homecoming Queens; Rock, Paper, Missiles;* and *Subverting Media: A Guide to Low Tech Information Activism.*

PBS Video
1320 Braddock Place
Alexandria, VA 22314-1698
Phone: 800-424-7963
Fax: 703-739-8131
Web site: www.pbs.org

PBS carries material produced for the Public Broadcasting System such as *From Swastika to Jim Crow; On Our Own Terms: Moyers on Dying;* the *American Experience* series; the *P.O.V.* series; and the *Frontline* series.

Select Media
18 Harrison Street, Suite 5
New York, NY 10013
Phone: 212-431-8923 or 800-343-5540
Fax: 212-334-6173
Web site: www.selectmedia.org
Contact: bwachter@usa.net

Select Media rents educational videos on the topic of Youth at Risk. Their titles include *Absolutely Positive; AIDS: Changing the Rules; The Ride;* and *Diary of a Teenage Smoker.*

Swank Motion Pictures
201 South Jefferson Avenue
Saint Louis, MO 63103
Phone: 800-876-5577
Fax: 314-289-2192
Web site: www.swank.com

Swank is a large distributor of feature-length fiction and documentary films licensed for public performance. Its documentary titles include *When We Were Kings; Roger and Me; Baraka;* and *The Cruise.*

Telling Pictures
121 9th Street
San Francisco, CA 94103
Phone: 415-864-6714
Fax: 415-864-4364
Web site: www.tellingpix.com

Telling Pictures distributes films produced by Jeffrey Freidman and Rob Epstein, including *Paragraph 175; The Times of Harvey Milk;* and *The Celluloid Closet.*

Third World Newsreel
545 Eighth Avenue, 10th Floor
New York, NY 10018
Phone: 212-947-9277
Fax: 212-594-6417
Web site: www.twn.org

Third World Newsreel carries many classic Newsreel titles such as *Wilmington; People's War;* and *Columbia Revolt,* as well as more recent work addressing issues for people of color in the United States, such as *Cuban Roots/Bronx Stories; Kabul, Kabul; Borne in War;* and *Imagining Place.* Third World also carries a large number of Latin American titles.

University of California Extension
Center for Media and Independent Learning
2000 Center Street, Fourth Floor
Berkeley, CA 94704
Phone: 510-642-0460
Fax: 510-643-9271
Web site: www-cmil.unex.berkeley.edu/media/
Contact: cmil@uclink.berkeley.edu

This Center, like most university media centers, specializes in films that can be used in support of instructional courses of all kinds. Like other centers, it has a generous collection of works that is of specific value in film courses and many titles primarily intended for other courses that are of special interest to the documentarian. Documentaries held include titles on Africa (Turkana Conversations Trilogy; *To Live with Herds; Under the Men's Tree*), social sciences (*Tatau: What One Must Do; Sunflowers; The Homeless Home Movie*), health and medical sciences (*Birth of Perception: The American Story on RU-486; Whose Body, Whose Rights*), and environmental science and issues (*Laid to Waste; Heart of the People*).

Video Data Bank
112 S. Michigan Avenue
Chicago, IL 60603
Phone: 312-345-3550
Fax: 312-541-8073
Web site: www.vdb.org
Contact: info@vdb.org

Founded in 1976 at the inception of the video arts movement in the United States, the Video Data Bank is one of the United States's largest providers of alternative and art-based video. The VDB distributes video art and documentaries made by artists and taped interviews with visual artists, photographers, and critics. It carries the work of video artists George Kuchar, Sherry Millner, Jim Cohen, Jeanne Finley, and Nelson Henricks, among others.

Viewfinders/ Uncommon Video, Inc.
P.O. Box 1665
Evanston, IL 60204-1665
Phone: 847-869-0600
Fax: 847-869-1710
Web site: www.uncommon-video.com
Contact: orders@uncommon-video.com

Viewfinders's catalogue consists of more than 7,000 titles. Upon request, it will also special order films not available in its collection. It carries a large number of documentaries produced for PBS, as well as theatrically released documentaries such as *Woody Allen: Wild Man Blues* and Nikita Mikhailkov's *Anna*. It also carries a number of documentary classics, such as *Victory at Sea; Night and Fog;* and *Shoah*.

Winstar Cinema
419 Park Avenue South, 20th Floor
New York, NY 10016
Phone: 212-686-6777
Fax: 212-545-9931
Web site: www.winstarcinema.com

Winstar Cinema distributes high-quality Art House fiction and documentary films licensed for public performance. Its documentary titles include *Beutopia; JS Bach in Auschwitz;* and *Wonderland*.

Wolfe Video
P.O. Box 64
New Almaden, CA 95042
Phone: 800-642-5247
Fax: 408-268-9449
Web site: www.wolfevideo.com

Wolfe Video distributes gay/lesbian films on videotape. Its collection includes both fiction and documentary. Its documentary titles include *Out of the Past; Stonewall; Eyes of Tammy Faye; Framing Lesbian Fashion;* and *The Castro*.

Women Make Movies
462 Broadway, Suite 500
New York, NY 10013
Phone: 212-925-0606
Fax: 212-925-2052
Web site: www.wmm.com
Contact: info@wmm.com

WMM is the largest distributor of women's media in North America. It carries more than 500 films by and about women, including many important documentaries such as *Blind Spot: Murder by Women; A Boy Named Sue; The Devil Never Sleeps; Hide and Seek; Surname Viet Given Name Nam;* and *Daughter of Suicide*.

Zeitgeist Films Ltd.
247 Centre Street, Second Floor
New York, NY 10013
Phone: 212-274-1989
Fax: 212-274-1644
Web site: www.zeitgeistfilm.com

Zeitgeist carries high-quality fiction and documentary films acquired for distribu-
tion at film festivals. Their collection includes the documentaries *Coming Out
Under Fire; The Gleaners and I; Let It Come Down: The Life of Paul Bowles;
Manufacturing Consent;* and *Buckminster Fuller: Thinking Out Loud.*

Zipporah Films, Inc.
One Richdale Avenue, Unit #4
Cambridge, MA 02140
Phone: 617-576-3603
Fax: 617-864-8006
Web site: www.zipporah.com
Contact: info@zipporah.com

Zipporah distributes all the films of Fredrick Wiseman, including *Law and Order;
Titticut Follies; High School;* and *Model.*

INTERNATIONAL DISTRIBUTORS

Australia

AIATSIS Film Unit
Australian Institute of Aboriginal and Torres Strait Islander Studies
GPO Box 553
Canberra, A.C.T. 2601
Australia
Phone: 02-6246 1111
Fax: 02-6261 4281
Web site: www.aiatsis.gov.au
Contact: adl@aiatsis.gov.au

AIATSIS is an independent Commonwealth Government statutory authority
devoted to Aboriginal and Torres Strait Islander studies. The AIATSIS Audiovisual
Archives hold the world's largest collection of film and video materials relating to
Australian Aboriginal and Torres Strait Islander studies.

Australian Film Institute
49 Eastern Road
South Melbourne, 3205 VIC
Australia
Phone: 613 9696 1844
Fax: 613 966 7972
Web site: www.afi.org.au
Contact: info@afi.org.au

The AFI was established in 1958, and is Australia's major distributor of Australian documentaries, short fiction, and animation. It operates the AFI Library, which holds Australia's most comprehensive collection of film and television literature.

National Film and Video Lending Service of Australia
Cinemedia Access Collection
222 Park Street
South Melbourne, Victoria 3205
Australia
Phone: 03-9929 7040
Phone: 800-803 758
Fax: 03-9929 7027
Web site: www.cinemedia.net
Contact: access@cinemedia.com

National Film and Video Lending Service of Australia is a distribution library holding approximately 14,500 titles. It contains an extremely comprehensive collection of films that covers the span of international cinema. The collection is distributed to registered borrowers throughout Australia.

Ronin Films
P.O. Box 1005
Civic Square, Canberra, A.C.T. 2608
Australia
Phone: 02-6248 0851
Web site: www.roninfilms.com.au

Ronin distributes educational films and videos in the territories of Australia and New Zealand, with a few titles available for international distribution. Its documentary subject areas include Aboriginal Australians, docu-dramas, East Timor, environment, health, history, gender and sexuality, France, Russia, war, and women's issues.

Austria

Austrian Film Commission
Stiftgasse 6
A-1070 Wien, Austria
Phone: 431-526 33 23-0
Fax: 431-526 68 01
Web site: www.afc.at
Contact: office@afc.at

Although not a film distributor, the Austrian Film Commission acts as an information clearinghouse for Austrian fiction and documentary films.

Sixpackfilm
Neubaugasse 45
P.O. Box 197
A-107 Vienna, Austria

Phone: 431-525 09 90
Fax: 431-525 09 92
Web site: www.sixpackfilm.com
contact: office@sixpackfilm.com

Sixpackfilms distributes European avant-garde films, many with a documentary import.

Canada

Groupe Intervention Video
5505 St. Laurent Blvd., Suite 3015
Montreal, Quebec H2T156
Phone: 514-271-5506
Fax: 514-271-6980
Web site: www.givideo.org
Contact: giv@videotron.ca

GIV distributes films and videos by women directors from Canada, the United States, and Latin America. Its documentary titles include *Boy, Girl; Breast Feeding: Who Loses, Who Wins; A Cancer Video;* and *Black Women of Brazil.*

Video In
1965 Main Street
Vancouver, BC V5T 3C1
Canada
Phone: 604-872-8337
Fax: 604-876-1185
Web site: www.videoinstudios.com
Contact: videoin@telus.net

Video In distributes the work of video artists primarily from the West Coast of Canada. Its library contains a large number of Canadian titles on social issues and gender politics, such as *Queen's Cantonese; Being Fucked Up;* and *Marking the Mother.* It also distributes approximately 160 American titles and a few international videos.

France

AMIP
52 rue Charlot
75003 Paris, France
Phone: 33 1 48 87 45 13
Fax: 33 1 48 87 40 10
Website: www.tvfi.com
Contact: amip@worldnet.fr

AMIP produces and distributes documentaries for the international television market. Its collection contains more than 500 hours of documentary programs on such topics as cinema, culture, history, biographies, and current affairs. Titles held include *Cinema of Our Time; David Cronenberg; Sugar Ray Robinson;* and *Tokyo.*

Light Cone
12 rue des Vignoles
75020 Paris, France
Phone: 33 1 46590153
Fax: 33 1 46590312
Web site: www.lightcone.org
Contact: ligtcone@club-internet.fr

Light Cone distributes experimental films and videos by Stan Brakhage, Chantal Ackerman, Caroline Avery, Pip Chodorov, Abigail Child, Maya Deren, Jonas Mekas, Jennifer Burford, Hans Richter, and Bill Morrison, among others. Many films in their collection have a documentary import.

Pathé International
10 rue Lincoln
75008 Paris, France
Phone: 33 1 40 76 91 69
Fax: 33 1 40 76 91 94
Web site: www.patheinternational.com

Pathé International is the distributor of films from the Pathé Group. Pathé International distributes feature films and documentaries in France, as well as internationally on such topics as sports, social issues, travel, ethnography, and adventure.

Play Film Distribution
14 rue du Moulin Joly
75011 Paris, France
Phone: 33 1 40 21 09 90
Fax: 33 1 40 21 88 44
Web site: www.playfilm.fr
Contact: playfilm@playfilm.fr

Play Film Distribution produces and distributes documentary films on such topics as ethnography (with a particular focus on Central Asia and Iran), the arts, cinema, history, biography, and current affairs. Its titles include *Paris Month after Month; Zinat: A Special Day; Rodchenko and the Russian Avant-garde;* and *Mokarrameh: Memories and Dreams.*

Germany

A.G. Dok
Im Deutschen Filmmuseum
Schweizer Straße 6
D-60594 Frankfurt Am Main
Phone: 49 69 62 37 00
Fax: 49 69 60 321 85
Web site: www.agdok.de

A.G. Dok is the distribution arm of the German Documentary Filmmaker's Association. It represents many important German documentarians who produce films on varied topics, including women's issues, war and peace, human rights, the arts, German reunification, music, and sexuality.

Athos Films International

GmbH Husemannstrasse 5
10435 Berlin, Germany
Phone: 49 30 443 97 69
Fax: 49 30 443 95 48
Web site: www.athos-films.com
Contact: production@athos-films.com

Athos Films distributes theatrical and television documentaries. Films are available on various media and can be ordered directly from Athos's Web site. Titles carried include *The Cruise; Burning Man 2020; 67 Ben Tsvi Road; Albania;* and *All the Way to America.*

Great Britain

British Film Institute Collections

21 Stephen Street
London W1T 1LN
Tel: 0207 255 1444
Fax: 0207 436 2338
Web site: www.bfi.org.uk
Contact: library@bfi.org.uk

British Film Institute Collections contains the largest collection of films and television titles in Europe, and includes the National Film and Television Archive. Its documentary holdings range from early historical Newsreels to important contemporary documentaries.

Cinenova

113 Roman Road
London E2 OQN
Phone: 0181 981 68 28
Fax: 0181 983 44 41

Cinenova is the United Kingdom's only film and video distributor specializing in work directed by women. Its catalogue includes films from Europe, Canada, and the United States, and covers issues that range from female sexuality to cultural identity and oral history. Its titles include *Great Dykes of Holland; Warrior Marks; Voices from Iraq;* and *Radio Earth Is on the Air.*

Lux Distribution

2-4 Hoxton Square
London N1 6NU
Phone: 020 7684 2844
Fax: 020 7684 2222
Web site: www.lux.org.uk
Contact: dist@lux.org.uk

Lux Distribution is Europe's largest distributor of experimental films and videos. Along with its comprehensive collection of British works are key pieces from the United States, Europe, Latin America, Japan, and Australia. Its collection includes works by Stan Brakhage, Alan Berliner, Ian Bourn, Annette Kennerley, Cathy Sisler, and Jack Smith.

Russia

Studio U-7 TV
P.O. Box 33
Ekaterinburg, 620219
Russia
Phone/Fax: 7 343 77 340 09
Web site: www.u7tv.e-burg.ru
Contact: u7tv@u7tv.e-burg.ru

Studio U-7 TV produces and distributes Russian documentaries on such topics as social and environmental issues, history, and ethnography; titles include *The Road to Mayak; Gods of Yamal;* and *Northern Sacrifice.*

Scandinavia

Danish Film Institute
55 Gothersgade
DK-1123 Copenhagen K
Denmark
Phone: 45 33 74 34 00
Fax: 45 33 74 34 01
Web site: www.dfi.dk
Contact: dfi@dfi.dk

The Danish Film Institute is a national agency responsible for supporting and encouraging film and cinema culture in Denmark. The DFI develops, produces, and distributes fiction films and documentaries.

INTERNET SEARCH ENGINES

Docuseek.com is useful for locating distributors of many social issue and educational documentaries. It currently searches the catalogues of Bullfrog Films, First Run/Icarus Films, New Day Films, Fanlight Productions, and Frameline.

Imdb.com (Internet Movie Database) provides film reviews and lists of casts and crews of well-known fiction and documentary films. It searches amazon.com for title availability on VHS and DVD.

Videoflicks.com is a leading online video retailer, offering more than 100,000 VHS and DVD film titles for sale.

Dvdpricesearch.com searches a number of online retailers, including amazon.com and buy.com, for film titles available on DVD.

Index

Page numbers in **bold** indicate illustrations.

Bill Nichols, an internationally recognized authority on documentary and ethnographic film, is Professor of Cinema at San Francisco State University, where he also directs the Graduate Program in Cinema Studies. He has published on a wide range of topics, from cybernetics and visual culture to New Iranian Cinema, and his anthology *Movies and Methods* (1976), helped define the new discipline of film studies. He is also the author of *Representing Reality* and *Blurred Boundaries* (both published by Indiana University Press) and editor of *Maya Deren and the American Avant-Garde.*